Treading the Deep

TREADING
THE DEEP

Inspirational Lessons on
Life and Leadership

COMMAND SERGEANT MAJOR (RET.)

BRADLEY
JONES

NEW YORK

LONDON • NASHVILLE • MELBOURNE • VANCOUVER

TREADING THE DEEP

Inspirational Lessons on Life and Leadership

Published in New York, New York, by Morgan James Publishing. Morgan James is a trademark of Morgan James, LLC. www.MorganJamesPublishing.com

Scripture quotations marked KJV are taken from the King James Version.

Proudly distributed by Ingram Publisher Services.

Morgan James BOGO™

A **FREE** ebook edition is available for you or a friend with the purchase of this print book.

CLEARLY SIGN YOUR NAME ABOVE

Instructions to claim your free ebook edition:
1. Visit MorganJamesBOGO.com
2. Sign your name CLEARLY in the space above
3. Complete the form and submit a photo of this entire page
4. You or your friend can download the ebook to your preferred device

ISBN 9781631957659 paperback
ISBN 9781631957666 ebook
Library of Congress Control Number:
2021946294

Cover Design by:
Rachel Lopez
www.r2cdesign.com

Interior Design by:
Chris Treccani
www.3dogcreative.net

Back Cover Photograph by:
Ileen Kennedy

Morgan James is a proud partner of Habitat for Humanity Peninsula and Greater Williamsburg. Partners in building since 2006.

Get involved today! Visit MorganJamesPublishing.com/giving-back

To all those with whom I've been privileged to serve and learn from, and to all those who sacrifice for God, family, and country.

CONTENTS

ACKNOWLEDGMENTS

It takes a lot of work and sweat to write a book. I thought being in basic training in the military was difficult. Writing a book definitely gives it a run for its money. I'd like to thank my editor, Ginger Kolbaba. Throughout the editing process I joked that she should have been a drill sergeant. She worked me hard, but I'm proud of the end result she helped me achieve.

Thank you also to the team at Morgan James for believing in this process and helping guide me throughout it.

I also want to thank the many family members and friends who offer unmitigated support for me through this rollercoaster ride called life.

To my kids—Matt, Adara, Mimi, Madyson, Eliza, and Daniel. I'm so proud that you chose me to be your father. Thanks for putting up with your dad.

To Jenne. Thank you for joining me on this journey called life.

CHAPTER 1

I Promise to Defend

———————

"Have you lived here in Portland your whole life?" the recruiter asked as we drove across the Ross Island Bridge that warm and clear morning of July 11, 1984.

"I've lived here most of my life, except for the six months I lived in Australia during my junior year of high school," I said, glancing at his clean, crisp uniform. I counted five stripes displayed on his collar before I quickly looked away. I was more than a little nervous as we wound our way into downtown Portland, Oregon—my first ride in a government vehicle—finally arriving at a nondescript building among familiar buildings I had walked past every morning on my way to school, but never knew what lay inside. Come to find out, this nondescript building was the Military Entrance Processing Station, or MEPS, as it's known to those who have willingly braved to enter therein.

We parked behind the building and walked inside. I surveyed the other young-looking possible recruits. They looked as nervous and uncomfortable as I felt. The recruiter explained that I needed to go through a physical examination before I could enlist.

"Are you sure you weigh more than 117 pounds?" He checked me up and down, a skeptical look covering his face.

"Yeah, I stepped on the scale this morning . . . 119."

"I sure hope so, because you wouldn't believe what happened with the guy we brought down here last week."

His words sounded ominous. I wasn't sure I *wanted* to know what happened with the guy. I inhaled deeply. *Man, I hope I'm not wrong*, I thought, because I was barely, *just* barely, above the military's minimum required enlistment weight for my height—117. On a good day, I weighed 120 pounds soaking wet.

"Yeah, that poor kid," the recruiter continued, shaking his head. He informed me that he and another recruiter had brought a below-minimum-weight prospective recruit to MEPS the week prior. During the ride from his home, they were feeding the young guy banana after banana. The guy valiantly ate eight to ten bananas and washed them down with water from two-gallon jugs they'd provided. "When the kid started to feel queasy, we repeatedly told him to hang on. We raced from the parking lot, arriving just in time to the main entrance where the poor guy couldn't hold back the tidal wave erupting from within. Right there, only steps from the entrance, he spewed everywhere. Partially digested bananas and water all over the glass doors and front step." He grimaced. "No way could he pass the weight requirement after that, so we led him back to the car with the consolation that we would try again later this week."

I shook my head at the recruiter's story. I may have been skinny, but I hoped enlisting would bulk me up. I thought of the high school upperclassmen I ran into after they graduated from basic. They looked so muscular and fit that I barely recognized them. *That's how I want to look. I just need to make this weight limit.*

Having graduated a month earlier from Clackamas High School in Portland, I knew I was not committed enough to more studying, passing, or paying for college classes, but I wasn't sure what I wanted to do. So I didn't think about it. I spent most of my time hanging out with friends when I wasn't working at my full-time job for a company that manufactured pitching machines and batting cages.

One day Doug, a company salesman in his late thirties, took me to lunch. "What are you going to do with yourself?" he asked.

The question pierced me. As much as I was trying to enjoy my job and time with my friends, I couldn't shake the nagging feeling that I needed to get out of Clackamas, Oregon, population twenty thousand, and do something with my life.

He looked at me expectantly. I wasn't sure what to tell him—I didn't even know myself. So I vaguely commented that I was kicking around the idea of joining the army.

"I think that's a great idea. Get out and see the world." He sipped his Coke. "You know, the lives of the guys you work with in the warehouse are about as good as they are ever going to get."

His pronouncement stunned me. I had become friends with many, if not most of them, but I had to admit, getting to know them, I knew he spoke realistically. Some of them had past brushes with the law, including prison time. I'd not thought that much about their lives—or mine as a parallel, but his words made me all the more anxious to break away from the familiar and comfortable.

"I don't have the money for college," I admitted. "And I don't really want to deal with four more years of school anyway." I paused. *So what do I want?* I wondered. "I want to go somewhere else and do something meaningful," I said, answering my thoughts out loud.

I had never previously considered the military as a way out, but I knew I felt strongly about my country and what it stands for. At sixteen I had an experience that made me realize just how deeply I felt about my country. I had the opportunity to live in Australia during the first part of my junior year in high school. My maternal grandparents moved to Australia when I was a toddler. During my sophomore year, my mom traveled there to visit her dad and stepmother. My grandfather's recent diagnosis of a blood disease inspired Mom to reevaluate the long-distance relationship she had with my grandfather. On the flight home she met John, an Aussie accountant from Adelaide, South Australia, who was traveling to America on holiday (as the Aussies would say). They hit it off—my parents were divorced—and after a quick courtship, they married . . . and that is how I found myself in Adelaide.

Leaving Oregon in the summer between my sophomore and junior years was gut-wrenching. My friends and I were all turning sixteen and getting our drivers' licenses and the freedom that they afforded. We could borrow our parents' cars to go to Friday night football games or on dates. Just when I was discovering freedom, I was packing up and moving to another country.

Whittling down personal possessions, I had the difficult task of figuring out what I really needed and what I could do without. I was left with only a fraction of the things I valued most—my record collection, my Santa Cruz skateboard with Tracker trucks and Kryptonic wheels, and the numerous concert shirts I'd collected. We boxed and shipped everything ahead of our move, knowing it would take several months before we saw them again.

Mom and I arrived in Australia in September 1982 and settled into a condominium in the foothills outside of Adelaide. I enrolled at Heathfield High School, attending the same school with the nieces and nephews of my stepfather, John.

School was serious business in Australia. It was a step up from the educational system I was accustomed to back home. Australian school systems hearkened back to the British education system where students wore uniforms and feared the headmaster. Heathfield had a semi-required uniform of gray corduroys and maroon sweater. (I am lost as to why they made us wear a sweater, given the warm climate of South Australia.)

For a time, I enjoyed the popularity of being the new kid from America and it did my heart good to know that all the girls, and I do mean *all* of them, were interested in hearing my Yankee accent. They all—even some of the guys—wanted to hear me talk.

And everyone wanted to know the same thing: "Have you been to Disneyland?" Not the question I would have expected, but yes, I had been to Disneyland.

Some thought the popular cult movie *The Warriors* was somehow based in reality, with more than a few people asking if there were really roving gangs in the bigger cities in the States. Alternatively, some thought everyone lived like the very wealthy Ewing family on *Dallas*, a popular television show at the time about a wealthy family of Texas oil tycoons, one of which was J. R., who was constantly deviously plotting against not only other competitors in the oil rich state, but members of his own family who got in his way. It made for good dramatic television, but was hardly the way my family—or any family I knew—lived.

Throughout my experience at Heathfield, I had a running mental picture with a narrative based on the video of Pink Floyd's "Another Brick in the Wall," where the experience of the young British student is depicted. The teacher delights in reading the young man's writings aloud, embarrassing him in front of the whole class.

Teachers in Australia had no qualms about calling out a student in front of the entire class, embarrassing them as a normal course of treatment. This longhaired kid from Oregon, who refused to wear the same uniform day after day, would have an experience with that concept soon enough.

One day one of my instructors asked me to speak with another teacher about an upcoming school activity day. I chose not to. The following morning the teacher asked me if I had done as he'd requested. His tone brought the attention of the entire class, and silently each student turned toward me conveying their interest in how I—the Yank—would handle being called out in front of everybody.

I ever so coolly told him that I had not spoken to the teacher the day before.

"Well, Brad"—his accent made it sound as though he was calling me Bread instead of Brad—"you're no longer in America, you're in Australia now, and here in Australia we do things and get them done on time."

With that, again, all eyes turned to me.

There's no way I'm letting this arrogant guy get the best of me, I thought.

I was sitting in a chair with an empty chair next to me. I slowly and very deliberately put my feet up on the other chair and crossed my legs. Then leaning back, I clasped my hands together behind my head. The picture of the ultimate, laid-back, nothing-gets-to-me Yankee. I looked up at him and said in the most matter-of-fact way, "Well, I guess I just haven't learned that yet."

The burst of laughter from the students was immediate and loud. But the teacher, with his face beet red, stood fuming and speechless. In an instant the tables had been turned.

From now on, he'll think twice before calling me out in front of a class-room full of students.

He walked out of the room, returning shortly to loudly tell me that the headmaster wanted to see me.

"Great, I want to speak to him too," I said, not missing a beat.

I left the classroom and made my way to the administration offices. The headmaster met me about halfway and in a respectful tone began a conversation with me about keeping my word when I tell someone I am going to do something. He was very principle-oriented, and I returned his respect, acknowledging that I could certainly do better. He then asked if I had anything else to say.

I told him I had no problem admitting when I was wrong, but there was no way I was going to keep my mouth shut when he openly criticized me and the USA! "He deserved every bit of disrespect for insinuating that we in America are lazy and don't get things done."

His eyes narrowed. "Don't you worry," he told me. "I will handle that issue, and no teacher at Heathfield will ever again criticize the United States."

As I walked away, I realized for the first time that I loved my country and would defend her when challenged.

I struggled with school that whole year. I missed my friends and the social scene back home. Their frequent letters described Friday night football and basketball games, dances, and the most gut-wrenching part, going out on dates since getting their driver's licenses. School was hard and I was struggling, so after only a few months at Heathfield, and much to my mother's disappointment, I dropped out and took a full-time job working in a mattress factory. Eventually, I summoned the courage to tell my mom that I wanted to return home. I knew it would break her heart, and I hated leaving her behind, but I reasoned that I needed to graduate from high school.

I returned home in early January 1983, living with my grandparents for the remainder of my high school career. Shortly after graduating in June 1984, my friend Paul, just days before he was due to ship out for basic, talked me into going to the recruiting station. He introduced me to the army recruiters who had worked with him on his enlistment. Of course being recruiters, they asked if I was interested in a career in the army. I was, but I still felt unsure.

They must have sensed it—they're good that way—and they talked me into taking the Armed Services Vocational Aptitude Battery (ASVAB) test. I figured I didn't have anything to lose, so I agreed. I scored high enough that very few jobs within the army were not open to me. I had no idea what career path I should choose. I looked at many different jobs, mostly in the emerging electronic technical areas. The one thing I knew for sure was that I had no interest in a career in the infantry. I wasn't kidding myself when I compared myself to people my own age—I didn't feel like I had the strength or stature to be successful as an infantryman.

But what job should I take? As I considered the possibilities, a vivid childhood memory came into my mind. My parents used to take our family to a parking spot next to the runway at Portland International Airport where we would sit and watch planes land and take off. I loved it. You would think that would translate into a desire to become a pilot, but an earlier experience flying to the Oregon coast through a terrible thunder and lightning storm in a small twin-engine Cessna cured me of any such aspirations. If I could work in the airline industry—and stay on the ground—that would be a perfect job for me.

So I began searching jobs in that field, and I came upon a radar maintenance technician—someone who worked on radar equipment to support flight operations.

Perfect!

That is how I found myself nervously riding with my recruiter to MEPS to receive a complete, and I do mean complete, physical examination. After I passed the weight "test," the recruiter led me to another room where I, along with about twenty other males, met the doctors who would examine us in very impersonal ways. After talking privately with a doctor, all the recruits came back together where we had to strip down to our underwear and stand with our feet on a line that formed a square, facing several doctors who stood inside the square to evaluate us. I felt uncomfortable and vulnerable standing in my tighty-whities. With arms hanging down, hands tightly clasped in front, I stared down at the floor. I was too embarrassed to look at any of the other recruits. I just ached for it to be over.

"Turn with your backs facing inside the square," one of the doctors told us.

What is this—some kind of line up for a firing squad? I wondered. We turned facing outward. The nervous tension in the room was palpable.

"Drop your underwear to the floor and bend over."

I don't imagine one could experience a more vulnerable moment. I closed my eyes and did as he commanded. I sensed one of the doctors come up and stand directly behind me. He paused for a moment, found or didn't find whatever he was looking for, and thankfully moved on.

The doctor who peered into my vulnerabilities made no disqualifying notes in my paperwork when I met with him privately. He indicated that I could put on some weight, but otherwise, said I was healthy enough for service. I was relieved when I was finally given the go-ahead to get dressed.

Back, fully clothed and standing again on the line, I wondered, *What are they going to do to us after that?*

"If you have smoked pot recently you need to tell us now!" a tall doctor with a commanding voice said. We all looked around the room at each other. Nobody moved. "If you have smoked any pot in the last couple months, you need to take a seat along this wall. . . . You had better tell us now because WE. WILL. FIND. IT. IN. YOUR. BLOOD!"

Several heads dropped, eyes aimed at the floor in defeat. They slowly and reluctantly made their way over to the chairs, knowing all eyes were glued to their every move. I felt sorry for the humiliation they had to be experiencing.

"Anyone else? Going once . . . going twice . . . nobody? Fine then, the rest of you go back down to the main-floor classroom for your swearing in."

The remaining seventeen of us civilians assembled in the classroom. There, in front of the Stars and Stripes, we raised our right hands. I felt a surge of pride as I pledged my allegiance. "I, Bradley Jones, do solemnly swear that I will support and defend the Constitution of the United States against all enemies, foreign and domestic; that I will bear true faith and allegiance to the same; and that I will obey the orders of the President of the United States and the orders of the officers appointed over me, according to regulations and the Uniform Code of Military Justice. So help me God."

I was officially in the army—Private Bradley Jones. I was so glad when we were finally able to leave that building. I enlisted into the Military Occupational Specialty (MOS) code, which identifies a specific job. I was assigned as a 26D Ground Control Approach Radar Repairman. Because this took some extra schooling, I had to wait for a school slot for that job to open, which meant I had to enlist into the Delayed Entry Program. Though I was now in the army, by enlisting in this particular program, I wouldn't go to basic for a few months. Some soldiers were shipping out immediately; those of us who were not were warned not to do any illegal drugs or get ourselves into trouble with the law.

Returning to work the next day, I made my way to Doug's office and proudly informed him that he was looking at a future radar technician. Doug came out from behind his desk and motioned for me to follow him. Outside in the parking lot sat his brand-new BMW glistening in the sun—a car I had secretly admired. Without warning, he threw me the keys.

"You drive," he said.

I could barely contain my excitement. We made our way to the freeway, where he told me, "Get on it." Music to my ears. I looked down and we were smoothly cruising at 100 miles per hour. I must have looked like a kid at Disneyland when we finally pulled back into the parking lot and into his space, which we seemed to have left only moments before.

I handed him back his keys and before we got out, Doug turned in his seat and stared me in the eyes. "Do you know who designed the ball-retrieval system in the batting cages we manufacture?"

"I can't say that I do."

"You know Dan, right?"

"Yeah, the guy who rides the Honda Interceptor motorcycle I wish was mine."

Doug laughed and nodded. "Yeah him. Well, he is the one who came up with that unique design based on his experience working on helicopters in the army."

My jaw dropped. "I did not know that."

"Brad, I know you may be nervous and even scared, but you're doing the right thing."

Those words stuck with me—especially because he had no idea how truly nervous I was—but for a reason beyond just enlisting in the unknown.

Unbeknownst to Doug—or anybody—was that I suffered from clusters of anxiety attacks and had since I was in the sixth grade. They would come unannounced in bunches lasting from several days to a full week. The thought of them coming on during basic training terrified me. In talking with others who had gone through basic, I knew I was in for a rollercoaster of stress and uncertainty. I worried that my anxiety attacks could keep me from becoming a soldier, making it so unbearable that I couldn't continue on.

When the attacks came, they felt like an adrenaline overload from our internal fight-or-flight mechanism suddenly entering the bloodstream causing rapid heartbeat, an overwhelming feeling of fear, and in some cases hyperventilation—all for no apparent reason. I was sure I must be going crazy, that something was seriously wrong with me. The thought of not knowing, or ever hearing about others suffering from the same thing, was a heavy burden I carried in silence.

As I thought about the prospect of dealing with those attacks during basic, I thought back to my first attack. It happened not long after a man propositioned me as I walked down the street in downtown Portland.

I was headed to buy skateboard parts from Cal Skates, the premier skateboard shop back then. I had to take a bus to get there and the bus stop was only a few blocks from the store. I got off the bus and began walking, not paying much attention to what was happening around me. As I pulled out a new pack of bubble gum from my pocket, I noticed someone was uncomfortably close behind me.

"Can I have a stick of your gum?" the man said. Not knowing what else to do, I held out a piece of gum to him, while doing my best to remain one step ahead. However, he didn't back away. Instead, he seemed to draw closer. "I like your hair. It looks cool."

I loved my long, feathered hair—the style that was all the rage. People frequently told me I looked like Leif Garrett, a popular teen heartthrob at the time. Looking over my shoulder, I politely acknowledged his compliment, and then sped up until I was forced to stop at a crosswalk.

Now he stood beside me. "I'm Alan," he said. "Yeah, I really like your hair. What style is that called?"

I mumbled my answer, wishing that the light would turn green so I could cross the street and get away from this guy.

"You like to party?"

That was when I realized he was after something more than conversation and a piece of gum. A tidal wave of intense fear washed over me, and my heart pounded in my chest so fast and hard, I was sure he could see my shirt move with each beat. Even at a young age, I'd considered myself a streetwise kid, but standing on the street corner, I felt paralyzed by fear and panic.

I felt like I was in one of those dreams where I open my mouth to call out to someone, but no sound comes out, or when I try to run, I can't seem to make my limbs follow—even though my mind is screaming, *Yell for help! Run, now! I need to get out of here somehow, someway!*

The thought suddenly came to me, *I should tell this dude whatever he wants to hear in order to get away from him.* I glanced around the crowded street corner and felt a ray of hope that he was not going to try to physically grab me in front of everyone. With so much fear, I actually wondered if I had the ability, despite my age and youth, to scream out if he did try anything.

Alan asked if I would meet him the next day at the bus stop where I had gotten off. As calmly as I could, I agreed.

He smiled and said he would show me a good time.

As soon as the light turned green, I booked across the street. Thankfully, he remained on the street corner. I continued up the next block, looking over my shoulder repeatedly, making sure he did not follow me. He finally turned and headed back down the block toward the bus stop.

I walked the rest of the way to the skate shop with an acute feeling of panic that would not subside. I couldn't believe I had gotten away from such a scary situation and an obviously demented and dangerous individual.

Once I purchased what I needed—without even looking around, which had always been my favorite part—I was faced with walking back to the same block to catch the bus home.

I decided to catch the bus from a stop several blocks farther down the street. I arrived at the stop and sat on a bench to wait for the bus to arrive. I had only been there a few minutes when Alan walked up with another young kid about my age, talking to him about meeting later. Nearly the same conversation he had with me.

Intense panic again washed over me. I wanted to get up and run but felt like any movement would draw his attention to me. They continued their conversation about meeting and partying as I sat paralyzed on the bench. As their conversation ended, Alan finally looked around and noticed me.

"We're still on for tomorrow, right?"

I managed to nod, and with that, he headed back down the street.

I was in a state of panic for the entire bus ride back to the southeast side of town, where we lived. I replayed the conversation repeatedly in my head, feeling an acute level of fear, the aftershocks of having narrowly escaped what, for me, could have been a life-altering situation.

Soon after, I had my first panic attack. Nothing was threatening me, but the fear I felt was reminiscent of what I had experienced that day in downtown. It is almost as if the level of fear feeds on itself, getting higher and higher with each heartbeat and breath of air. From that point on, the panic attacks appeared with no warning. Fortunately, they came in clusters, giving me periods in between—sometimes lasting months—of respite from the paralyzing and debilitating disorder.[1]

I shook my head from the memory and thought toward my future and my upcoming basic training. I could only pray that they wouldn't spring up on me. One thing I knew for sure, though: I had no idea how I was going to handle all the physical, mental, and emotional stress coming in the days ahead.

CHAPTER 2

Shipping Out

———————

The new recruits flew commercial from Portland, Oregon, to Columbia, South Carolina, heading to Fort Jackson. On the plane, our group of half a dozen sat together near the front. I had a window seat next to Rich Nelson, also from Portland. Rich was not happy to be on his way to basic. Honestly, neither was I. We both knew how uncomfortable the days ahead would be. Rich was unhappy for another reason, though. He claimed he tried to tell his recruiter that he wanted out of his enlistment. According to Rich, the recruiter told him he had to ship out for basic since he signed a contract, and to work it out when he got to Fort Jackson.

Yeah, I thought, *I'm sure the drill sergeants will be happy to help you with that issue as soon as you tell them what your recruiter said.*

We arrived late in the evening after a short bus ride from the airport to the base. We were herded, along with several other busloads of recruits—approximately 120—into a large auditorium-style room, where a female in uniform instructed us to take a seat.

I stuck close to Rich, figuring that sitting next to him, if and when he tried to tell them what he told me on the plane, would somehow, in their

15

eyes, make me look better. Although, before shipping out, Rich shaved his head, anticipating what was coming for those of us with long hair. I, on the other hand, kept my long hair, which suddenly had me wondering if it wasn't me making Rich look good. Looking around the room, I was relieved to see that plenty of others had long hair too. Rich and I sat near the front along with the others from our flight. We'd only met one another earlier that day, but somehow staying close to familiar faces felt more comforting.

In walked four similarly dressed soldiers, three male and one female. By their expressions, they were all business. I instantly sensed the tension level ratchet up. The shock of someone else taking complete control began to set in. This sure wasn't high school! Looking around, I could see the same apprehensive expression on many faces.

We waited in silence as other recruits filled the remaining seats. Among the recruits on our bus ride, the conversation was lively, flowing freely. Now no one spoke aloud, preferring to whisper, as if everyone sensed that talking aloud would somehow draw unwanted attention.

The female sergeant addressed the group first. "WELCOME TO FORT JACKSON." Her voice thundered. Even though her announcement wasn't terrifying, the level of her voice certainly was. She shouted every word.

"IN ORDER TO COMPLETE YOUR IN-PROCESSING TONIGHT, WE NEED TO COLLECT SEVERAL FORMS YOU SHOULD HAVE CARRIED WITH YOU!" She spoke to us as though she were talking to a bunch of unruly grade-school kids, repeating directions several times.

"PLEASE LISTEN CAREFULLY SO WE CAN GET THROUGH THIS PROCESS QUICKLY. IF YOU HAVE QUESTIONS, PLEASE RAISE YOUR HAND AND ONE OF OUR CADRE WILL ASSIST YOU. THE FIRST FORM WE NEED FROM YOU IS . . ."

As she continued to shout, I realized this was the first of many commands—and that even though she said "please," it wasn't a request.

After handing in the required paperwork, the next order of business was to pass through what they called the "amnesty room."

"EACH OF YOU WILL ENTER THE AMNESTY ROOM ALONE," she continued in a shout. "THIS IS YOUR ONE AND ONLY OPPORTUNITY TO DISCARD ANY CONTRABAND, DRUGS, OR WEAPONS YOU MAY HAVE BROUGHT WITH YOU!"

Seriously? I thought. *Who would bring drugs or weapons to basic training?* I soon learned that wasn't the only prohibited items. Food and candy were considered contraband and were strictly off-limits. As the sergeant read off the list of prohibited items, I heard a few recruits quietly groan.

"IF AFTER PASSING THROUGH THE AMNESTY ROOM YOU ARE FOUND IN POSSESSION OF EITHER WEAPONS OR DRUGS, YOU WILL BE SUBJECT TO SEVERE CONSEQUENCES, WHICH CAN INCLUDE FORFEITURE OF RANK AND/OR PAY, AND THE STRONG POSSIBILITY OF BEING DISHONORABLY DISCHARGED. PLEASE KEEP THESE THINGS IN MIND AND START OFF YOUR MILITARY CAREER BY DOING THE RIGHT THING!"

When it was my turn, I entered an empty room with a hole in the wall at about shoulder level. I didn't have anything to discard, but the hole piqued my curiosity. I walked over and looked through it. Sitting on the ground was a trashcan close enough to drop things into, but beyond reach should anyone decide to search through it.

I strained my neck to see what was in the trashcan. There was mostly what looked like candy and other items of food, but nothing I could see like weapons or drugs.

What a smart, ingenious way to get soldiers to get rid of prohibited things, I thought and then walked to the door on the other side of the room and exited.

After passing through the amnesty room, one of the cadre sergeants was waiting at the exit door instructing the males to go back into the auditorium. The females were diverted to a different room. It was already getting late when another sergeant read from a master list. His voice thundered too. "THE FOLLOWING PERSONNEL WILL FOLLOW SER-GEANT SMITH. WHEN YOUR NAME IS READ, PLEASE GATHER IN THE FOYER. YOU WILL NOT BE COMING BACK HERE, SO MAKE SURE YOU GATHER ALL YOUR BELONGINGS. IF YOU BROUGHT IT IN, THEN YOU NEED TO CARRY IT OUT!"

Again, I knew his politeness in saying please wasn't actually him being polite.

My name was announced in the third group, along with Rich's and about twenty-five others. I was secretly glad that Rich was in my group, since I'd at least know one person—even though he believed he was going to quit as soon as he could.

Waiting for us in the foyer was Sergeant Moyer. He stood every bit of 6'5" with enormous hands and an exceptionally deep voice. None of us was exactly sure when we would see our first drill sergeant. Sergeant Moyer told us to follow him to where we would spend the night. Together we exited the building. Outside he put on a baseball-style cap. I had seen pictures of drill sergeants that my friend Paul had sent me, and I knew they wore the Smokey-Bear-style hat.

Sergeant Moyer must not be a drill sergeant, I thought. Nonetheless, his sheer size and demeanor commanded respect.

He led us down the sidewalk, into a building, and up to the second floor where we found giant rooms filled with rows of bunk beds separated by wall lockers.

"This is where you will sleep," he told us, now without shouting. "Each bunk already has blankets and linen on top. The latrines are located between the bays. Your platoon number is fifteen. Take care of any personal hygiene matters and then try to get a good night's rest. Tomorrow will be a busy day. If you have any personal issues, I will be downstairs in my office all night. Other recruits will be coming in throughout the night, so make sure you keep any gear you have off the unoccupied bunks. Any questions?"

No one had any. I think we were all too scared.

The first night's sleep was not a good one. I chose a top bunk and tried to doze. I awoke to another group of recruits arriving and filling up the remaining empty bunks.

It was still dark when a shrill female voice came over the intercom loud enough to wake the dead. "FIFTEENTH PLATOON . . . FIFTEENTH PLATOON . . . SOMEBODY BETTER ANSWER ME."

The recruit closest to the intercom finally managed to say, "Yes, ma'am?'

"THAT'S YES, SERGEANT," the shrill voice responded. "UNDER-STAND?"

"Yes, ma'am—err, um, I mean, Sergeant."

"TAKE CARE OF YOUR PERSONAL HYGIENE AND BE DOWN ON THE QUAD AT 0530!"

A mixture of "Yes, ma'am—yes, Sergeant!" came from nearly everyone in the room.

"What time is it?" I asked as I jumped off my bed and grabbed my towel and soap.

"Five," my bunkmate mumbled, still half-asleep.

Five o'clock. I couldn't remember the last time I'd been awake that early—and since my body was still on Pacific Time, it was actually two o'clock my time. I moaned, wishing I could get even just another hour of sleep.

Outside, I took a moment to look at the surrounding buildings where we were staying. Since we'd arrived after dark the night before, I hadn't had the opportunity to take in the scope of the first military base I had ever seen. The buildings were part of a large U-shaped structure with a giant courtyard in the center. The ground level had open breezeways large enough for several platoons. Each morning we assembled in the breezeway to receive instructions on where we were going and what we were doing that day. Now I stood with my platoon and got our instructions. Our first stop—"chow hall," a large dining facility at the top of a hill. Good thing, since my stomach was growling. Inside the chow hall entrance, we found people waiting for us—and they seemed only too happy to shout

out commands. "GET IN LINE!" and "MOVE UP AND MAKE YOUR BUDDY HAPPY!" which meant tighten up the line. It was amazing how many could fit together when properly motivated.

Breakfast was, for me, the go-to meal of the day, so I looked forward to that first meal. Chow hall food wasn't bad—but it wasn't good either. I hated cheese and any food that was made or laced with it—and they were serving some cheese-covered hash-brown casserole dish that didn't look all that appetizing. When going through the chow line you got what they gave you. And as soon as the servers laid eyes on this skinny kid, they heaped on an extra helping. I lacked the courageous humor to say, "Cheese, me-no-likey."

I struggled during chow time. Not only with eating the cheese-covered food, but with keeping up with the others. I am a very slow eater. As hard as I tried, I could not keep up with other recruits who practically inhaled their food without ever tasting it.

After breakfast, we had an appointment with a room full of barbers. Each one held an electric razor, and the efficiency they employed to shave a recruit's head was impressive. In only a few quick passes, they completely removed even the longest hair. Before going to the barber, I never realized how much we identify people by their hair, and after it was all shaved off, we had a hard time recognizing each other.

What can happen in 30 seconds at the barber

I had never felt cold air on my head before. Now without my gloriously long mullet, I was shocked how much a head of hair protected a head from the cold air.

After the barber, we moved to another building where we stood in a long line to receive clothing, then another building and another long line for the equipment we needed for the next eight weeks. Our first few days at basic was a lot of standing in long lines.

At the end of one of the lines was terror, however. We assembled at the Troop Medical Clinic (TMC) to learn we were getting our shots and vaccines. I am not fond of needles or the prospect of getting a shot, let alone multiple shots, but I quickly found out I was not terrified like some of the others who broke out in a cold sweat over it.

With jackets removed—we were finally dressed in our camouflage green uniforms called Battle Dress Uniforms (BDUs)—we moved slowly in a single line toward two medics, one on each side, each holding large vaccine guns. The guns looked like a torture device from *Star Wars*, glossy and black. With each shot, they made the pressurized air release noise similar to when you remove the air hose after pumping up a tire.

Like watching a gruesome train wreck, I couldn't take my eyes away from the soldiers in front of me. Several flinched when the guns were placed, one against each upper arm, causing the gun needle to rapid-fire in succession and leaving a trail of bloody vaccine tracks on their upper arms. Two recruits passed out. Seizing the moment, medics quickly administered the required shots while they were down, followed by smelling salts to revive them.

On day four, we packed our newly acquired gear into our two duffel bags with our dress uniforms—fresh from being tailored—on top. We could feel the inevitable coming. The "Come to Jesus" experience we hoped to survive: meeting the drill sergeants whose sole mission in life was our pain and misery as they molded us into warriors . . . even soldiers. We were all told to eat lunch and then assemble back in the airway by our duffel bags, which all sat in neat rows.

I wasn't sure I'd be able to eat with my stomach reminding me of what was ahead, but I forced it down and then exited the chow hall with a group of about ten recruits—based solely on the proximity of our bunks. We began the two-block walk back to our bags. As we crested the hill that overlooked the barracks area, we saw inside the large courtyard numerous trucks with trailers in a semi-circle. The trailers, which we learned were referred to as "cattle cars" were there for us. I wondered how so many recruits would be able to fit in each.

Next to the trailers stood a group of supremely confident-looking men clad in their dress uniforms arrayed with rank stripes down their sleeves, chests full of medals, and the one defining item we had all been waiting for, dreading really—the unmistakable Smokey Bear hat, that identifying trademark of the modern army drill sergeant. They were an impressive sight. Their eyes raked over our group and they seemed to ooze with antic- ipation. Then they quite literally appeared to take on the movement and characteristics of a school of sharks, circling prey right before a feeding frenzy.

"Oh no!" several recruits audibly gasped. My stomach lurched. We had just realized the sharks were between us and our duffel bags. We had to walk right through the center of circling predators. Several had what looked like sawed-off baseball bats in their hands. As we got close, we realized they wanted us to look at them, going out of their way to position themselves in our field of view, taunting us, daring us to see who had the guts to look directly at them. I looked down . . . around . . . *anywhere* to avoid looking in their direction.

As I walked by, I looked up quickly, and just as quickly, looked away. There was no way on God's green earth I was actually going to make eye contact with any one of them as much as they wanted us to. They shook their heads and pointed at us. "YEAH, I GOT YOU," they yelled. "YOU'RE MINE!"

My heart raced like a thoroughbred as I quickly found my gear and stood next to it. Sergeant Moyer, who had been in charge of us up to this point, stood before us and bid our group goodbye and good luck.

A stocky, unhappy-looking drill sergeant approached us with an expression that conveyed, *You don't want any part of this.* Only, it would have been, "YOU DON'T WANT ANY PART OF THIS." In a loud, authoritative voice, not screaming by any means but in a tone that pierced me to the core, he said, "I WANT A FORMATION WITH FOUR EQUAL RANKS!"—lines—"IN FRONT OF THAT CATTLE CAR RIGHT NOW!"

We started moving, but clearly not quickly enough.

"WHAT ARE YOU WAITING FOR, AN INVITATION? MOVE, MOVE, MOVE! GOOD LORD ALMIGHTY, I'VE NEVER SEEN PEOPLE MOVE SO SLOW IN MY WHOLE LIFE!"

We broke into a run, recruits flying all over the place, falling over each other, getting up, falling again, trying desperately to assemble into a formation as quickly as possible. We were a mess, nobody seemed to know who to follow, and some guys arrived onto the quad and tried starting a line, while others were doing the same thing. Lines moved, tried to combine, and then moved again.

The drill sergeants shook their heads. "YOU'RE MOVING WAY TOO SLOW. WAY! TOO! SLOW! GET BACK TO YOUR BAGS AND LET'S TRY THAT AGAIN!"

We could not move quickly enough, let alone organize ourselves into four ranks on a designated spot.

The futile formation drill lasted several agonizing minutes, until finally, standing in a quasi-formation, they told the first rank to go get their bags and come back to their position. I was in the second rank, and when it was our turn, I got to where my bags had been, only they were not there!

The sweat of anger and agony burst from every pore in my body. *Who's the mother-loving moron who grabbed my bags?* I wasn't sure what to do and I felt the clock ticking against me. I could just grab someone else's bags—giving some other poor, unsuspecting recruit the same situation I now faced—or I could do the thing I dreaded more than anything in all eternity: approach and actually verbalize my dilemma to someone who was busy stoking the "fear of God" burning inside me.

I swallowed hard and ran up to the drill sergeant doing all the yelling. The instant I was next to him, I went to the position of Parade Rest (feet shoulder-width apart, hands clasped together and placed in the small of my back). He glanced at me with a look that said, *Just what in the world do you want?* Before he could say anything, I said, "Drill Sergeant, someone else has my bags!"

He turned toward the formation and screamed, "FOR THE LOVE . . . WHO PICKS UP BAGS WITH SOMEONE ELSE'S NAME ON THEM? FIRST RANK! CHECK THE NAME ON YOUR BAGS!"

Sure enough, a recruit sprinted past me, dropping my bags at my feet and continuing over to the remaining bags.

I was surprised when the DI looked down at me and said—*without* shouting, "Get back in formation."

"Moving, Drill Sergeant!" I said and hightailed it back to my spot.

After everyone finally had the right bags, the DI pointed at the cattle car. "YOU GOT TWO SECONDS TO GET ON THIS CATTLE CAR! MOVE! MOVE! MOVE!"

I've never seen so many recruits hit a doorway at the same time. I could not help but think of contests to see how many people could fit into a phone booth or a Volkswagen Beetle. Chaos again ensued. After several attempts at getting on the cattle car and having to get off for being too slow, around forty of us were finally allowed to stay on. The inside was lined with boards for bench seating. The benches were close enough to each other that everyone's knees were constantly knocking together and we could reach out and put our hands on the shoulders of the recruits sitting directly across from us. The drivers fired up the trucks and pulled slowly out of the courtyard.

No one spoke the entire ride to our new barracks. We all were too focused on heaving to catch our breath. Sweat poured down our faces. We sat in a wide-eyed state of shock, looking at each other with *Oh no, what have I done?* expressions on our faces. After a short trip of a mile or two, the trucks stopped in front of a huge brick building with the same open breezeway on the ground floor.

The door swung open and a DI stepped up and inside the car. "YOU GOT TEN SECONDS TO GET OFF THIS TRAILER AND NINE OF THEM ARE GONE!"

Ten bodies hit the doorway at the same time, getting nowhere fast. I waited, knowing my body weight was no match for some of the bigger, stronger recruits. As we exited, we were met by several drill sergeants shaking their heads and yelling. "YOU ARE ALL MOVING LIKE YOU'RE IN SLOW MOTION! WHAT IS WRONG WITH YOU PEOPLE? NOW GET YOUR SORRY A***S BACK ON THE TRUCK . . . AND DO IT AGAIN!"

Finally, our sadistic drill sergeants must have grown tired of their fun and told us to assemble into a formation in the airway. Other platoons were doing the exact same thing, and as we ran, drill sergeants standing in the breezeway met us and told us to go back and try again, because . . . we were too slow. While heading back I saw two recruits, running full speed, slam into each other and fully knock each other to the ground. They quickly got up as if nothing had happened and took off in different directions.

A number of us made it into the breezeway. We stood at attention, trying to make ourselves invisible. A recruit in front of me had three different DIs in front of him, all standing with their faces only inches away from his, screaming at him for something he had done, or not done, fast enough. I watched as giant beads of sweat popped out on his head. He looked terrified—and then he began to sway. Seconds later, he lost consciousness and hit the ground with a loud thud.

I thought the drill sergeants would help him up or show some level of concern. But they stood over him and debated among themselves whether they should bury him right there. My only conscious thought was to hope they would not look over to where I was standing and decide I was their next victim. Luckily, they saw something else that caught their interest and moved off in another direction.

Finally, the majority of the platoon assembled properly in formation in the breezeway. Everyone was gasping for air. The drill sergeants walked around the formation, pacing up and down between our ranks (lines). "I HAVE NEVER SEEN A GROUP MOVE SO SLOWLY. YOU HAVE TO BE THE SORRIEST, SADDEST, WORST GROUP OF RECRUITS WE HAVE EVER SEEN. YOU HAD BETTER GET YOUR A***S IN GEAR IF YOU HAVE ANY HOPE OF SURVIVING THE NEXT TEN WEEKS!"

One thing everyone quickly learned in basic: the drill sergeants owned everything that existed. It was their wall, their floor, their grass, their dirt, their air, and their sky. Later that evening as our drill sergeant, a Sergeant First Class (SFC) named Drill Sergeant Kiker, was showing us how to properly make a bed, he looked up at me leaning against a wall with my hands in my pockets.

"JUST WHO DO YOU THINK YOU ARE LEANING ON MY WALL WITH YOUR HANDS IN YOUR POCKETS? YOU THINK YOU JOINED THE AIR FORCE?"

I jerked my hands out of my pockets feeling completely embarrassed with everyone's attention on me and waiting to see what he would do next. Thankfully, it was late and he let it go.

Sometime during that initial introduction to our drill sergeants, one of them yelled at some poor recruit to "BEAT YOUR FACE, PRIVATE!"

Beat your face? I thought. *What does that mean?*

The poor guy was already a human bundle of nerves resting precariously on a bed of pins and needles and he didn't know how to respond. We all watched as he stood there, eyes darting around the room for any sign of someone to step up, rescue him, and to tell him—and everyone else—what "beat your face" meant. The moment of silence lingered long enough that it broke its own sweat . . . anticipation dripping slowly . . . only we were not the hostile witness being hammered by the prosecuting attorney in a Smokey Bear hat.

Then the recruit did what came naturally to his mind—he began slapping himself in the face.

The DI, who had been standing several feet away, took two astonishingly rapid and direct steps toward the terrified young guy from the South. "WHAT ARE YOU DOING TO YOUR UGLY FACE, PRIVATE? TRYING TO IMPROVE IT? YOU CAN'T IMPROVE UGLY! NOW HIT THE DECK AND START DOING PUSH-UPS . . . UNTIL I GET TIRED!"

The realization came like a Christmas present. *Ohhhh, I get it!* "Beat your face" was Fort Jackson's colloquial and comical way of telling us to do push-ups, and lots of them.

The amount of fear and sweat in the room was both palpable and growing more offensive with each passing moment.

"YOU GUYS ARE STINKING UP MY BARRACKS. BEAT YOUR FACES EVERY LAST ONE OF YOU FOR THE FUNKY ODOR YOU'VE ALLOWED TO PERMEATE MY BARRACKS!"

While we were still down trying our best to continue doing push-ups, he began pacing up and down the aisle way.

"EACH AND EVERY ONE OF YOU WILL TAKE A SHOWER TONIGHT. YOU WILL WASH YOUR NASTY, GOAT-SMELLING BODIES, USING SOAP—SOMETHING APPARENTLY MANY OF YOU ARE UNFAMILIAR WITH. YOU WILL FAMILIARIZE YOUR-SELVES WITH THE MIRACULOUS BENEFITS OF SHAMPOO AND SOAP. YOU WILL EACH TAKE NO MORE THAN ONE MIN-UTE IN THE SHOWER—THIS IS NOT A HOWARD JOHNSON HOTEL. IT IS NOT A BURGER KING EITHER—YOU CANNOT HAVE IT YOUR WAY!"

I would have laughed at his reference to the fast-food restaurant's pop-ular advertising slogan if I weren't so exhausted—and scared of the consequences.

"NOW, WHEN I GIVE THE COMMAND TO 'RECOVER,' YOU WILL MOVE IN AN ORDERLY FASHION TO YOUR WALL LOCKERS AND GET YOUR PERSONAL HYGIENE ITEMS. YOU WILL THEN PROCEDE INTO THE LATRINE FOR SHOWERS AND OTHER PERSONAL HYGIENE ACTIVITIES, INCLUD-ING BRUSHING YOUR TEETH AND APPLYING A GENEROUS AMOUNT OF MUCH-NEEDED DEODORANT. PERSONAL HYGIENE WILL BECOME A NEW AND GLORIOUS HABIT FOR EACH OF YOU EVERY SINGLE DAY! IS THAT UNDERSTOOD?"

"Yes, Drill Sergeant!"

"WHAT WAS THAT? THAT'S ALL YOU GOT?"

"NO, DRILL SERGEANT!" we yelled, matching his sound level.

"SOUND OFF LIKE YOU GOT A PAIR!"

"YES, DRILL SERGEANT!"

"REC—" He stopped himself from giving the command, because a few recruits began to jump up.

"WHO TOLD YOU TO MOVE? I DIDN'T SAY RECOVER. GET BACK DOWN AND EVERYONE BETTER JUST KEEP ON PUSH-ING! YOU ARE, BY FAR, THE WORST RECRUITS I HAVE EVER SEEN IN MY ENTIRE CAREER AS A DRILL SERGEANT. AT THIS RATE WE WILL BE HERE DOING PUSH-UPS ALL NIGHT!"

I didn't know anyone could yell so strongly and consistently.

My ears were ringing and my arms were doing their own brand of screaming at me. I hadn't ever done that many push-ups before—and my body didn't like it at all.

Finally, after numerous false starts and enough push-ups to make us all want to puke, we were allowed to recover!

Before lights out, Drill Sergeant Kiker read off a list of personnel who had Kitchen Police (KP) the next day. We were to awaken earlier than the rest of the platoon and report to the chow hall for the day. When he called my name with about ten others, I breathed a silent sigh of relief. I was going to miss the first full day of basic.

I volunteered to run the giant dishwasher and spent the entire day with the noise from the dishwasher, rather than a screaming drill sergeant, caressing my ears. When our shift ended, the sergeant in charge told us to go back to the drill sergeant's office and report in. The chow hall sat on the ground floor of the massive barracks complex that housed not only the four platoons from our company—Delta Company, 7th Battalion, 2nd Brigade (D-7-2)—but four other companies as well.

The walk back to our company area through the breezeway was not far. About halfway there, before rounding the final corner, we stopped as a group.

"Does anyone know how to properly report in?" I asked. Everyone shook their heads. Despite knowing we were walking into the lions' den, we formulated a plan—we would line up, single file, in front of their office door. Whoever that unlucky person was at the front of the line would convey that our group had completed KP duties—hopefully in a way that would avoid drawing any wrath. Being day 1 of basic, I could tell everyone was as nervous as I was. We knew we were way out of our element, but what choice did we have?

The office door had a large windowpane that provided an obstructed view into their office. From outside we could see them sitting at their desks, feet up, smoking, while talking and laughing together.

We randomly formed a line in front of the door. The unlucky first recruit swallowed his fear and looked back at us. "Here goes nothing," he said. His knock instantly stopped their animated conversation inside.

"ENTER!"

He stepped through the door, which automatically closed behind him. We could see him perfectly through the glass, but we could not hear what was said. Suddenly, he was down on his chest, then on his back, then he was doing push-ups, then running in place, followed by down on his chest and on his back repeatedly.

We couldn't help but laugh among ourselves at his predicament. Until, that is, the door opened and the recruit, now sweaty and out of breath, came out. Before he could tell us anything, one of the DIs yelled, "NEXT!"

One by one each recruit went in, endured an almost-identical aerobic abuse, and emerged a heaving mass of sweat. We asked each one what they said, and with info from each victim, we formulated what the next recruit should say. I was moving closer and closer to my turn in the torture chamber. We could see the DIs were relishing each recruit's fruitless attempt to report.

One recruit got worked over much more than the rest. When he finally came out, we asked why he was in there so long.

"I called our drill sergeant 'Drill Sergeant Kicker,' and he went nuts on me! He yelled, 'It's pronounced like hiker with a *k*!' He made me do all those exercises while telling me over and over, IT'S NOT KICKER, IT'S KIKER, YOU THINK YOU CAN REMEMBER THAT, PRIVATE?"

We couldn't help ourselves, we all burst out laughing. I was finally next in line when Drill Sergeant Kiker with a "K" emerged. "GET UP TO THE PLATOON BAY AND GET READY FOR LIGHTS OUT!"

"Yes, Drill Sergeant!" Wanting nothing more than to escape from the lion's den, we took off racing each other back to the barracks. Inside, everyone was busy showering and getting ready for lights out. I was eager to know how the first day had played out.

"So what happened today?" I asked the recruit bunking next to me.

"We marched to a nearby parking lot and spent the entire day doing push-ups, squat-thrusts, and flutter-kicks because nobody could stay in step while we marched up and down the length of the parking lot."

"What are squat-thrusts and flutter-kicks?" I asked.

"Oh, don't worry, you'll find out."

That's what I'm afraid of, I thought as I rolled over on my bed and fell asleep.

CHAPTER 3

What Makes a Soldier a Soldier

The next day, I was introduced to squat-thrusts and flutter-kicks, both of which were used when we had performed so many push-ups nobody had any arm strength left. They were all equally torturesome. Squat-thrusts are the motion of squatting down until your palms touch the ground, thrusting your legs back—now you're in the push-up position—and then immediately bringing your legs back up under, now squatting again, followed by standing back up. Flutter-kicks are nothing more than crunches performed while on your back with your legs elevated, feet moving up and down in a scissor motion. The torture was remaining in that position until everyone's feet were off the ground. Moans and groans were common.

After breakfast and barracks cleanup that first Sunday, Drill Sergeant Kiker asked the platoon if any of us wanted to attend church services. Nearly every hand went up. "OH, YOU ALL NEED JESUS NOW, HUH?" That church service was the most peaceful hour any of us had experienced in what seemed like years. I'd never seen so many heads bowed down—including my own—in silent contemplation.

Those first couple of weeks, we marched to a large parking lot where we learned drill and ceremony. Over and over we practiced how to properly assume the different positions, including attention, saluting, and parade-rest, facing movements—pivoting to the right or left from the position of attention—and marching as a platoon. Doing all these things in unison was an exercise in sweat and pain, with an added measure of Drill Sergeants Brown and Kiker's nose-to-nose "encouragement" providing motivation sautéed in adrenaline. Drill and ceremony were the logical places to start, as they were our introduction to hearing commands and executing movements, some more complex, with timing and precision.

It was not pretty at first. However hard we tried to execute movements in unison, someone in the platoon always seemed to mistake their right from their left, or vice versa.

"NO, NO, NO, NOT THAT LEFT! YOUR MILITARY LEFT!" There was no hiding when practicing a movement to the left or right when one or more in the formation mistakenly turned the wrong direction.

"YOU *DO* KNOW YOUR LEFT FROM YOUR RIGHT, DON'T YOU?"

"Yes, Drill Sergeant!"

"WELL, HOPEFULLY THIS WILL REMIND YOU. FRONT LEANING REST POSITION, MOVE!" Some days we spent more time in the front-leaning-rest position—a fancy term for the push-up position—than actually doing drill and ceremony.

While marching, some recruits bobbed their heads up and down drawing immediate attention from our drill sergeants, who had a field day screaming at us. "WHO'S BOBBING UP AND DOWN IN MY FORMATION? YOU ARE NOT BACK HOME ON THE BLOCK!"

Drill Sergeant Kiker had a habit of asking recruits, "WHY DID YOU JOIN THIS MAN'S ARMY? YOUR MOMMA DON'T LOVE YOU ANYMORE?" or "WHAT IS YOUR MAJOR MALFUNCTION?"

Each movement or maneuver was preceded by a block of instruction, describing step-by-step—referred to as "by the numbers," followed by actual demonstrations. The drill sergeants were seasoned soldiers who made it look easy, providing an example of how movements were supposed to look when performed correctly. During the hours we spent practicing, we made so many mistakes that eventually—sweaty and exhausted from hours of punishment for the mistakes of a few individuals—tempers began to boil over. Following an exhaustive time doing push-ups, or some other equally painful exercise, we were given another opportunity to "get it right." Back down doing push-ups again for yet another recruit's mistake, someone would start by muttering a comment. But then the longer the time went when we were still paying for somebody's mistakes, the mutters escalated. "C'mon, dude, get your s*** together!" The dynamic within the platoon created a tangible, performance-based pressure-cooker.

The tension level was unlike anything I'd ever felt before. And we *all* felt it. I may have been young and naïve, but there was no mistaking the deeper lessons we were being taught. They were breaking us down in order to rebuild us into a cohesive team. The tension gave me ample motivation to make sure I was not the one causing everyone to suffer for my mistakes. Unfortunately, certain recruits seemed incapable of avoiding the unwanted attention their mistakes brought, no matter what we were doing. From then on, they suffered under a near-constant scrutiny from our drill sergeants. It took great effort to remove yourself from their crosshairs once you were in them. Near the middle of basic, I knew I had been successful at blending in and remaining anonymous when Drill Sergeant Brown looked at me one day and said, "Jones? Where have you been hiding all this time?" My answer, "Doing what I'm supposed to, Drill Sergeant!"

Ultimately, all the pain and suffering bore fruit. As a platoon, we began to move in unison from one movement to the next. Crisply snapping each movement when commanded by our drill sergeants, "PRESENT ARMS." Saluting. "ORDER ARMS." Bringing the right saluting arm back down. "PARADE REST. RIGHT/LEFT FACE. FORWARD MARCH!" We began to look impressive as we performed complex movements in unison, executing each one with sharpness and precision.

While marching, either Drill Sergeant Brown or Kiker called cadences that the platoon repeated as a way to keep everyone in step with one another. Singing cadences at the top of our lungs became a source of competition between platoons as we frequently passed each other marching from place to place. Some cadences were clever, some patriotic, and some crude, though nobody seemed to mind. I began to feel a level of pride I had never felt before as I joined in and sang,

MAMA, MAMA, CAN'T YOU SEE . . .
WHAT THE ARMY'S DONE TO ME!
THEY TOOK AWAY MY FADED JEANS
GOT ME WEARING ARMY GREENS!"
THEY TOOK AWAY MY CADILLAC
GOT ME PACKING ON MY BACK!

We were transforming into a unit with a singular purpose. A platoon whose potential was growing bigger than the sum of its individual parts.

After eight to ten days of actual basic, and much to our surprise, our drill sergeants informed us that training was shutting down for Christmas. *Christmas exodus* was the term they used and they told us, "You don't want to be here."

Before arriving I figured basic would continue through Christmas. From the looks on everyone else's faces, they thought the same. I relished the thought of going home—real food, a good bed, sleeping in, privacy in the shower. But I didn't have enough money to get from South Carolina to Oregon—especially on such short notice. Airfares during Christmas would be way too much for me to afford. But I knew I couldn't stay on post.

When we arrived, we'd received a partial paycheck, but even that wasn't enough to cover the airfare. Some guys mentioned taking a bus. The bus fare was more in my price range, but it meant that the first three days of my time off would be spent riding a bus across the country.

I hopped on one of the buses heading west, which contained only fellow recruits, mostly from Delta Company, and many from (my) 3rd Platoon.

Before we left, Drill Sergeants Kiker and Brown were adamant that we remain in our Class-A uniforms the entire time in transit. It took only a few hours, and a pep talk from an understanding bus driver, to convince us that no drill sergeants were hiding in the bus's cargo hold, waiting to climb up from below and torture us for not obeying orders. One gutsy recruit finally made his way to the small bathroom at the back of the bus, and after a few minutes, a smiling civilian emerged. The rest of us looked left, then right, then with the coast clear, we grabbed our backpacks and headed toward the back to see how quickly we could follow Clark Kent's example, only narrowly avoiding another incident like the one getting off the cattle trailer during that initial drill sergeant encounter.

Just before leaving Fort Jackson, I purchased a Walkman from the Fort Jackson post exchange. Having left all my cassette tapes back home in Oregon, I purchased one cassette along with the Walkman—U2's *Unforgettable Fire*.

With nothing to do but listen to the music and stare out at the landscape for hours on end, I found myself transfixed by America's beauty. This was the first time I listened to an album repeatedly until I became familiar with each song. The lyrics of "Pride (In the Name of Love)" struck me as particularly poignant while crossing Georgia and passing the majestic oak trees there: "In the name of love, what more in the name of love?"

I was crossing through the exact area where Martin Luther King Jr. was born and raised, listening to a song written by an Irishman, feeling inspired by his life and sacrifice, to pen the lyrics to a song about one of America's greatest treasures. On and on I listened as the message from the lyrics and songs hit me like a sledgehammer. I stared, transfixed by the beauty of the rolling countryside throughout the southeastern states. I loved this country. And now as a soldier, I was offering myself to serve her with everything I had.

The comforts of home, family, and friends were a double-edged sword for me. I thoroughly enjoyed relaxing whenever and wherever I felt like it, but I could not shake the nagging thought of the trouble that awaited me having to return and finish the majority of basic.

With only a couple days remaining before boarding another bus for three days, my family pitched in and purchased a one-way flight back to South Carolina. I could not have felt more grateful for the extra time.

The day of my flight, I debated whether to board wearing my Class-A's. I rationalized that I could just change in the airport bathroom once we landed in Columbia. I was about to pack my uniform into my suitcase, when the thought occurred to me, *What would I do if my luggage is lost, or is delayed during the layover in Chicago?* Knowing that wasn't a chance I wanted to take, I donned my uniform and headed for the airport.

I was grateful I listened to my conscience. Walking off the plane in Columbia, I was stunned to see several uniformed drill sergeants waiting as we walked through the doorway into the terminal.

"Move out to that area and take a seat," one of them said, looking at me and pointing to a section of seats where a few other recruits, all in the Class-A's, were seated.

Behind me, several recruits emerged into a full-blown firestorm. Their shaved heads were a dead giveaway. The drill sergeants were in full attack mode. "ARE YOU RETURNING TO BASIC TRAINING?"

The look of shock on their faces indicated they were.

"WERE YOU, OR WERE YOU NOT, INSTRUCTED TO TRAVEL IN YOUR CLASS-A UNIFORM?"

None of them could formulate an answer other than, "Yes, Drill Sergeant."

One drill sergeant peeled off from the others and practically marched them over to where a few of us were sitting.

The drill sergeant pulled out a clipboard he was carrying and pen at the ready. "WHAT'S YOUR NAME? WHO IS YOUR DRILL SERGEANT? WHAT COMPANY ARE YOU IN?" Finally, after he'd gathered the information, he pointed to the chairs. "SIT HERE, AND

DON'T MOVE FROM THESE SEATS. DO YOU UNDERSTAND ME, PRIVATE?"

"Yes, Drill Sergeant."

The recruits could not hide the acute regret they were feeling. I could not help thinking, *That could've been me.* The section began to fill; a mixture of recruits in uniform, grateful they'd followed directions, and a handful of sad, dejected-looking recruits dreading the trouble and additional punishment that awaited them. Looking around, I had that giant knot in the pit of my stomach as I thought, *I would've rather never left than have to return knowing what I was walking into.*

That night's sleep was like that first night in the reception-and-processing barracks. Not good. The next morning at 0430 the lights came on in the barracks and in walked both Drill Sergeants Kiker and Brown.

"WELCOME BACK, LADIES! JUST ROLL ON OUT OF BED AND BEAT YOUR FACE UNTIL WE GET TIRED! DID ANY OF YOU MISS US?"

"Yes, Drill Sergeant."

"YOU THINK THAT WEAK ANSWER IS GOING TO WORK?"

"NO, DRILL SERGEANT!"

"I THINK WE MAY HAVE TO DRUG TEST EACH AND EVERY ONE OF YOU! I THINK ALL THE PARTYING AND DOPE SMOKING HAS AFFECTED THE MOTIVATION LEVEL YOU HAD BEFORE YOU LEFT! WHO'S MOTIVATED?"

"WE ARE, DRILL SERGEANT!"

"SOUND OFF LIKE YOU GOT A PAIR! I DON'T KNOW, DRILL SERGEANT BROWN, BUT I THINK WE ARE GONNA HAVE TO START AGAIN FROM SQUARE ONE!"

I knew I should have continued doing push-ups, flutter-kicks, and squat-thrusts while I was home. I ran a couple miles on the beach at the Oregon coast once, and my muscles screamed at me for not doing more.

Thanks to our drill sergeants' determination, we quickly got back into the swing of things at basic training and soon we had moved on to phase 2, which was Basic Rifle Marksmanship (BRM). Nearly all of us were giddy to get our hands on our first weapon, the M-16A1 rifle. The M16A1 5.56mm rifle was a lightweight, air-cooled, gas-operated, magazine-fed, shoulder- or hip-fired weapon designed for either automatic fire or semiautomatic fire (single shot) by using a selector lever. The army now issues soldiers the M-16A2, which when fired on automatic fires a three-round burst.

Finally being issued a weapon, and the opportunity to learn its components and functioning, was the unspoken turning point in going from being a civilian to becoming a soldier. At least in my young mind, this was the mental concept of what makes a soldier a soldier.

The process of drill and ceremony had instilled in us the absolute necessity for timely and precise execution to commands, as a precursor to the training and use of the very first weapon many of us ever handled, let alone used as a means to defend something. In addition, drill and ceremony was based on the cumulative efforts of the entire platoon functioning as a unit. Before moving on to BRM, we were paired up with another recruit identified as a battle-buddy. How Raymundo Martinez became my battle-buddy was pure coincidence due to standing next to each other in formation that day. I had only really noticed him since his bunk was directly across the aisle from mine and we hadn't really ever talked that much. But I couldn't have asked for a better battle-buddy and friend. Ray was from a small town on the outskirts of San Antonio, and he had a heart and sense of humor as big as the state of Texas. He was shorter than I was, but I could tell by his already stocky build that he'd grown up working hard.

My battle buddy Ray Martinez and I

Many times, when I was physically spent and ready to give up, Ray would look over and say, "C'mon, dude, keep going. You can do it." Even though I could see how much he was also straining to continue, he would say something encouraging and grin, which always helped me dig deep for the determination to continue. Having Ray as my battle-buddy, with his easygoing demeanor and hilarious sense of humor, got me through the early days, which were physically and mentally hard for me. It wasn't that I was out of shape, it was simply that I did not have the physical stamina the others seemed to have. Watching Ray taught me that no matter what, we could always smile and never give up.

The first block of instruction on the M-16 was how to disassemble and reassemble the weapon. Next we were taught the purpose and use of the front and rear sight apertures, including proper sighting, trigger squeeze, and breathing discipline.

The classes and practice finally led up to us firing our weapons on a range, which for me, was beyond exciting. To get to the ranges, we would either ride in the cattle cars or march. It was winter in South Carolina, which meant the weather could be bitterly cold one day and warm the next. That made it tricky to try to predict how to properly layer our clothing.

I never did find a balance with clothing layers that kept me warm without making me sweat too much. I either layered too heavy or not enough. Mostly, I just froze. I had very low body fat, which meant once I got cold, I stayed cold. The only thing that warmed me up again was a hot shower.

Despite constantly freezing, I still couldn't wait to get out onto a rifle range and practice marksmanship. I couldn't get enough of lining up on the firing line and attempting to hit forty out of forty pop-up targets. Each time, I was beyond giddy when I heard my lane score announced over the range loudspeaker, "Lane 7 . . . thirty-six out of forty" or "Lane 11 . . . thirty-eight out of forty." Sometimes I was disappointed when I scored only in the low thirties, but I knew I always had another chance to improve the next go around.

The day for M-16 weapon qualification finally arrived. The excitement and adrenaline were tangible. As my heart pounded and my breathing quickened, I fired and qualified expert my first attempt, which allowed me to spend some much-needed time in the warm-up tent.

I could tell I was putting on weight as I progressed through basic. I ended up having to get a completely new set of camouflage clothing. I was certainly getting stronger with all the push-ups and other exercises required each day.

Six weeks into basic we reached the final phase, which consisted of practicing thirty-one common tasks until we could execute each one to standard. The tasks included a proficiency in handling first aid, in which we had to apply a pressure dressing, treat for shock, splint a limb, and apply a tourniquet. For our weapons, we had to clear a jammed M-16, employ a fragmentation grenade to take out enemy position, and a host of other tasks we had to master in order to graduate. Each of us was issued a "smart-book" we were required to carry with us at all times. It was a bible of sorts, with instructions and drawings we were encouraged to study during downtime between training events.

After many hours and days of practicing each task, we were able to execute most with minimal errors—even with the added stress of the all-seeing eyes of a drill sergeant as he hovered close by. Punishment, usually in the form of push-ups, gave us the motivation to perform each task mistake-free. When we satisfactorily accomplished a task, we received a verbal "GO!" from a drill sergeant, as opposed to, "PRIVATE, YOU ARE A NO-GO AT THIS STATION. NOW WHAT IS YOUR MAJOR MALFUNCTION?"

"I don't know, Drill Sergeant."

"YOU DON'T KNOW. WELL, ALLOW ME TO HELP YOU FIGURE THAT OUT AND IMPROVE YOUR MOTIVATION. DO YOU KNOW HOW I'M GOING TO DO THAT, PRIVATE?"

"Yes, Drill Sergeant, by having me beat my face."

"WELL . . . IF YOU'RE NOT A HIGHLY INTELLIGENT INDIVIDUAL, PRIVATE. YOU ARE ABSOLUTELY RIGHT, SO GO AHEAD AND GET ON DOWN WITH YOUR HIGHLY INTELLIGENT SELF AND BEAT YOUR FACE FOR BEING SO SMART!"

Some lessons hit home as I watched mistakes fellow recruits made and the suffering that followed. One time we marched to a training area where stations were set up that allowed us to practice numerous tasks in cold and overcast conditions. I liked this particular training setup since we could practice, repeatedly, those tasks we struggled to perform to standard. One of the more complex and time-consuming tasks was to employ an M18-A1 Claymore mine. Claymores are used to reinforce a perimeter surrounding a fighting position or a larger operational area. The Claymore is a directional anti-personnel mine that fires seven hundred steel balls embedded in a layer of composition (C-4) explosive, initiated by a handheld electronic blasting cap. Used extensively in Vietnam, it proved effective when the enemy drew near, or were about to overrun a position. Proper setup, aiming, and detonation are critical.

The beginning of our task included inventorying a bandoleer containing the mine and all necessary accessories, before performing a circuit test using the wiring, blasting cap, and firing device. After completing the circuit test, all accessories were reloaded into the bandoleers, which were then carried—along with our weapons slung across our backs—as we low-crawled on our stomachs ten to fifteen yards to the spot where we emplaced the mine.

Waiting behind a wall of sandbags, we watched as Private Ratliff low-crawled to the designated spot. His M-16 was slung across his back by a nylon sling. Just before he began removing the contents of the bandoleer, he grabbed his M16 and slid the sling up and over his head.

Why is he doing that? I wondered. Private Ratliff then committed the most egregious, offensive sin one could commit in all of basic. He placed his weapon on the ground next to him.

The sin, drilled into us until we were blue: "YOU WILL MAINTAIN PHYSICAL POSSESSION OF YOUR ASSIGNED WEAPON AT ALL TIMES. THIS MEANS YOU CARRY IT IN YOUR HANDS OR SLING IT ACROSS YOUR BACK. YOU NEVER, EVER PUT YOUR WEAPON DOWN!"

With Drill Sergeant Town next to us, there was no way we could warn him of the imminent tornado headed his way. With a long blade of grass hanging from his mouth, Town looked down at his feet and slowly shook his head back and forth. For a moment, he seemed to be contemplating his next move rather than jumping up immediately as we expected him to do. Drill sergeants, having seen it all, are usually very quick when they see something that needs correcting, and which they can administer with their own brand of humorous dialogue (yelling) while they "smoke" a recruit. This time Town's reaction seemed to be in slow motion.

Private Ratliff was too busy aiming the mine to notice when Town slowly stood, quietly walked over, and loomed over him. Ratliff immediately noticed the shadow covering the sun from his view. He must have sensed his imminent demise, because he immediately tried reaching for his weapon. Town beat him to it, snatching it up by the barrel. Without a word, Town spun a full 360 degrees like an Olympic discus thrower and hurled the weapon spinning in the air like a helicopter blade. It was an impressive distance worthy of a medal. We looked at each other surprised that an M-16 could fly that far. Then he turned his attention back to Ratliff. "NOW, LOW-CRAWL OVER THERE AND BRING IT BACK!"

Ratliff spent the remainder of the morning crawling on his stomach—leaving a long and winding snail trail in his wake—until he finally reached his weapon. He rested for a few moments before crawling all the way back to where Town was waiting. But Town wasn't finished with him yet. While Ratliff was busy low-crawling and keeping his head down, a drill sergeant walked over, picked up the weapon, and removed the bolt. He then disassembled it into pieces, giving each piece to a different drill sergeant. Ratliff, exhausted from the long journey, stood while Town looked him up and down. "PRIVATE, PERFORM A PROPER FUNCTION CHECK ON YOUR WEAPON!" (The purpose of a function check is to confirm the weapon is operational. A step-by-step procedure, vital to being a soldier.)

Fortunately, for him he quickly recognized a problem. "Drill Sergeant, my weapon is malfunctioning."

"WHY IS YOUR WEAPON MALFUNCTIONING, PRIVATE?"

"Uh, I think the bolt is missing, Drill Sergeant."

"ARE YOU ABSOLUTELY SURE, PRIVATE?"

"Yes, Drill Sergeant."

"WELL, YOU MIGHT WANT TO CHECK WITH ALL THE OTHER DRILL SERGEANTS OUT HERE TODAY AND SEE IF THEY KNOW WHERE YOUR MISSING BOLT COULD BE!"

He spent the next hour going from one drill sergeant to the next, doing push-ups, squat-thrusts, and flutter-kicks before they would give him the single pieces they had in their pockets.

He was finally able to piece together the bolt to complete the function check.

"ARE YOU EVER GOING TO LEAVE YOUR WEAPON UNSE-CURED AGAIN, PRIVATE?"

"No, Drill Sergeant."

"BECAUSE IF I FIND YOUR WEAPON UNSECURED LIKE THAT AGAIN, I WILL SEND THAT BAD BOY TO THE MOON .. . AND YOU WILL LOW-CRAWL TO THE MOON AND BACK TO GET IT . . . DO YOU UNDERSTAND ME, PRIVATE?"

Much of the physical conditioning during basic prepared us for a twenty-mile road (ruck) march. A ruck march was marching single file with a full complement of gear, which included our web belt with full canteen, our rucksack—military backpack—loaded with fifteen to twenty pounds of gear, our helmet (called a steel pot—this was before Kevlar helmets), and finally our individual weapon, which we carried in our hands. The morning of the road march dawned cold and rainy. Even though we had ponchos to cover us from the rain, I knew once we started down the shoulder of the road I was in for a long, cold, shivering day. We were in two long columns, one on each side of the road. I was on the right somewhere in the middle of the line. By the time those in front of me trampled on the rain-soaked dirt shoulder, it was already a sloshy mud soup for my footsteps. My feet were soaked and freezing, like walking on two blocks of ice.

Basic was the crucible that tested our ability to withstand physical and verbal abuse, designed to push recruits to the breaking point and then some. One day I learned the hard way how much a person could physically do with the proper motivation and fear.

Rounding a corner with several other recruits, we practically ran over Ratliff who was being punished for something. A puddle of sweat was on the floor below him. We laughed just as Drill Sergeant Brown stepped from behind a pillar.

"OH, I KNOW YOU'RE NOT LAUGHING AT HIM, BECAUSE THAT WOULD MEAN YOU WANT TO TAKE HIS PLACE!" He had us line up and he continued as he paced back and forth in front of us. "YOU THINK IT'S OKAY TO LAUGH AT SOMEONE WHEN THEY'RE GETTING SMOKED?" Then he ordered us to attention with our arms extended in front of us. He grabbed our weapons and placed them on top of our extended arms.

As we stood for long, aching minutes, he spoke of how much he disliked unmotivated soldiers, how we had within us the ability to choose whether or not we would make our time in the army successful, and the key to that success was to be motivated. "I KNOW YOU'RE NOT THINKING OF GIVING UP AND LETTING YOUR WEAPONS FALL TO THE GROUND. DON'T YOU EVEN THINK ABOUT LETTING THAT HAPPEN. KEEP THOSE ARMS UP. RAISE 'EM UP! KEEP 'EM UP!"

To add more misery, he had other recruits who were standing nearby place their weapons on our trembling arms.

"DON'T YOU GIVE UP ON ME. YOU NEED TO SHOW ME WHAT YOU'RE MADE OF. SHOW ME WHAT MOTIVATED SOLDIERS CAN DO!"

My face felt fiery as I groaned and strained with every ounce of strength I never knew I had in me.

Finally, after what seemed like an eternity, he let us place the weapons on the ground. He continued to pace back and forth. "YOU DIDN'T THINK YOU COULD HOLD THOSE WEAPONS UP THAT LONG, NOW DID YOU?"

In unison, we shook our heads. "No, Drill Sergeant!"

"DON'T YOU EVER FORGET THIS. EACH ONE OF YOU HAS THE ABILITY TO ACCOMPLISH WHAT SEEMS IMPOSSIBLE WHEN YOU CHOOSE TO BE MOTIVATED. IT'S A SIMPLE CHOICE TO MAKE EVERY DAY COUNT BY BEING A MOTIVATED SOLDIER!"

As we made our way back to the squad bay, we all looked at each other, dumbfounded over what we had just endured. It was brutal what I'd gone through, but I knew that drill sergeant was right. And I knew his was a lesson I would never forget. He instilled pain in me—but he also instilled a belief that I could do more than I expected of myself. I could be pushed or I could choose to push myself beyond any mental or physical limit. It was my choice.

Basic training resulted in tremendous physical changes in pretty much everyone. Those who showed up overweight graduated with a completely new self-image—that of the fit person they probably always wanted to be. Like me, those who showed up skinny and weak developed muscles from endless push-ups, flutter-kicks, and whatever else the drill sergeants could dream up.

One highlight for me came in our final basic weeks. It was a warm sunny day and we were in an unfamiliar training area forested with tall pine trees reminiscent of home. Teamed up with our battle-buddy, we were being tested on a combat tactic made famous during WWII, and executed to near perfection by members of Easy Company 506st Para- chute Infantry Regiment following the D-Day invasion. The boys from Easy Company executed a textbook assault on an enemy-fixed position by a numerically inferior force. The Brecourt Manor Assault has provided, for generations of soldiers that followed, an invaluable model to emulate. The objective is to move with speed, using covering fire on an enemy position, allowing you and your buddy short leap-frog-type bursts of speed, until you arrive close enough to disable the machine gun nest with a grenade.

Before beginning the assault, Ray and I were briefed using a terrain map showing where the enemy machine-gun bunker was located just beyond the tree line. Verbal communication and hand signals for when Ray would move under the covering fire I provided, and then he would do the same for me, were paramount to our ability to safely maneuver toward the objective. Drill sergeants with whistles paced along the route approaching the bunker. Their all-seeing eyes watched our every move, making sure we signaled and put necessary covering fire on the bunker, before, during, and after our buddy moved from one position of cover—behind a tree or mound—to the next.

As we stood on the ready line for our turn, I could feel the adrenaline surge coming on like a hurricane. Ray and I knew the bigger the burst of speed moving from cover to cover, followed by diving headfirst like a baseball player sliding into home plate behind the next covered position, the better. Our training taught us that slowing down when moving under fire could be fatal. Our momentum and speed were a serious force to overcome once we arrived at the next position. The way to overcome that force was by thrusting the butt of our M-16 into the ground to help absorb some of the energy from such a sudden stop. Our drill sergeants demanded a fully committed headfirst power slide when it came to hitting the ground. The mantra was: *I'm up, I'm moving—the enemy can see me. I'm down, he missed.*

We were purposefully kept away from this particular training area, so we were seeing the terrain features and bunker approach possibilities for the first time. The noise coming from the bunker was the unmistakable sound of a machine gun screaming as it poured rounds down range. The deafening noise simulated the total chaos and sensory bombardment of combat. It sounded as if there were two machine guns blasting. The bunker sat low to the ground with an earth-and-shrub covering. It was barely noticeable among the surrounding terrain features. Low and long slit-like openings running along three sides gave the enemy a wide field of view. It was easy to see how someone, not completely alert when approaching, could easily overlook it.

With Ray, I knew we had a decent chance at executing the assault error-free. We were in sync during our practice runs. The armorer walked over with two fully loaded thirty-round clips, one for each of us. We function-checked our weapons, then loaded the magazine. It was game time.

Ray looked at me. "C'mon, brother, let's do this."

We gave each other one final high-five then took up our starting positions, about ten meters between us. Facing us, about ten yards back, stood Drill Sergeant Welcome, leaning forward with his hands on his knees.

Beyond I could see Drill Sergeant Kiker pacing up and down, flanking my side of the approach, and Drill Sergeant Brown flanking Ray's side.

Drill Sergeant Kiker moved into position. "SHOW US WHAT YOU CAN DO, JONES!"

I looked at Ray. "BUDDY READY?"

"READY!"

"MOVING" I jumped up, just as Ray began firing on the bunker from his position, and sprinted as fast as I could, zig-zagging around and over low bushes and dead wood. The position of cover I was aiming for was behind a large pine tree, hoping the pine needles mixed with tree bark and dirt would provide some cushion. I figured if I dove for the base of the tree like a running back diving for the end zone from three yards out, there would be no doubting my commitment level. Pine needles, dirt, and bark flew as my body came crashing down at the base of the tree. I slid farther than I intended, but not far enough to expose myself to the bunker's field of view.

Drill Sergeant Kiker positioned himself just beyond the tree, like an umpire bent at the waist and ready to make the close call at home plate. Was I safe or out? I immediately scrambled to put myself in position to put covering fire on the bunker for Ray. Only then did I look up through a cloud of dust at Kiker grinning, "Nice landing, Jones." Delivered in a *normal tone.*

From Ray, "BUDDY READY?"

"READY!"

"MOVING!"

I was already heaving for air when I began squeezing the trigger, giving Ray the same protective fire he gave me. I timed each shot between gulps of air. I heard Ray approaching like a freight train. With gusto, he dove and hit the ground, throwing up a wave of debris followed by an impressive cloud.

I hope my wave of debris and dust cloud was as cool as that, I thought.

One other thought raced through my mind: *This is absolutely the most exciting, adrenaline-soaked thing I've ever done. What an incredible rush— providing covering fire to keep my buddy alive, and he's doing the same for me.*

With our drill sergeants tracking us, Ray and I made the next several three-to-five-second rushes, putting us into position to finally assault the bunker. It was my job to deliver the final blow, eliminating the enemy and silencing their machine gun. Ray was covering me from the far side of the bunker, I just had to get around to that side as quickly as possible.

The noise from the machine gun was even louder being this close, but it meant that I didn't have to worry too much about the sound of my footsteps and heavy breathing. I instinctively stayed low as I ran as fast as I could around the backside, where I slowed and dropped to my knees and into a low-crawl position. I had a good angle on the opening behind some low foliage, but I still needed to get closer to insure my one grenade went through the opening and didn't ricochet off, leaving us to take the brunt of the blast.

I glanced at Ray. He nodded, willing me to go for it. I waited for a burst of fire from the machine gun only a few yards away. On the next burst I quickly crawled until I was perpendicular to the opening. I had to demonstrate for our drill sergeants standing close by that I knew how to properly handle and throw a grenade. If I fumbled with it, or didn't extend my arm once I pulled the pin, it was game over, and after getting this close, I couldn't let that happen to Ray and me. I pulled the pin, extended my arm, and rolling to my left, I lobbed the grenade. It sailed right through the opening. A direct kill shot.

Drill Sergeant Kiker blew his whistle. "JONES, YOU AND MARTI-NEZ . . . ARE A GO AT THIS STATION!"

Ray and I jumped up and yelled, "YEEEEEAAAAAAHHHHH!" We threw our arms around each other as if we'd just won the Super Bowl. All those days training in the cold and rainy weather, mud soaked and freezing, had paid off. I was so happy I could feel myself getting emotional. It seemed natural, but I didn't want either drill sergeant to see what I was fighting to hide. I put my arm around Ray, and together we walked off, side by side, on a cloud of satisfaction and adrenaline.

Completing basic training was a major accomplishment in my young life. I was proud of all the hard work and sweat I had endured during those formidable months in South Carolina. Through it all, I knew I was taking with me an important life lesson: that despite reaching my limits, mostly physically, I could *never give up.* It isn't the biggest or the most physically talented who claim the privilege of graduating, it's the ones who may not look physically like a soldier but who absolutely refused to quit or give up long after they had reached their limitations.

The night before graduation, we received back our civilian clothes. For the first time in ten weeks, I put on a pair of Levi's that were now way tighter. Even my T-shirt seemed to stretch over my upper body. I stepped on a scale and weighed 145 pounds. Having arrived at the post weighing barely 120 pounds, I felt transformed. The transformation was even evident in Rich Nelson who, despite all his efforts to convince anyone who would listen that he shouldn't be there, ended up sticking it out and graduating after all.

Graduating was a proud and emotional, albeit solitary, experience for me. Nobody from my family was able to make the trip. Marching across the parade field that day, though, I never felt more confident in who I was: Private Bradley Jones. Citizen . . . defender . . . soldier. It connected the dots from who I had been to who I had become.

CHAPTER 4

Training for My New Life

My buddy Ray and I stood in the breezeway saying our good-byes. "I won't miss this place," Ray said and nodded around him. "LET'S GO, LET'S GO, LET'S GO!" he said in his best drill sergeant voice.

We laughed. The breezeway was where things reached a delirious fever pitch during that first day of basic, coming face to face with our drill sergeants. We landed here after that ride over in the cattle cars. We were scared silent before holy hell broke loose. Holy, because it was a "Come to Jesus" moment for many of us, and hell because it had been the scariest experience of my life.

"Yeah, but we survived it, didn't we?" I said and playfully punched his shoulder.

We laughed again and then looked away from each other. This was harder than I expected. We had both received our assignments and this was where our time together was coming to an end. Ray's assigned unit was only a few blocks from where we were standing. His unit trained soldiers in the supply and admin MOS's (Military Occupational Specialty).

He pulled out a piece of paper from his pocket and handed it to me. His new address was written on it. "Write me, and I'll write you back," he said. "Let's keep in touch, dude—I mean, buddy."

"Thanks for being funny when I wanted to give up," I told him. "Your humor got me through some challenging moments."

"You bet. I hope to see you again sometime down the road. You're always welcome at my family's ranch in Texas."

We hugged, and I felt as though I was leaving my own brother behind. We'd experienced a lifetime in only ten weeks. I wished we could have continued as battle-buddies during this next phase.

If I ever find myself fighting in a war, I would want Ray by my side.

Out on the street an army of Greyhound buses sat idling. Most of us were heading to other bases.

The radar repairer MOS I signed up for fell under the aviation branch, headquartered at Fort Rucker, Alabama, but the training was at Fort Gordon, Georgia, home of the Signal Corps, a mere seventy miles away. Signal (communications) operations and training focuses on operating and maintaining tactical and strategic transmission and switching equipment, network control facilities, single and multichannel high-frequency radio systems, and maintenance of tactical and defense satellite communication systems. I was scheduled to spend the next twenty-two weeks training. Though I was glad to start my next phase of military service, I dreaded having to start again. With life in the army, from one day to the next, our locations and circumstances can change completely, leaving behind experiences and people only photos and memory bring to life. And that's where I found myself as I gave Ray a last look and then stepped onto my bus.

The ride to my new "home" was subdued as I stared out the window at the passing landscape, deep in my thoughts. I wondered what training, platoon, and barracks life would be like in this next phase? I also wondered how I would be treated, now that I was considered a soldier?

Pulling into Fort Gordon, the bus slowly made its way to a large parking lot with a sign that said "Reception and Processing Area." I grabbed my bags and joined a couple hundred brand-new soldiers decked out in our dress green Class-A uniforms and spit-shined shoes, fresh from the ultra-controlling environment of basic training. Those first few minutes with this new group were a shock—albeit a good one—to my senses. The first being that no one met us and yelled, "FORM UP!" or "MAKE A LINE!"

It was Saturday, and the soldiers who seemed to be in charge led us to familiar-looking barracks, designated as transient quarters by a sign out front. These leaders actually *spoke* to us, instead of screaming. "You will stay here until Monday when you will move to your assigned units based on the particular training you signed up for," the soldier told my group. I felt inclined to stick with soldiers from my platoon, not wanting to separate from familiar faces.

A group of us grabbed our gear and set up in empty eight-man rooms next to each other. Unpacking our personal items, I noticed the soldiers who led us to the barracks and rooms did not stick around. No one was hovering close by, and we were suddenly and unexpectedly on our own. I felt a level of freedom that seemed unfamiliar and unpredictable, which made me wary that the honeymoon could suddenly end at any moment.

We were politely instructed—politeness seemed almost foreign—to remain in the area around the barracks where we could change out of our Class A's and into our camouflage Battle Dress Uniforms (BDUs). We wasted no time changing into the clothing we had spent ten weeks growing accustomed to.

After changing, we returned to the area outside the barracks. I looked west down the sidewalk where several rows of barracks stretched as far as I could see.

Within the walls of the brick city Fort Gordon, Georgia 1985

Directly across from us, in an open third-floor barracks window, a soldier sat between two large stereo speakers watching all the foot traffic below. The local rock station was blasting from the speakers. We took a moment to stand in awe at the blatant level of freedom on display. The deejay announced over the radio, "The local weather for this fine Saturday in Augusta will be sunny and warm with highs in the mid-sixties. Here's Foreigner from their album *Agent Provocateur*." The song "That Was Yesterday" began to play. I'd heard it before, only this time, in this moment, the words spoke to me as never before.

No more hiding in yesterday
'Cause yesterday's gone.

The words echoed my thoughts and feelings. Memories of my life and family back home flooded my mind. Memories that suddenly felt so close, but at the same time seemed a lifetime ago. Looking at the sea of barracks, I thought, *Man, that* was *yesterday . . . and yesterday's gone.*

To our right sat the army chow hall. It would be our next stop on this unfamiliar base stretched out before us. We were eager to see if the chow we had been eating during basic compared to the food from this chow hall. The food quality may have been the same, but the atmosphere—minus the drill sergeants constantly yelling for us to "FINISH UP AND MOVE OUT!"—was certainly a step in the right direction.

Each army barracks has a room called a "day room" much like a common area found in on-campus housing at universities. Generally located on the first floor, they are outfitted with televisions, an occasional pool table, and crude chairs and couches where soldiers can relax. As I entered the day room after dinner, my eyes instantly went to the large television at the far end of the room. For the remainder of the evening I was awe-struck at finally being allowed to watch television again. Not so much the shows, they were pretty much the same, it was the commercials that seemed more up front and in your face. After only two months away, they seemed somehow new and different.

When Monday arrived, we were given our unit assignments. One by one my platoon mates set off to their new homes. Most shared an MOS with someone else in the group, except for me. I was the last remaining soldier.

"What training are you here for?" the sergeant asked me.

"I'm here for 26D Ground Control Approach Radar Course, Sergeant."

He looked at me with a sympathetic expression. "Oh, you're one of those guys who will be here for a while."

Not what I expected to hear, but he pointed me in the direction of my new home.

Delta Company 5th Battalion 1st Training Brigade—or D-5-1, as we were called—was located about a half mile down a long row of red-brick barracks buildings. And I'd have to walk it.

I picked up my gear and walked alone as I passed barrack after barrack, looking for the D-5-1 sign out front. It was odd to suddenly be alone after ten weeks of being drilled with, "WHERE'S YOUR BUDDY? FIND YOUR BUDDY! TAKE CARE OF YOUR BUDDY!"

When I finally found my new home, I was relieved to see a group of soldiers like me—fresh from basic. A guy in civilian clothes walked up to me. "Are you a 26D?"

Not knowing who or what rank he was, I answered smartly, "Yes, Sergeant."

He smiled and grabbed one of my duffel bags. "Follow me."

I followed him to the third floor and into an eight-man room with four bunkbeds. He threw my duffel bag on an empty bunk and pointed to an empty wall locker. "Put your gear in there." He started to walk out, but before he could get to the door, I asked, "Is there a formation to march to the chow hall for dinner?"

He burst out laughing. "No, dude, just put on some civilian clothes and grab dinner on your own."

Wow, this is almost too good to be true.

Putting on civilian clothes and being able to walk alone to the chow hall went against all the programming from basic, but was glorious nonetheless. Returning to my new home on the third floor, I found a few of my new roommates casually sitting while they spit shined their boots. Not wanting to be the odd man out, I pulled out my own shoeshine kit and joined in on the activity. It felt comforting to share this simple experience as we talked about spit-shining tips and crazy experiences from basic training.

Right in the middle of my first real opportunity to hang out in a relaxed atmosphere, through the open windows, the first notes of Taps began to play over the loudspeaker system. Suddenly, everyone in the room leapt to their feet and saluted. Throughout basic we'd been taught repeatedly that we never salute indoors unless reporting to a superior officer. Though I knew I didn't need to salute right then, I couldn't help myself and followed their example. So I also jumped up and snapped to attention quickly bringing my hand up for a crisp salute. Only when I jumped up, I neglected to first take care of two containers that were on my lap—one with black polish and the other, the lid, filled with water. When I hopped up, both containers hit the floor spraying water everywhere.

We stood for a split second and looked at each other, until the others could no longer contain themselves. They burst out howling at my expense. "Oh, dude, that was the funniest thing I've ever seen!" they all said. "Dude, you should've seen the look on your face!" They were beyond giddy that they were able to get me, "the newbie," to follow their example without even thinking. Obviously, I was embarrassed, but could not help laughing along, seeing how hard they were laughing at my expense.

On the third floor, where I lived, our platoon sergeant, Sergeant First Class Louis B. Thompson, was not your typical loud platoon sergeant. He was a bespectacled African American who spoke in an intelligent professor-like manner. His reaction when someone upset him was always entertaining: "Get yourself out of that bunk and wait for me in my office where I will help you plan your weekend!"

Everyone had the utmost respect for Sergeant Thompson and his thankless job of corralling a large platoon of soldiers, representing nearly every background and culture America had to offer. Each morning, Sergeant Thompson would open each door, turn on the lights, and announce in a pleasant tone, "Good morning, gentlemen. PT formation in fifteen minutes." At the same time, we could hear the other platoon sergeants on the floor below banging pots and pans and trashcan lids to wake up their soldiers. My new buddies and I would look at each other and comment how grateful we were for Sergeant First Class Louis B. Thompson!

Sergeant Thompson's stock went way up one afternoon when he passed my room and heard music coming from the boom box I'd recently purchased. He stuck his head in. "Who is this?"

"It's a new cassette by a group called Aerosmith."

He gave me a look that said, *Are you kidding me?*

"Have you heard of them?"

He stepped into the room. "*Of course* I've heard of Aerosmith! Steven Tyler, Joe Perry, Tom Hamilton, Brad Whitford, Joey Kramer."

My jaw dropped as he listed the band members' names.

He saw my surprised look. "I'm from Detroit, and if you're from Detroit, you know about Aerosmith!" I admired Sergeant Thompson more than he knew, but I honestly could not grasp a black man from Detroit—where Aerosmith had a huge following among autoworkers since their songs could easily be heard over the factories' heavy machines—knowing anything about a rock band from Boston that were revered by a nearly all-white audience among the youth of the '70s and '80s. The associations in the army were opening my mind in more ways than one.

Behind the rows of barracks sits Barton Parade Field, a grassy field long enough that one lap around is nearly four miles. Each morning at 0530 our company assembled into a formation and marched several blocks to the field along with literally thousands of other soldiers. The field was equipped with elevated platforms where each platoon sergeant stood over-looking the whole formation as we went through the daily routine of physical training (PT). Even though we were being trained in a highly technical field, we were still required to maintain the physical standards required of soldiers serving in combat arms (armor, infantry, artillery) career fields. PT formations are expected, in fact, highly encouraged, to "sound off," while counting the repetitions of each exercise. It was something carried over from basic that showed off our motivation level.

If our platoon sounded off in a manner that showed low motivation, which usually happened on Mondays after our weekends off, then additional exercises could quickly cure that malady. With so many units on the field at the same time, the cumulative noise rising up along the entire field was impressive, akin to the noise level from a crowd in a large stadium. It was a contest nearly every day to see if our platoon could sound off louder than the adjacent platoon.

At some point during the noise and motion, Reveille, our early-morning wake-up call, played, which signaled the start of the duty day and the raising of the Stars and Stripes. At the opening notes, the platoon sergeant would call the whole formation to attention and have us do a facing movement pointing the platoon toward the flag. The thousands of soldiers from all the companies and platoons running the length of the entire parade field saluted when we heard the order, "PRESENT ARMS!"

Suddenly, the thunderous noise rolling across Barton Field fell silent, with each soldier standing at attention, paying respect to the flag of this great nation.

I found myself often thinking, *Wow, this is America. I am part of something larger than myself . . . something inherently good and somehow sacred.* It awakened deeply patriotic feelings within me. For a time, I kept those feelings to myself until one evening I decided to share them with a group of fellow soldiers. I was completely surprised when nearly all of them said they experienced similar feelings. They too felt deeply patriotic as they stood in the silence of those early mornings on Barton Field.

After that first weekend and after I'd completed my in-processing to Delta Company, I was ready to begin my training. Of the twenty of us in our training, I was the lone newbie among my roommates, who were all well into their training, including a couple who were close to graduation.

The next afternoon, we gathered in formation and met our new platoon sergeant, Sergeant First Class Ortega, who announced that for the beginning classes, known as Common Basic Electronics Training (COBET), our classes would start in the afternoon and continue into the late evening. "While on this schedule," he told us, "you will be referred to as Nighthawks."

The ten weeks of COBET were broken up into classes covering basic electronic theory, followed by component (circuits) theory, digital logic, and radio/antenna principles. In the beginning, I felt completely lost, having literally zero experience with or knowledge of any of the equipment and theories. But I managed to successfully get through COBET—which for me was a major accomplishment.

Delays between classes ending and the next one starting were common, some lasting two weeks or more. During delays, we were farmed out for grounds beautification details. After morning PT, personal hygiene, barracks clean up, and breakfast, we marched over to a shack where we reported for that day's duty, referred to as TAC-Detail. Pretty much everyone loathed it. Soldiers would do just about anything to avoid going, including telling their platoon sergeant they were not feeling well and getting a permission slip to go to the medical clinic on sick-call. Others would simply drop out of the formation when the platoon sergeant who was marching us wasn't looking. All of these avoidance tactics were well known, and actually had a name for them—*shamming*.

In the lexicon of military life in 1985, the word *shamming* took precedence among many new words, becoming an instant favorite in our everyday vocabulary. No matter the conversation, the insertion of the word *shamming* was a prerequisite whenever and wherever possible. During formations when a sergeant asked, "Where's Private so and so?" The entire formation in unison would reply, "Shamming, Sergeant."

"Why are you late for formation, soldier?"

Again, the entire formation would say, "Because s/he was shamming, Sergeant!"

At the slightest indication that somebody was not doing his or her part, that person was labeled a shammer. It did not matter where someone was or what that person was doing, whether it was something legitimate or not, as far as we—really, everyone—were concerned, that person was obviously, and unequivocally, shamming somewhere.

The second most-used phrase in 1985 mil-speak was *8-up*, signifying someone's displeasure or dislike for someone or something, anything, really. The answer to why a soldier couldn't pass a PT test? It was obvious, he was 8-up beyond belief. When after an all-day GI party, we learned we had to prepare the barracks for an upcoming inspection, well, that was simply 8-up. He's all 8-up, she's all 8-up. Conditions, standards, rules, and regulations—8-up covered them all.

By now we got to know most of the students who were close to finishing the radar portion of school, the class we were eagerly anticipating. We saw how excited they were to be close to graduating and know where their duty station was. Some were going to Korea and Germany. I looked forward to one day being in their position.

When the first day of radar class finally arrived, I couldn't have been more excited. *Finally, I'm getting to the meat of my training.* Brant Hall, the building where this class was held, sat directly across from our barracks. It had three two-story halls surrounding a giant hanger in the middle. About halfway down each hall were double-doors leading into a hanger large enough for several radars in one section while two rows of helicopter airframes took up the rest of the space. There were Blackhawk, Huey, and Apache airframes that caught everyone's attention.

The opening lecture covered radar theory and concepts for two separate radar systems. One system was a tactical radar, meaning it was transportable by either ground vehicles or helicopter; the other was a fixed-positioned radar system, similar to what would be used at an airport.

Our instructors were all combat vets having served tours in Vietnam. They described helicopter insertions into dense jungles with their field gear and the equipment they set up to establish an active runway in a nearby clearing. Once they got the radar system up and running, a C-130 cargo plane would come in low and huge parachutes would deploy out the back cargo door, which pull a large shipment of supplies on giant pallets. These pallets hit the ground at more than 100 miles per hour, skidding along the clearing before finally coming to a stop.

Within an hour or two, infantry units from the army and marines emerged from the jungle tree line, having been hidden there the whole time. They converged on the shipments and resupplied their food, ammo, and whatever gear they needed before vanishing back into the tree line like the baseball players in the movie *Field of Dreams.*

I could have listened to their stories all day. They sounded so cool and adventurous.

That afternoon our three primary instructors led us into a large hangar attached to the building where we had our classrooms. There, on a large custom-made tripod, stood the AN/TPN-18A tactical radar system. It was smaller and more compact than what I had imagined, but what it lacked in size, it made up for in buttons and dials on the front panel. The electronics were housed in a large square box, about the size of a large refrigerator, with a large dish—the part that spins on top called a wave-guide—and a curved banana-shaped dish, about the size of a large surf-board, mounted on the side. It had a thick black power cable coming from the back, which ran across the floor like a giant snake to a large receptacle on the wall. This thing could not just plug into a regular 110-volt outlet. Located at the end of the cable was a plug about the same diameter and length as a liter bottle of Coke.

I watched transfixed. *Someday that will be me*, I assured myself, as an instructor hit a power switch, bringing the radar system to life. Light illu-minated the front-panel buttons and dials, and from behind the panel, we could hear the hum of internal circuitry.

Pulling open the front panel, Sergeant First Class Beck pointed to several large components. "The current running through these compo-nents will kill you instantly if you make contact with it. It will cook you from the inside out in a fraction of a second. You never *ever* lose respect or focus for the killing potential this radar has." He then grabbed a long rod with a cable attached. "This is a grounding rod, before you ever do *anything* inside this, or any other radar, you always use the grounding rod to discharge any remaining current once the system is shut down for maintenance. I want you all to see this." He took the grounding rod and pointed it inside the radar. "Located in the bottom toward the back you can see the high voltage power supply." He was slowly moving the tip of the rod toward the component to which he was referring.

When the tip was within a few inches, several blue arcs appeared from the top of the power supply going straight into the rod with an unmis-takable crackling noise—just like how downed high-voltage power lines sound when they are discharging in the movies.

"The lightning you see will be the *last* thing you see before you depart this earth if you're not careful."

I thought it was awesome and scary all at the same time. And I couldn't help my eyes from bulging slightly as I tried not to smile and yell out, "Cool!"

We learned first about the tactical radar transmitter, followed by the receiver section, covering functional areas and identifying major signal paths in each section. We were given large fold-out schematics that initially looked *beyond* complicated, but through our own color-coding efforts, they became valuable resources. At the completion of each section, the instructors installed bad components or "bugs" into that section of the radar, and one by one, we had to troubleshoot the problem.

Again I found myself struggling to keep up on concepts others seemed to grasp more easily. Intuitively knowing where and what to look for when a particular function of the radar system was not working did not come easily. This only added to my anxiety. I was determined to ask questions of both classmates and instructors to keep up with a firehose's worth of information. One of our instructors always said, "Find out what's good, so you can find out what's bad." Valuable advice, especially since I had no prior experience with electricity and electronics in general.

Talking with classmates about my insecurities, one of them asked me, "Didn't you ever tear into something that was broken to see what was inside—what made it work?" I thought back on the times I could have torn a broken appliance apart to see what was inside, but chose not to.

At the end of each section, we had to pass a final troubleshooting exam in which we had to trace signal paths and check voltages in order to identify the bad component. If we passed, we moved on to the next section. If we failed, we "recycled" back to take the class all over again. Despite my efforts, I failed that first section. I couldn't believe it. Everyone else in the class passed and moved on to the receiver section.

The class behind us had just started that first radar section. I would be joining them, but before moving to that class, I found myself in the office of the MOS course manager, a bespectacled E-8 Master Sergeant, for an interview. "Do you *want* to be here?" he asked, catching me completely by surprise.

I sat for a moment, a myriad of thoughts running through my head. *I can't believe he's asking me this. I volunteered for this training, why would I want to quit now?* Finally, I answered, "Yes, absolutely, I came here because I want to be a radar repairman."

He had interviewed other students after they'd failed, and I knew that several students had informed him they no longer wanted to continue, requesting to be discharged from the army under Chapter 11—soldier cannot adapt to military life. We were all coming to terms with what we learned from fellow students at or near graduation—and the reality was that finishing up the entire course was taking the average student much longer than the twenty-two weeks annotated in our enlistment paper-work. The ones who requested a discharge were unwilling to continue at the thought of being in a training status for such an extended period. They were willing to take their chances forging a path back home as a civilian.

For me, the thought of such a long school was definitely daunting. Delta Company housed soldiers being trained in several other aviation-related career fields. We watched the arrival and departure of many soldiers as the months passed. Some we knew in passing, while others became close friends we stayed in contact with through letters from their new duty station. The letters gave us a window into their lives and experiences in places like Germany and Korea, places we eagerly anticipated just as soon as we could finish our training. They left, while we continued to remain behind.

Now sitting in front of the master sergeant in that interview, the reality struck me that I had minimal options back in Oregon. So I did my best to convince him that I would do whatever it took to graduate.

It was depressing to think about close friends and classmates continuing on without me. We started out together and it was not easy to accept that they would finish and ship out before me. I was grateful, though, that I bonded quickly with my new classmates. They readily accepted me. I felt much more relaxed re-taking the tactical radar transmitter portion again. At some point during the lectures and following troubleshooting exercises, something clicked within me. I think it may have been that I took to heart the previous advice to find what's good (working) to find what's bad. A level of confidence came to me that seemed to slow things down during, what would previously be, moments of stress.

The final exams for the remaining radar sections were still stressful; having already failed one, I could not fail another and remain in the course. If I did, my only options were to re-classify into a different MOS or get discharged. I did not want even to consider the thought of being discharged and returning home. And settling for a less-technical MOS was a thought I hated even worse. No, I signed up to repair radars and I was determined to do everything within my power to make that happen. I pushed myself to ask questions during practical troubleshooting exercises, even requesting additional troubleshooting time from our instructors.

The instructors assured us the "bugs" they were using for practical exercises and exams were ones we would see once we were working on the radar systems at our permanent-duty stations. The extra trouble-shooting paid off, providing me a measure of confidence as each exam approached—and I passed!

During the final exam on the tactical radar, I was troubleshooting a problem in the portable trailer that contained the scope and other peripheral equipment. I followed the problem to a set of drawers already placed on top of the cabinet for ease of tracing voltages and signal paths. I reached for the edge of a particular drawer attempting to flip it over when I was hit by a disconnected component wire, which sent 250 volts up my right hand and arm. They quickly went numb. I stood there and shook my hand as though I had smacked a finger with a hammer.

Behind me, I could hear both instructors laughing. "Did you find the bug, Jones?"

"Yes, Sergeant, I think I found it." For the next twenty minutes, my writing hand stayed completely numb, depriving me of the ability to write the answer on the test sheet. Fortunately, they allowed me to submit my answer verbally. Still laughing, they were at least sympathetic enough to write the answer for me. Before sending me back to class, one of them told me, "You should have seen the look on your face!"

Troubleshooting the tactical radar

The second radar, a fixed-position system, was older and more temperamental. With this system, we transitioned from new integrated circuitry to one based on old technology. Inside the front cabinet door were drawers containing large and small tubes, which made the radar glow with an orange luminescence.

In class we learned about components that stored voltage or current for later discharge based on timing. The stored-up energy is referred to as "potential." Even though a piece of equipment sat unplugged for quite some time, it still had the potential to reach out and bite some unlucky and unsuspecting individual.

Toward the end of the final radar class, we each received Permanent Change of Station (PCS) orders, which told us where the army was sending us. I was to report to a unit in Germany. I couldn't have been more excited. I was already a huge Volkswagen fan, having bought and driven two VW Beetles by then. I had already planned on buying a VW Rabbit GTI, a fast and sporty hatchback. Now I could buy one in Germany and bend some needles flying down the German autobahn, which has no speed restrictions.

Prior to shipping out, I flew home to Oregon on Christmas leave and shared the exciting news with my family. They made sure I had plenty of warm clothing for Germany's cold and snowy winter conditions. I finally felt I had accomplished something significant. My family was genuinely excited for me. I could tell my grandparents, whom I lived with for my junior and senior years of high school, and particularly my grandfather, was proud that I ventured out and was making something of myself.

After Christmas break I returned to my post for my last two weeks of class before shipping out to Germany. Now *I* would be the one saying goodbye to soldiers with many months remaining, including a couple soldiers from my original class who had later failed a section and were recycled back to a class behind the class I was soon to graduate with.

The first day back in class our entire group of instructors uncharacteristically gathered in our classroom where they announced that the department of the army had come to a decision regarding our MOS: they were adding an additional ten-week navigational-aids (Nav-Aids) equipment course to our already long radar training.

Previously, the Nav-Aids course had been taught to returning graduates, after six to twelve months of experience working on the radar system at their duty station. We had already been there long enough to see a few graduates we met just after arriving when they returned for the extra course. As soon as we saw them, we peppered them with questions, "Where are you stationed? What's it like there? What's the army like at your duty station?" They related how cool it was to finally be doing our job maintaining the radar systems, and how army life at a duty station was so much better than what we were experiencing. "Just hang on and get through the course." It had given me hope for better days ahead. Now I sat in stunned silence, feeling gut punched.

Upset by the news, we couldn't help ourselves as we complained. "We've already been here longer than any other MOS, and now you're telling us we have to stay here even longer? Why can't we just go to our units and return like others have?"

Our instructors understood and even sympathized with our borderline insubordinate feelings, but in the end, they were powerless to change anything. The army decided to combine the two courses, and we were the sacrificial guinea pigs.

Despite the shock, we accepted our temporary setback, and as good soldiers are known to do, we saluted and moved out, setting our sites on graduating after one more class—ten weeks away.

At least we don't have to return to being in a training status again, I reasoned to myself.

Fortunately, the ten additional weeks passed quickly, our platoon sergeants granting us a bit of latitude for having been there now nearly a full year. I received new PCS orders—this time to Fort Huachuca, Arizona. So much for all the warm clothing for Germany I'd received at Christmas. The only comfort I found was that nobody in our class received orders to Germany. With the exception of two going to Korea, we were all going to stateside posts.

To my surprise, shipping out of Fort Gordon and no longer being in a training status gave me mixed feelings. Most of the time there, all we talked about was finishing school, getting out of Augusta, Georgia, and getting on with life. For so long I could not wait to put Fort Gordon and my training in the rearview mirror. Despite those strong feelings, and with only days left before shipping out, I suddenly and surprisingly realized how much I was going to miss this place, especially the close friendships I'd developed among classmates and fellow soldiers with whom I'd been honored to serve. The bond of brotherhood/sisterhood that developed serving beside each other day after day, sharing each other's burdens of physical, mental, and emotional strain, formed a strong bond between us.

It was cool and cloudy in March 1986 when I was scheduled on an early-morning flight from Augusta, Georgia, to Tucson, Arizona. I couldn't take my eyes off the mountain range when I stepped off the plane, and a feeling washed over me that's hard to describe. It was as if I could look at both the past and future while standing in the present. The past had been a monumental grind at times, but I persevered and made it. Looking at those mountains, I felt like their beauty and grandeur represented the potential of my future. I was alone, but not lonely, standing on the summit of that moment, looking up and forward, to climbing to the next.

CHAPTER 5

Leading by Example

T he desert vistas up ahead were now shrouded in a black abyss as dusk gave way to darkness. The lights of Tucson slowly faded behind us as the shuttle van carrying me and one other soldier headed east on I-10 for about forty miles, before turning south on Highway 90. Up ahead, headlights from oncoming cars were the only visible things as the highway climbed toward an invisible rise. Cresting the rise, the curtain of darkness was pulled back revealing thousands of tiny lights ahead.

"Those are the lights of Sierra Vista and Fort Huachuca," the driver pointed out, referring to my new "home."

To me the lights appeared to be only a few miles away. We continued toward them for several more minutes, but they didn't seem to get closer. "How far away *are* those lights?" I asked.

The driver chuckled. "About twenty miles. You don't have desert vision yet. At night out here, things appear much closer than they really are. Your desert vision will kick in before you know it."

The driver wasn't kidding. Thirty minutes later we pulled up to a red-brick, three-story barracks, identical to the one I'd moved out of the day before. The driver turned to both of us. "Which one of you has orders to 11th Signal Brigade?"

"I do, Sir," the other solder said. I watched as they both disappeared into the building, each carrying a duffel bag.

After a few moments, the driver returned. "The EPG barracks are not far from here," he told me, referring to the Electronic Proving Ground. Stopping the van in front of an identical red-brick, three-story building, he turned to me. "This is your new home. Welcome to Fort Huachuca." He carried one of my duffel bags as we made our way to the entrance.

Straight down a short hallway, the building opened into a foyer where two soldiers in uniform sat behind a desk. "Signing in, Private?" a sergeant there asked.

"Yes, Sergeant," I said, taking a look around while he pulled out some paperwork. A long hallway led down the length of the building with office doors on one side and mailboxes on the other. Across from the desk, a doorway led into a large day room, where I could see a pool table and chairs facing a television.

"Where are you coming from, soldier?"

"Fort Gordon, Sergeant. I just finished training as a 26D ground/control approach radar repairman." I felt proud to share my new title whenever I could.

"Well, congratulations, that's awesome. Welcome to EPG." He showed me to my temporary room—I'd receive my permanent room on Monday—and explained where things were on the post, such as the chow halls (there were two—one of each side of the barracks) and Operations, then left me to settle in. Since it was the weekend, I had time to get acquainted with the post before having to report to my new assignment Monday morning at 0730.

Early the next morning, I headed toward one of the chow halls and stopped dead in my tracks. The desert landscape surrounded us, and everywhere I looked I saw nothing but barrenness. Directly behind the post to the west sat the jagged and rocky formations of the Huachuca mountain range. Looking east, the desert floor gradually sloped down to a point, then gradually rose to another mountain range. The expanse between the two went on for what seemed like hundreds of miles. Bare and brown. I grew up in Oregon's Willamette Valley, where everything is some shade of green. Tall, mature trees block the overall view. To the east, on clear days, I could see Mount Hood, but mostly it was shrouded in clouds. The harsh-looking rocky and drab landscape of southeastern Arizona, with its many shades of brown, was unlike anything I had ever seen.

EPG barracks lower left

With a slight breeze blowing, I could feel the dry morning air warming as the sun continued to rise in a cloudless sky. The change from the humid air I'd grown accustomed to, after a year in Georgia, was instantly noticeable. Looking up toward the foothills leading into the nearby mountains, I could see trees in the canyons that looked like bushes from where I stood. Waking up with dried blood in my nose that morning I realized, *This hot and dry desert air will take some getting used to.*

On Monday morning, promptly at 0730, I walked into Operations, orders in hand. The office was divided by a long counter with a small waiting area, where I stood, on one side, and several desks on the other side.

One of the staff members looked up when I walked in. "Can I help you?"

"Yes, Sergeant, I'm Private Jones. The CQ told me to report here."

"Is this your first duty station?" she asked.

"Yes, Sergeant, I just completed AIT at Fort Gordon. Here's a copy of my orders." I handed her my Advanced Individual Training papers.

She took the copy and scanned for info that apparently indicated the company and section I was assigned to. All I could decipher on the page was Fort Huachuca and EPG; all the other alphanumeric info was meaningless to me. She picked up the phone and dialed a number. "Will you send up a sponsor," she said to whomever was on the other end of the line. "You have a new soldier here in Operations."

She hung up and turned her attention back to me. "They're sending someone up. Let's get you a room number and keys to where you'll be living."

My room, located on the second floor, was empty but already had two soldiers living in it. It was technically a four-man room with four beds and four wall lockers. Since the room had only two occupants, they'd arranged it to give them the most privacy. Just inside the door two wall lockers formed a wall to the left with two beds up against the wall on the right. The lockers and beds formed an alley around which the room opened to another partition of wall lockers perpendicular to the windows, which created a space of privacy on each side where their bunks sat against the walls. I had my choice of one of two bunks beyond the privacy zone nearest the door.

The supply sergeant who escorted me to the room commented that she had avoided adding another person to this room as a favor to one of the soldiers, whom I think she liked, but could no longer avoid giving them another roommate. I looked around and wondered what rank my new roommates were, and how they would react to a wrench (me) being thrown into their living arrangement.

After throwing my gear onto one of the empty bunks, I returned downstairs to Operations where a soldier from the section, who identified himself as my "sponsor," Specialist Kevin Pease, was waiting for me. I was assigned to work in the Reliability, Logistics, and Supportability Branch (RLSB) of the army's Electronic Proving Ground (EPG). We made small talk about where we were from on the short drive down to the compound where my section was located.

That's odd, I thought as I looked around at the building where I'd be working. It was nowhere near the airfield.

"Is there another shop closer to the airfield?" I asked.

"Nope, this is the assigned office for all of us." His expression changed to one of understanding of what I was really asking. "Being assigned to this section means you probably won't be working the MOS you trained for."

In less than thirty seconds, I found out my assignment was to work in a section that tested and evaluated electronic equipment for the army under Test and Evaluations Command (TECOM). After a year in radar school, and much to my chagrin, the army was asking me to embrace and do a completely different job from the one I'd signed up for.

After all the time and effort I put into my studies to finally work in the career I'd just spent a year training for—and now I'm not even going to put it all to use? I felt frustrated and stunned.

My first official day on the job—and just before I walk into it—I learn it isn't the job I expected. *So what job* am *I signed up for?*

I nervously stepped through the open door into the office of E-8 Master Sergeant (MSG) Jack Crumling, Non-Commissioned Officer in Charge (NCOIC) of RLSB. I stood at parade rest and cleared my throat. "May I speak with you, Sergeant Crumling?"

"Absolutely. Take a seat, Private." He motioned me over to one of the two empty chairs facing his desk. I could feel the sweat on my palms when I pulled my hands apart from behind my back. I took the nearest seat, the one on the right, and sat ramrod straight.

On his desk, directly in front of me, was a triangular wooden plaque that stated, "MSG JACK CRUMLING: THE BOSS" on a gold plate. I shifted nervously.

The wall behind his desk held numerous framed certificates and several wooden plaques, also with gold plates, attesting to his long career and many accomplishments. He maneuvered his lanky, more than six-feet-tall frame into his chair and looked expectantly at me. His salt-and-pepper hair surrounded a shiny, bald dome, which I later learned brought him the affectionate title of "Chrome-dome" from members of his section. His neatly trimmed mustache had more dark hair than gray, but was way more impressive than the patch of peach fuzz growing under my nose. He wore wire-rimmed glasses with square lenses.

Deep down I knew sharing my feelings was taking a big risk. I was treading in new and unchartered waters. I didn't know what to expect and was well aware that he could react angrily to my complaint, exercising the monumental gap in our rank, and could tell me, "Quit your sniveling and do the job the army sent you here to do." Or he could just as easily dismiss my feelings outright with little or no reaction. Sort of a *Not my problem* kind of approach.

Here goes. I swallowed hard. "Sergeant Crumling, I don't really even know where to begin." I paused. "I just endured a yearlong ordeal to graduate from radar repairer school. I got orders to finally leave Fort Gordon and come here, and then I find out I'm not going to do the job I just sacrificed and trained for. I'm now supposed to do something totally different? To say I'm completely shocked and utterly disappointed would be putting it mildly."

He listened patiently as I shared my feelings, nodding every now and again. "I understand your disappointment, but allow me to share with you the opportunities that come with working in the Test and Evaluations environment. Here at EPG, the army brings in soldiers from different high-tech MOS career fields. This creates a well-rounded knowledge pool for testing and evaluating cutting-edge systems and equipment. When we've done our job, that equipment will eventually get fielded and will ultimately shape the modern battlefield."

He knew how to communicate, especially with young soldiers like me. His years and experience gave him a level of patience and foresight that instantly drew me in with his fatherly approach.

"I have no problem if you want to go down to the radar lab at the airfield and see about transferring to that section," he said. "As a matter of fact, I will take you down there myself to talk to the NCOIC. C'mon, we can use one of the section vehicles parked outside."

Relief washed over me when it became apparent he actually seemed to care about my feelings.

"So, Brad," he said as he drove, "Where are you from?"

I was surprised that he called me by my first name. *But with his rank he can call me whatever he wants.* But I appreciated that he seemed interested and was carrying the small talk.

After a brief ride, we arrived at the radar lab. It sat alone in a tan brick building close to the aircraft hangers and other structures that dotted the runway flight line. Inside, it took my eyes a moment to adjust from the bright sunlight outside to the lower lighting inside. Standing beside MSG Crumling, I glanced around the large main room. It had two large garage doors that opened up to the flight line. Lab counters, just like the ones we used in school, lined the walls adjacent to the garage doors. The lab counter upper-shelves contained test equipment I instantly recognized.

This is home. I could see into several adjoining offices to our left. We interrupted a lively ping-pong match taking place on a table in the center of the room. Two soldiers were battling it out, while half a dozen soldiers watched from swiveling stools, surrounding the table.

MSG Buck Halsey came out of his office to greet us. "Hey, Jack, what brings you down to the radar lab?"

"Hey, Buck, I brought one of your own to see about him possibly transferring down here to work on radars. This is Private Jones, fresh from the 26D course."

MSG Halsey extended his hand to me. I did my best to match the strength of his grip as we shook. Before I could say anything, he told me, "You don't want to transfer down here. All radar maintenance has been turned over to civilian contractors since they designated this runway as an alternate landing-strip for the space shuttle. We're all waiting for PCS orders to other posts. There's nothing for you to do down here."

I looked up at Sergeant Crumling and could only shrug.

"Are you assigned to work for Jack in RLSB?" MSG Halsey asked.

"Yes, Sergeant, I am."

"Well, I'm sure Jack has shared with you what a great opportunity you have to do something totally unique for the army. The best advice I can give you is to stay in Jack's section and sink your teeth into that job. Jack will take good care of you."

"Yes, Sergeant. Thank you."

Back out in the parking lot, my mind was still swimming as I tried to take it all in and come to terms with such a drastic turn of events. "Sergeant Crumling, thank you for bringing me down here. I hope you're not mad at me for wanting to see for myself?"

"Not at all, Jones. I don't mind doing my job taking care of soldiers."

We hopped into the military truck and headed back to my new section.

"In 1980 when Ronald Reagan was elected, he gave the word to open the financial flood gates to the Department of Defense," MSG Crumling said as he drove. "When that happened, many items already in the design or development stages were suddenly given the go-ahead. Funds poured in to defense-contracting companies like never before. Ideas and giant 'What-ifs' that lingered in minds and on drawing boards suddenly got the jumpstart they'd been waiting for. Here at EPG, you will have the opportunity to be involved in testing and evaluating the latest advancements in technology and capabilities as it relates to electronic gear and gadgets. The systems I've personally seen and been involved with here are going to revolutionize not only the battlefield, but our world also."

The sting of not working on radars was fading fast, and I became caught up in the insights he was sharing.

"Would you like to see some of the gizmos and gadgets?"

"Sergeant, I thought you'd never ask."

He explained that Remotely Piloted Vehicle (RPV) development was well underway, with several prototypes being tested in a hangar on a remote corner of the base called Black Tower. The equipment to control and monitor the UAVs, large and cumbersome by today's standards, looked similar to the control positions NASA employees used during the Apollo missions, but even then, it was awe inspiring. Launch and retrieval equipment, the size of semi-trailers sat outside beside the hangar. Inside the spacious building, I could see a flurry of activity taking place as civilians and soldiers worked on each one of the three or four large prototypes. I could have stayed and watched all day, but Sergeant Crumling motioned me back to the truck.

We drove back the way we came for several miles before turning right and driving up a road into a canyon. After rounding several corners, a large building, tucked neatly into one side of the canyon wall, came into view.

"This is the facility where they're testing super-secret night-vision goggles, NVGs, that make the pitch black of night look like day," he said.

"You mean like the starlight scope we looked through in basic, Sergeant?"

"Something like that, but *way* better."

In my excitement, I purposely kept pace with Sergeant Crumling to keep myself from sprinting to the building entrance. The work space inside looked similar to the radar lab with work benches and test equipment. Several soldiers stood immediately as soon as they saw Sergeant Crumling. Their supervisor came out of his office. "Hey, Jack, to what do I owe the pleasure?"

"Just giving a new soldier the grand tour."

They walked into the office together. I got the sense they wanted to talk privately. I looked at each soldier as they looked at me—all of us silently making our rank checks. Each one outranked me, but not by much.

Several pairs of NVGs were on the workbench. I motioned toward the goggles. "Have you used them?"

"Yep," said one, as they all nodded.

"Are they cool?" I asked.

"They are so far beyond cool, it's not even close."

"Are you in RLSB with Sergeant Crumling?" another one asked.

"Yeah, I guess so. I just got here from AIT."

Another spoke up. "One of my roommates is in your section. From what I've seen, people in your section get to travel—TDY—quite a bit."

I wanted to hear more about the goggles, but I wasn't sure what I could ask, or how much they could tell me. "I'm just trying to come to terms with doing a different job from the one I just spent a year training for."

They nodded collectively. "Dude, we all felt that way coming here as our first duty assignment," a different soldier said, seemingly speaking for the group. "But this job will give you a front-row seat to the world of R&D-Research and Development. You will see things very few people get to see, and if you decide to get out after your enlistment, the contracting companies we work with will be standing in line to hire you. Most of the civilians on this base are prior military. If you play your cards right, you can chart your future here."

For the first time, I felt a wave of hope mixed with relief wash over me. And for the first time I thought, *This is where I'm supposed to be.*

Each one-of-a-kind test facility employed a mix of soldiers and civilians working together, testing equipment in ways that were nothing short of mind boggling. There were test facility chambers that grew mold on equipment, simulating a humid jungle environment. Others were designed to sandblast, shake, and bake equipment, simulating a desert environment. During the tour, I was stunned by the advanced capabilities of equipment and systems in the design-and-development stages. This level of sophistication was beyond anything I had ever seen.

After the tour we pulled into the Haze Hall secure compound where the RLSB offices were located. MSG Crumling pulled the truck into a parking spot, and after shutting it off, he turned to me. "Well, what did you think?"

The only thing I could offer was, "Unbelievable." I knew deep down he had gone out of his way to personally give me a vision of the possibilities ahead, and because of that, I felt a sense of loyalty to him as a leader and mentor I could trust.

He smiled. "So are you on the team?"

"Yes, Sergeant Crumling. I am on the team."

He was MSG Crumling in uniform, but he was Jack during off-duty hours. Why he took an interest in a previously long-haired punk kid from Oregon, I will never know. But from the very beginning, Jack trusted me to run special errands for him. Whenever he needed me to run an errand, he yelled, "Boy!" from his office.

"Your daddy wants you!" a soldier would say and most of the others would look at me with a grin.

I would walk into his office and under my breath, so only he could hear me, I'd whisper, "What do you want, old man?"

My comment always brought a smirk to his face, which then he quickly erased.

I always did exactly what he asked, because I realized he trusted me. But that didn't stop me from, on occasion, returning and reporting that I had delivered the paperwork to the wrong section. On those occasions he would come after me. "Why you little s***. I guess you don't appreciate those mosquito wings on your collar anymore!"

I couldn't help laughing as I stayed one step ahead of his outstretched arms.

Though I was serious about my job and I loved being in the army, I was far from a model soldier, still susceptible to making poor choices, which Jack was more than willing and able to bring to my attention. Being on the receiving end of a controlled-burst ass-chewing from Jack—along with other soldiers—when we failed to live up to something that upset him was the last place any of us wanted to be. Jack could chew us up like no other—not a tirade by any means, but an extremely effective form of communication, informing us in unmistakable terms how he felt. In those moments, I seemed to unconsciously go to the position of Parade

Rest—standing with my arms behind my back, hands clasped together—until he was finished.

Looking around at the others, I noticed all of us had our heads down, our eyes facing the ground. We all seemed to be feeling the same thing—the effects of having let him down. Deep down, we all truly wanted to please him.

Jack followed up one particular ass-chewing by sharing a principle of his leadership: "Once I'm done chewing ass, as far as I'm concerned the matter is over and done. I don't hold on to anger or carry a grudge. I'm willing to put the matter behind and move forward, as long you understand my expectations, and choose to act accordingly."

And he meant it. The moment these encounters ended, a smile would come back to Jack's face, and he would treat us as if nothing ever occurred.

Even so, the experiences of being in Jack's crosshairs, and the resulting sense of self-disappointment lingered long after, because I knew he really liked me. One particular time, we were gathered in his office to hear the results after he and the Chief had inspected our rooms in the barracks. For the most part he was pleased at how clean and orderly we kept our rooms. Suddenly, his tone changed and his words became sharp. "And if I ever find FTA or anything derogatory on any walls or wall lockers again, that soldier will forfeit pay and lose a stripe." We all looked around at each other, only I knew who he was referring to. "Any questions? No?" And with that he ended the meeting.

I felt terrible for putting him in that position, because I completely deserved to be called out in front of my peers. I had put up those letters using black electrical tape on the side of my wall locker big enough for everyone to see. It was an acronym common in the army in those days with a double meaning: one was "Fun, Travel, and Adventure." The other was "'F' the Army." I walked out of his office, with everyone except me wondering who the guilty party was. I walked outside alone, profoundly feeling the sense that I had let Jack down by doing something so impulsive and stupid. And the worst part was that I couldn't do anything to take it back. I leaned against the side of the building and looked out across the base to the Huachuca Mountains and the crystal-clear blue sky beyond.

How could I have been so stupid?

Suddenly, the office door swung open, and Jack came out. Our eyes met, and I felt like he could sense what I was feeling. He slowly sauntered over to me and leaned his back against the wall beside me. Looking down, he scratched at some gravel with his shoe.

After a moment in which neither of us spoke, he finally said, "You okay?"

"No, Jack, I can't believe how stupid that was. I was mad about having twenty-four hours of CQ duty in the middle of a holiday weekend," I said referring to Charge of Quarters duty in which I had to man the front desk of the barracks. "That's when I put those letters on my wall locker. I know by doing that I put you in the worst possible position."

"Are you still mad?"

"Not anymore."

"It's pretty simple from here," he said. "Take it down. I was mad at you, yes, but I did some pretty dumb things when I was young too. The things that tend to teach us the greatest lessons are the ones that hurt the most. It's over and done with, so let's put it behind us."

As if my admiration and respect couldn't go any higher—he'd just made it go up even more.

"Thanks for coming out here and talking to me, Jack. I apologize for doing that."

He nudged my arm. "Forget about it." The smile came back to his face, and again it was as though it had never happened.

Living in the barracks as a single soldier can be pretty one dimensional with only beds and a couple desks with chairs in each room. A few soldiers, having served overseas, returned with state-of-the-art hi-fi stereo systems, which we all admired for their ability to shake the building to its very foundation. Personal televisions were not yet common. The day-room had one community television, but very few hung out there, preferring to watch in a room lucky enough to have a roommate who had one and was generous with its use. Other than that, we had a full gym across the parking lot, with a pool, weight room, and basketball and racquetball courts.

The bottom line is barracks life could be boring at times. Acquiring a vehicle is pretty much standard for soldiers living in the barracks. My section was comprised of those of us—about 25 percent—who lived in the barracks, while the other 75 percent lived either off post or in on-post housing. Marriage was required to avoid living in the barracks.

That spring, in 1986, a new soldier arrived from Fort Gordon, coming from D-5-1, the same company where I'd spent a quarter of my enlistment. He was a young guy, like me, full of juice, and ready to take on the world. And his name was Bobby Franklin. He arrived at the base with his bullet bike, a Yamaha GPZ 1100.

As I got to know Bobby, I learned that he grew up in a family who raced at Indianapolis Motor Speedway and Daytona Raceway. He knew car and motorcycle engines forward and backward. Racing was in his blood.

Soon after settling into our section, we learned just how much he knew. One day our "Chief"—the Officer in Charge (OIC)—was telling us that he wanted to make his brand-new IROC-Z Camaro faster. He explained his opinion that lowering the engine temperature would raise the horsepower.

"Chief, that's not the way you make it faster," Bobby said casually, but respectfully. "If you want to make it faster, you need to raise the engine temp, not lower it."

Chief's, and pretty much everyone else's, eyebrows went up at Bobby's sheer audacity.

"I know for a fact that lowering the temperature of the engine will drive up the horsepower," Chief argued.

"Absolutely not, Chief," Bobby countered. "You couldn't be more wrong. Raising the temperature is the only way to do it." The exchange began near the end of the duty day and continued on after the office emptied. Neither wanted to concede the point.

Later, Bobby caught up with us at dinner and told us what happened after we left. "He got really frustrated and told me, 'You're just a punk kid. What could you possibly know about engine theory? I have a close friend who's an engineer in Detroit, and I'm sure he'll agree with me on how to raise the horsepower.' Well, I didn't appreciate what he called me and I lost all military bearing. I told him, 'Chief, if you would just shut up for a moment and listen, you just might learn something!'"

The other soldiers and I froze. "You told him to shut up?" *Well, it's been nice knowing you*, I thought.

"Yeah, he was pretty stunned," Bobby continued. "He told me, 'All right, smart guy, you prove me wrong.' So I grabbed a piece of paper and wrote ten reasons why my approach was correct."

"That was gutsy," one soldier said.

Bobby gave us a half smile. "I told him, 'You take this list and talk with your engineer friend, and if he's as smart as you say, he will agree with me on all ten points.'"

The gauntlet of *I know more than you* had been thrown down by a young-gun soldier to an older and more experienced leader, who could have rained down hell on Bobby, with or without being proven wrong.

"You're confident this engineer is going to agree with your list?" we asked him.

"Oh absolutely, I know I'm right."

"Okay, but be careful in the future," we warned him. "He can take it out on you in some other way."

The Chief apparently called his engineer friend, and in a private exchange between the two, a very humbled Chief admitted the engineer agreed with Bobby on every one of the ten points. Without missing a beat, the Chief adopted Bobby's way of raising the horsepower as if it had been his opinion all along. He never retaliated against Bobby, but he never gave credit to Bobby either, even though we all knew who was schooled in the end.

I loved weekends on a military base. They are quiet and peaceful unlike the weekdays where there's plenty of hustle and bustle. Weekends at Huachuca were no exception, sublimely warm sunny days spent sleeping in, relaxing with friends, having barbeques, and taking time to wash and wax our cars. Nice cars are in abundance parked outside the barracks on military bases.

Most single soldiers live in the barracks, which allows many to purchase the latest craze in cars and motorcycles. Big blocks, small blocks, fast or efficient, the parking lot was full of cars that represented an extension of the many different senses of style and taste. My roommate Tom served a tour in Germany and shipped back a Mercedes Benz sedan when he returned stateside. My other roommate Andy had a Nissan 280ZX turbo that came with a hefty $350 monthly payment, an amount that blew our minds at the time. Admiring all the new sleek cars, I couldn't resist jumping in and buying one of my own—a used but sporty 1983 Volkswagen GTI.

One lazy Saturday afternoon in early June, as my roommate Andy and I waxed our cars in the parking lot, Bobby emerged from the barracks and made his way to us.

"Either of you been to Tombstone yet?"

I waited for Andy to answer first, since he was nearing the end of his four-year enlistment, having been stationed at Huachuca for more than three years. "I've been there a few times," Andy said. "It's pretty cool."

I had yet to venture out to see the town famous for the gunfight at the OK Corral. "I haven't been there yet," I said, leaning against my finely waxed GTI.

"Well, I'm riding out there to check it out. Anyone want to ride out with me?"

Andy declined. But with nothing better to do, I agreed. "Yeah, I'll go."

Bobby returned a few minutes later with an extra helmet, and before long, we were enjoying the freedom and warm wind of the open road.

Soon we were on the outskirts of Sierra Vista passing more and more open land, unique to the desert landscape of the southwest. After turning left onto Charleston Road, Bobby leaned forward, shifted, and rolled the throttle back. The bike leaped forward as if it wanted to pull out from under us.

The rapid acceleration sucked the air right out of my helmet. I glanced over Bobby at the speedometer and was shocked to see we were going 150 miles per hour. The sound and force of the passing air was like a tornado. Even though it was strapped, I thought for sure my helmet was going to fly off my head. It felt as if someone was reaching over the top of it, trying to pull it off from behind.

At 150 miles per hour, it is literally like being in another dimension. Objects on your left and right rush past your peripheral vision in a blur. The dashed white line running down the center of the road appears as one continuous line. I was out-of-my-mind petrified, but rather than scream at Bobby to slow down, I wrapped my arms around his waist in a death grip. The road stretched straight out in front of us for several miles. The moment we turned onto Charleston and began accelerating, I looked ahead and saw a car near the end of the straightaway just starting to disappear from view. Looking up, a car appeared out of nowhere, coming toward us. My life suddenly flashed before me as Bobby veered the bike into the opposite lane. In that split second, I thought we were going to hit the car head on. The wind *whooshed* as we shot past the car. In a split second I realized it was the car I had seen earlier when we started accelerating. It was traveling the same direction we were. We overtook it so fast, I thought it was going the opposite way.

When the straight section ended, the road twisted and turned. On long sweeping curves, Bobby slid himself off the seat like he was taking a corner at Laguna Seca Raceway. I had no idea what I was supposed to do. Was I supposed to slide down toward the inside of the curve keeping my body in line with his? I resigned myself to staying on the seat with the bike, holding onto Bobby's waist with my outstretched arms. At every curve he gunned it, taking them as sharp and as low as possible. Coming around another curve, we came up behind a motorhome.

Okay, he has to slow down now. There's another car coming the opposite way.

Only Bobby gunned it, threading the needle as we shot through the narrow gap between both vehicles.

Finally, the town of Tombstone loomed in our sights. I was never so glad to be back on city streets traveling at a prudent 25 to 30 miles per hour. We made our way to the main street where Bobby brought the bike to a stop.

I wanted to kiss the ground. I pulled my helmet off and looked at Bobby, who sported a sly grin. "Don't you ever, *ever* do that to me again."

He threw back his head and laughed. "I hope I didn't scare you too bad."

Working in the same section, Bobby and I became close friends. And in all our adventures together, I *never* got on a motorcycle with him again. Fortunately, for both of us, he knew I was serious, and we rode back to base staying close to the posted speed limits.

CHAPTER 6

Into a Headwind

M y first project was to test a simulator for REMBASS (Remotely Monitored Battlefield Sensor Simulator), which Raytheon, a defense contractor and industrial corporation, designed and built. The actual REMBASS equipment consisted of sensors that soldiers placed in the ground to detect enemy troop, vehicle, and tank movements. The simulator trained soldiers on how to operate the system, avoiding the lengthy and cumbersome task of having to set up the sensors and involve actual troops, vehicles, and tanks. The Raytheon contractors, who were quick to point out that Bruce Springsteen was wearing a red REMBASS ball cap in his MTV video for "Glory Days," taught us how to operate and maintain the simulator.

According to testing criteria, someone within RLSB (Reliability, Logistics, Supportability Branch) was required to evaluate the maintenance procedures in the simulator's technical manual (TM).

When Jack asked our group who wanted to handle it, I announced, "I'll do it." I could tell by his look that he was pleased to see me jump in and get involved in an ongoing project.

Jack gave me the go ahead and assigned Sergeant (E-5) Roger Melvin, a seasoned and experienced evaluator, to supervise and mentor me through the process.

The one and only photo of Roger and Jack

Roger was a lanky Midwestern farm boy, well over six feet tall, who had an air of confidence that transcended those who outranked him. With his personality, confidence, and quick wit, he was clearly the center of attention in the office. He stood always ready with a humorous comment or banter, especially with the senior leaders in the section, which frequently cracked everyone up and made even tense situations bearable. He was easy to like, so I was glad I got him as my supervisor.

The project focused on evaluating and performing each maintenance function according to the task directions in the TM. If anything needed to be tweaked or fixed, I could use only the tool kit provided with the system. It was my initial exposure to evaluating procedures from a manual and recording the results in a technical writing format. Not exactly stuff of war stories, but I thought it was interesting to learn how the mechanics of these war machines worked.

During the evaluation, I identified several tasks I was not able to perform with reasonable effort or that required tools that were not included in the tool set. From there I took photos and wrote Test Incident Reports (TIRs) to address these issues. Roger was patient with me, imparting advice and latitude during the process. He helped me compile all the TIRs and write the final report, which we submitted to a technical writing team for their evaluation.

The team complimented my work. Even though Roger was ultimately responsible for the quality of the final report, he deflected the credit, which he certainly deserved, to me. Working with Roger gave me confidence, especially as I was starting a new and unanticipated career path.

We became close friends, hanging out after work and on weekends. Roger loved four wheeling in his 1983 AMC Eagle, 70s classic rock—especially Bachman-Turner Overdrive and The Guess Who—but most of all, he loved golfing. Roger became like a big brother to me, including me in frequent golf outings with other seasoned evaluators, whom I looked up to for their knowledge and experience.

One afternoon, I saw Roger on the phone. As soon as he saw me, his face went blank. "Jones, you need to report immediately to Captain

Covington's office," he said. Captain Covington was the EPG Company Commander (known as the CO or Company Officer). Roger offered no other explanation.

Driving to the barracks, I couldn't shake the nervous feeling in the pit of my stomach. *Did I do something wrong? What could this possibly be about?* I couldn't think of anything I'd done that would require me to report to the CO.

The CO and First Sergeant's offices were co-located in a cubby just down the hall from Operations. The CO's door was to the left and it was open, whereas the First Sergeant's door was straight ahead and closed. From the hallway, I could not see into the CO's office, which only added to the feeling that I was walking into an ambush.

Finally, I willed myself to step into the CO's open doorway. I was surprised to find Jack standing behind Captain Covington who was seated at his desk. Both looked up from the paperwork they were reading. I scanned their faces for an indication of why I was there. Both wore serious, all-business expressions.

"Come in PFC [Private First Class] Jones," Captain Covington said.

I stepped forward and saluted. "PFC Jones reporting as ordered, Sir."

He returned my salute and looked up at Jack.

Jack came around the desk and grabbed my left collar where my PFC rank was pinned. "You won't be needing these anymore." He removed the black metal rank pins from each collar.

What did I do? I don't even know what I did wrong and now I'm being demoted?

The company clerk entered the office and began reading a citation. "Attention to Orders!" Jack and Captain Covington, who now stood, both snapped to Attention. I had never been in trouble before, but whatever it was, it certainly sounded serious . . . and official.

"The Secretary of the Army has reposed special trust and confidence in the patriotism, valor, fidelity, and professional excellence of Bradley P. Jones," the clerk continued. "In view of these qualities and his demonstrated leadership potential and dedicated service to the United States Army, he is, therefore, promoted to the rank of Specialist."

My heart was pounding like a jackhammer. *Did he just say something about a promotion?*

Jack smiled. "Had you scared, didn't we?"

I was so shocked and relieved at the same time I could only nod.

Captain Covington congratulated me with a handshake and certificate of my promotion.

Once outside, I shook Jack's hand again. "Thanks, Sergeant Crumling . . . for scaring me to death."

"Brad, I did this for you early in your career, earlier than most. From here on, you have to earn your promotion to Sergeant."

Shaking hands with Captain Covington,
Jack is standing just to my left with a huge grin

I was stunned and amazed to have a highly respected leader believe in me from the start. "Thank you, Sergeant, I appreciate your trust in me."

"Keep up the good work, Brad," he said, before turning on his heels and walking off.

I couldn't help but wonder why he took such an interest in me. I knew I probably would never get the answer, but I was humbled and honored just the same.

Jack had gone out of his way on my behalf in other ways, not just my early promotion. After we had a conversation about my AIT experience and the change the army had made to my MOS, Jack took it upon himself to correspond with TRADOC (Training and Doctrine Command), petitioning them to grant me additional promotion points for having completed the extra ten weeks of Navigational-Aids equipment training while at Fort Gordon. Jack fought and won sixty additional promotion points for me.

And now this promotion.

Roger laughed and congratulated me as soon as I returned. "Had you going, didn't I?"

I laughed and nodded, grateful to have Roger in my life as well.

One morning, not long after my promotion, as I was walking from the guard shack to the office, I noticed half a dozen pick-up trucks with large, square, windowless boxes in each truck bed parked nearby. Roger came out of the office door. "Hey, you want to give me a hand inventorying the equipment that just arrived from Florida?"

"Sure," I said and walked to the equipment.

Before Roger joined our team in Arizona, he and other team members, including Duane, John, and Vic, worked in Florida on a project called JTIDS, Joint Tactical Information Distribution System. JTIDS was a radio frequency distribution system designed to provide multiservice (all branches of the military) encrypted, tactical datalink communications, using similar technology found in today's cell phones.

"This is the computer that syncs up with the other rigs using that extendable antenna outside," Roger explained of the electronic equipment once we were inside one of the trailers. It all looked so cool and new age to me, different from anything I'd ever seen. Roger pointed to each component and briefly explained its function.

"Look," he said finally. "I talked to Jack, and he OK'd my request to have you assigned to the JTIDS project. I just received orders for a special overseas assignment. I leave in a couple months."

I was stunned, and all I could think to say was, "Thanks for looking out for me." I was just getting comfortable with things and suddenly everything was changing again.

I realized that he hadn't given me information about the equipment because he thought I'd be casually interested. He was giving it to me because it was my next assignment. I began paying more detailed attention as he taught me how to initialize the system and sync up with other mobile JTIDS rigs spread out across the valley. He also told me of the upcoming trip back to Florida for further testing in early '87 that had me excited to be on the project.

Despite our close friendship—from my viewpoint—Roger did not hesitate to call me out when I needed it. He reminded me one day that as a sergeant, he outranked me, and he expected me to meet certain expectations. I was supposed to meet him by the JTIDS rigs at 1300 following lunch that day. On the way out of the chow hall, I ran into Staff Sergeant Diaz who wanted me to go with him to the PX (Post Exchange). Rather than tell him I was supposed to be somewhere at 1300, I reasoned that since he outranked Roger, and had asked that I accompany him, my going with him would be okay. I thought I was in the clear all the way up to the moment I arrived by the equipment at 1345 and saw the look on Roger's face.

"Where were you?" he asked.

I looked down and folded my arms behind me. "At the PX with Staff Sergeant Diaz."

"Oh, and you think because you were with him, you can just disregard the direction I gave you to meet back here at 1300?"

I had nowhere to hide and knew better than to try to talk my way out of what I knowingly and rightfully deserved.

"When I tell you to be somewhere, you better be there. Do I make myself clear?"

"Yes, Sergeant, it won't happen again."

He further explained that if I wanted a good reputation as a hard-working go-to soldier, a reputation he had, I needed to be a man of my word. Thankfully, Roger's leadership style was similar to Jack's, and before long, I knew he was no longer mad when his wickedly funny sense of humor returned. However, the disappointment I felt left a lasting impression that I did not step up and say something when I should have.

With Roger's departure date getting closer, I felt like I was losing my best friend. At a barbecue the night before he was scheduled to leave, I asked to speak to him privately. I felt awkward, in the modern world of machoism, trying to express what I was feeling. "I don't really know what to say or how to say it, but I want you to know how grateful I am for all the time you've taken to teach me about what we do here. I definitely look forward to catching up with you again as soon as you return from the Philippines."

"Me too," he said. "Me too."

By the time Roger shipped out, I was a fully integrated, albeit non-contractor trained, member of the JTIDS test team. We spent the next couple of months driving the JTIDS rigs out to various predetermined locations, some way out on the farthest reaches of the base, where we would initialize and synchronize with each other, setting up a communications net to test. Testing consisted of, among other things, using large airborne equipment to jam the net and recording the time it took for the net to rebuild on large tape drives.

It didn't hurt that the officer-in-charge (OIC), assigned as the overall project supervisor, was a smart and very attractive lieutenant named Stephanie Rainsford. With her long cascading blond hair, which she let down after duty hours, she reminded me of Bo Derek from the famous 1979 sex comedy *Ten*, but without the beads. More than that, she was nice, easy to talk to, and well-liked and respected by everyone on the team. I knew the system well enough to be noticed by Lieutenant Rainsford. I also recognized that I was not the only one secretly smitten with her, and that even worse, she was way out of my league.

As the promised sun and surf of Florida drew closer, several more soldiers from my section were assigned to the project, receiving their OJT by other members of the team, as there wasn't time for anyone to attend contractor training before the equipment needed to be packed up and shipped to Eglin Air Force Base, Florida. The group of soldiers from my section were replacing previous team members, like Roger, who were shipping out to other assignments, or ETS'ing (Expiration Term of Service) altogether.

After cleaning and parking the rig, my squad leader came over. "Hey, before you take off, Jack wants to talk to you."

I walked into Jack's office. He was on the phone and motioned for me to take a seat. When he hung up, he paused for a moment and looked at me as though he were waiting for me to say something.

"Sergeant Parson said you wanted to speak to me?" I finally said.

"Yeah." He paused briefly again. "We've had a situation come up and we need you to fill an open slot in an upcoming PLDC class at Fort Bliss, Texas."

He was sending me to Primary Leadership Development Course (PLDC). PLDC was the first course that trains specialists and corporals (E-4s) in the fundamentals of leadership. From what I could tell, most soldiers took the course near the end of their first four-year enlistment, if they were planning on reenlisting, or after they reenlisted. I was only halfway into my first enlistment, so the opportunity to go came early and unexpectedly.

"The class starts in January," he continued. "Which means we're taking you off the JTIDS project."

The promised sand and surf of Florida vanished, ripped from my mind like a thief stealing my car. I looked down to gather my thoughts and compose myself. "I thought Bennett was going?" I said.

"She has chosen to ETS rather than attend the course. You were next in line behind her."

I leaned back in the chair and looked up. My mind suddenly flashed back to my surprise promotion that Jack orchestrated and the promotion points he fought to get me.

Now respectfully and valiantly, I attempted to convince Jack that remaining on the project through operational testing in Florida was in my best interest. "What about all the hard work Roger invested in training me?"

"The project will go on and be just fine. Plus, Roger would agree with me that this opportunity is more important than working on your tan in Florida."

"How 'bout I go to this course as soon as I get back?" I knew I was pushing him, at least as far as I dared, without crossing the line. The last thing I wanted to do was say something that would make him question the confidence he had placed in me. Had this turn of events come from anybody other than Jack, I didn't think I would have handled myself nearly as well.

Jack remained firm. "Brad, in my experience, when these opportunities come, you have to jump on them. It may be hard for you to see now, but this is about your career and your future."

The next morning when I told Lieutenant Rainsford that I was being taken off the project, she gave me a glimmer of hope when she dropped what she was doing and straightway went to see Jack. She offered to give up two other soldiers from my section, if she could keep me. Jack said the same thing to her. "This is about his future."

My last day on the project was just before I returned home to Oregon to spend Christmas with my family. During my time home, I enjoyed myself and catching up with everyone, but I couldn't completely relax. I was silently dreading what lay ahead. To make matters worse, the day before I was supposed to leave home for Arizona, my car ended up in the shop for repairs. I called Jack and explained my situation.

He extended my leave, but made it clear that I had to be back before a certain day. "Before you depart for PLDC, the new Command Sergeant Major wants to personally inspect each of you, along with your TA-50 gear." TA-50 gear included gas mask, tent, sleeping bag, pistol belt, canteen, magazine pouches, and rucksack, among other items. The inspection was called a "showdown," where we stood by our equipment displayed on the floor in a prescribed layout configuration.

Sensing his urgency, I reassured Jack that as soon as my car was out of the shop, I would be on my way.

By the time my car was finished, I was due back to base—1,200 miles away—by midnight the next day.

It was dusk, twenty-two hours later when I stopped for gas at the California-Arizona border and called Jack from a pay phone.

"Where you at, boy?"

"I just crossed the Arizona border."

I could hear the clear sense of his relief through the phone. "Listen, the first thing I want you to do in the morning is get a good haircut."

"What about going to Supply to sign for my TA-50 gear?"

"Don't worry about your equipment. Your squad leader, Tom, already went to Supply and signed for all of it. He is going to do the layout while you're getting a haircut. You hear me? A *good* haircut. Understand?" Like many soldiers, I was continually pushing the limits of army regulation 670-1 with my hair length. Jack had been fairly tolerant with me and others up to a point, but I could tell from his tone that he wanted me well "within" standards for the next day's showdown.

"Yes, Sergeant, I understand."

"Okay, then we'll see you in the morning."

I pulled into the barracks parking lot close to midnight and spent the next two hours shining my boots and pressing my uniforms. Finally, at 2:00 a.m. I crawled into bed.

The next morning I walked into the barbershop at the PX and told the woman I was going to a leadership school and needed a good haircut. All that feathering-length hair I had worked so hard to grow ended up on the floor. She sheared off more hair than I felt was necessary, but on the bright side, Jack would be pleased.

Five of us were heading to PLDC. So each of us stood by our equipment, which was laid out on green army wool blankets. The air in the room became electric the instant Command Sergeant Major (CSM) Ted Harris walked in and scanned over the room and its occupants. Harris was new to EPG, having arrived only a month before. He was still in the process of getting the lay of the land, and the rumors were not positive about him, which made everyone uncertain about how his leadership style would translate in the test and evaluations environment. Before his assignment to EPG, he spent his career coming up through the ranks as an MP (Military Police). He was a veteran of two tours in Vietnam, the second of which, he personally ran a POW camp of captured Viet Cong soldiers.

CSM Ted Harris

He exuded confidence and displayed an uncanny sense of when minutia was in the air. In other words, we could not BS him. He was 5'9", about 185 pounds. While he was not physically imposing by any means, what he may have lacked physically, he made up for in sheer presence.

He had an aura unlike any leader I had ever encountered. He carried a swagger stick—a shiny ten-to-twelve-inch stick made of stainless steel. It looked like a giant shiny nail that he would use to tap on walls, desks, whatever happened to be nearby. By the looks on certain faces, his tapping drove them nuts.

He frequently wore the Class B (less formal) uniform—green dress pants with light green short-sleeved shirt. Jack wore the same uniform almost every day with his E-8 rank displayed on black boards attached to his shirt's shoulder. Harris's shoulder boards had the same amount of stripes as Jack's, but inside the rockers and chevrons was a star surrounded by oak leaf clusters that spoke volumes.

It was the first time I had ever seen a senior leader make experienced, mid- and upper-level NCOs visibly nervous. Harris wore high-gloss, black, low-quarter shoes. Each shoe had metal pieces attached to the toe and heel that made a tapping sound when he walked. A sound everyone came to recognize.

With his years of experience, including combat, he was all about taking care of soldiers. Some did not like him or his style, feeling that he was not a good fit for the environment we worked in. They felt he was more suited for the Combat Arms units, like Infantry or Artillery, not a unit like EPG. Even though he wasn't universally liked, *everyone* respected him. The only person who didn't seem nervous around him was Jack.

Harris slowly walked around the room, his shoes tapping with each step. He paused in front of each soldier—standing ramrod straight at Parade Rest. Looking them up and down, he checked their personal appearance. "Are you ready to be an NCO?" he asked one soldier.

"Yes, Sergeant Major," the solder said, his voice quivering.

"Uh huh." He pursed his lips and nodded slightly as he glanced down at his equipment. I glanced down at my gear, gear I had not personally checked out, including a gas mask, which requires a fitting.

When he finally got to me, I felt myself stand a little straighter.

"Jones, are you ready for this?"

"Yes, Sergeant Major, I believe so," I managed to say without my voice cracking from nervousness.

He seemed ready to move on after looking me over. I almost inwardly sighed with relief, thinking I was in the clear when he used his swagger stick to point toward my gear. "Jones, how about you put on your gas mask for me?"

I couldn't believe it. Of all the soldiers in the room, he asked me to try on my gas mask. *There's no way he could know what I went through to get here, or that I didn't check out my own gear . . . could he? Man, I hope this mask fits.*

As soon as I slipped on the mask, I realized it was too big. I hoped he would not notice.

He did. He turned to the group of leaders in the room. "How is this soldier going to survive a chemical attack in combat with the wrong size gas mask?"

His question went unanswered with blank stares prevailing among the group of leaders.

I certainly was not going to open my mouth. Immediately following the showdown, I drove to Supply with Tom and traded my mask for one that fit.

The next morning, I departed for El Paso, Texas, and Fort Bliss—home of the army's noncommissioned officer (NCO) academy, and the place that would be my home for the next month.

Fort Bliss is the home to the army's Air Defense Artillery (ADA) branch, specializing in anti-aircraft weapons such as surface-to-air missiles. The ADA motto is "First to Fire" in reference to their anti-aircraft batteries being the first to fire in World War II against the Japanese. Fort Bliss is also the home of the United States Army Sergeants Major Academy (USASMA). USASMA is the premier leadership school for senior noncommissioned officers of all US military branches and numerous allies and their senior military leaders.

Before reporting to the PLDC building number and address I was given, I stopped at the PX for one last breath of freedom before the lockdown I had been warned about. After the PX, I reluctantly drove to the building, which was literally a repurposed prison complete with surrounding walls and guard towers. I was assigned, with most soldiers from other bases, to stay in a refurbished World War II building a few blocks away. The building had sloped bomb ramps leading down into the rooms where we slept. The classrooms and instructor offices were above.

First thing the next morning, during a formation with all of our gear sitting at our feet, Sergeants First Class Washington and Sellers introduced themselves as our platoon sergeants, along with several others who would be our instructors. One by one, Sergeant Sellers held up each item that Sergeant Washington called out as instructors walked up and down each rank to verify that we all had produced the required item. Soldiers who didn't have an item, such as a tent-half, or gas mask, were told to pack up and leave.

These guys are not playing around.

After the showdown, we marched in our highly spit-shined boots and starched uniforms to a nearby obstacle course. Only for this course, we would be low-crawling the entire length. The dirt was light and chalky, like talcum powder. They had us form two lines about ten yards from a large dirt mound. The first ones in line were allowed a short burst to run up the mound at the sound of the starting gun. At the top they began low-crawling down the mound. At quick intervals the next soldiers in line sprinted to the top of the mound, but those who tried to extend their run farther down the other side were punished by being made to return to the starting point where they had to low-crawl from there.

I was halfway back in the line, so when it was my turn, I faced a giant cloud of dust, which already hovered over the mound and beyond. I sprinted up the mound and dropped onto my chest feeling dirt slide inside my jacket and T-shirt. I crawled down the other side, right into a long sunken pit with just enough room to crawl on my chest under a mosaic of barbed wire above me. I could taste the gritty dirt in my mouth.

When I crawled out from under the last strand of barbed wire, I jumped up for another quick three-to-five-second rush straight into the next long pit of low-strung barbed wire. For this one, we crawled on our backs. I felt waves of dirt sliding down and sticking to my sweaty back. Cadre paced up and down on the outside of each pit igniting and dropping extremely loud explosives into detonation holes beside each pit, screaming for us to keep moving.

On the final stretch everyone had slowed down considerably due to fatigue. I crawled up next to a female who had completely stopped. She looked at me through a dirt-encrusted face. "I can't go any farther." Just then another soldier crawled up on the opposite side of her. Together we locked our arms in hers and pulled her the rest of the way.

Finally able to stand, I looked around at the others. Everyone was coughing up dirt and inspecting the holes in their previously starched and pressed uniforms. I glanced down at my own pants with blown-out knees, and my once highly spit-shined boots, which were no longer black. The black leather toe portion was completely worn down to the tan leather beneath. The boots I'd worked so hard applying hundreds of coats of black Kiwi were ruined, as were pretty much everyone else's.

The cadre had us students gather around them in a horseshoe-shaped gaggle where the head platoon sergeant spoke. "Now that you've completed our obstacle course, you do not want to get kicked out of this course and have to do that all over again."

Well, on the bright side, I thought, still spitting dirt out of my mouth, *at least the worst part is over.*

After marching back, we were allowed to shower and change before going to our first class. Our instructor, Staff Sergeant Berry, outlined the course curriculum, which included classroom lectures on the fundamentals of leadership, followed by practical exercises.

Some skills were individual, like Land Navigation and taking and passing the Army Physical Fitness Test (APFT), but others involved leading squads and/or platoons of soldiers while marching and administering organized PT (Physical Training), among other things. In order to graduate from the course, we had to pass individual evaluations demonstrating each skill.

One by one each of us were placed in various leadership positions and evaluated on our performance. We studied the role of the NCO as it evolved from the pre-Revolutionary War period through the World Wars, and how those roles contributed to the post-Vietnam NCO of the 1980s. Between and after class periods, we practiced leading others in Drill and Ceremony (D & C) and conducting PT. Initially, leading others in D & C and PT were stressful "on-the-spot" moments where coordinated squad/platoon movements relied on specific commands issued in a certain sequential order. As the days passed, our class coalesced and we encouraged one another to overcome our initial nerves and gain confidence.

Entering week two, I was selected to serve as a quad leader, while we studied the purpose and use of training schedules, to insure required unit training events were conducted and accomplished. Accordingly, at the end of each day, I briefed the class on the next day's lectures and what materials to bring, followed by upcoming events later in the week. Everyone was eagerly anticipating the upcoming twenty-four-hour pass starting Saturday afternoon. It was our chance to unwind in off-post hotel rooms and refresh ourselves for the week ahead.

Leading up to that Saturday, I briefed the class numerous times on the release and return times for that weekend's twenty-four-hour pass. Sunday's return formation was listed at 6:00 p.m. on the training schedule. It's what I had been briefing all week. Just before releasing us Saturday afternoon, however, Sergeant Sellers announced that Sunday's return formation time was changed to 5:00 p.m. Along with everyone in the formation, I heard it, but for some reason, in my mind, it never replaced the time I had been briefing all week.

When I pulled into the parking lot fifteen minutes prior to 1800 (6:00 p.m.), I noticed one of my classmates, who was the acting platoon sergeant, watching me carefully. He waited for me to park and exit my car, then he shook his head as I approached. "Where were you?" he asked with a stern tone. I must have had a quizzical look on my face because before I could answer, he said, "The return formation was forty-five minutes ago. I've been looking all over for you."

"What?" I said as panic set in.

"You have to immediately report to the CQ up at the prison."

I ran to my car before he could say anything more. As I drove up the road, my heart raced while I tried to think of something I could say to the Charge of Quarters to make this nightmare go away.

The staff sergeant at the CQ desk looked up as I approached. "Are you the soldier reported AWOL from the 5:00 p.m. formation?"

"Yes, Sergeant," I said, swallowing hard. "I'm the one." I couldn't think of anything else to say.

"What's your name and student number?"

"Specialist Bradley Jones, student number 071."

"Okay, I'm logging that you were fifty-seven minutes late. Go ahead and return and report to your platoon sergeant."

That evening, every nightmare scenario played out in my mind, making sleep impossible.

The next morning, class started off like normal. At our first break, however, our instructor told me to report immediately to Sergeant Washington's office."

I knew it was game-time. The dreadful feeling in the pit of my stomach grew worse.

"You want to explain to me why, according to last night's CQ log, you were fifty-seven minutes late for formation?" Sergeant Washington said after I entered his office.

I had tossed and turned all night considering what I would say at this moment. I finally concluded that attempting to offer some excuse would only make my predicament worse. "Last week as squad leader, I briefed Sunday's formation time listed on the training schedule every day to my class. That original time stuck in my head. So the reality is . . . I have no excuse, Sergeant."

He looked at me as if waiting for something more. When I remained silent, he looked back down at the counseling statement laying on his desk. "I've already annotated in the purpose block the reason for this counseling. And since you have no excuse, I have no other choice than to recommend you for dismissal from this course." He wrote those words in the Plan of Action section and passed it to me. "I need you to read this, then sign it."

"Recommend Specialist Jones's dismissal for failure to follow course instructions/standards," it read.

I signed, too overcome by anxiety to say anything more.

"You need to take this counseling statement and report to Senior Platoon Sergeant Ramirez's office at the prison."

Standing in front of Master Sergeant Ramirez was no less intimidating, and again, I offered no excuse. He filled out another counseling statement, also recommending me for immediate dismissal.

From his desk he pulled out a piece of paper containing a cumulative demerit chart. He informed me that for every thirty seconds late, I received one demerit, but that it doubled every thirty seconds. So the count goes up exponentially from one, two, four, eight, sixteen, thirty-two, sixty-four, and so on. The chart went only so high, and I was way beyond the last column of the numbers on the chart.

"You have accumulated more than two million demerits, Specialist Jones. Anything over fifty is grounds for dismissal. How many demerits do you currently have?"

"I have about twenty-five, Sergeant."

"I hope you're proud of the fact that you have catapulted yourself beyond everyone in this course with well over 2,000,000,025 demerits."

I didn't know what to say.

"I suggest you pack up your personal belongings right after you report to the Commandant, who's waiting to see you in his office."

Two weeks into my training and I'm already getting kicked out.

By far, one of the most intimidating experiences for a young soldier is having to report to a Command Sergeant Major, the Commandant of the entire NCO academy—and he was already expecting me. I knocked three times loudly on his office door and waited. After a long pause, a gruff, irritated voice said, "ENTER!" Inside the room I immediately noticed the distance between the door and the front of his desk was only a few feet. There was no maneuver space or "safe zone." He had his large desk pushed toward the door so that he had all kinds of space behind, leaving little to no space for those with the unfortunate experience of standing on this side.

I stood at attention and saluted. "Specialist Jones reports to the Commandant as ordered."

He returned my salute. "Stand at Parade Rest." He had all the counseling statements spread out on his desk. He glanced at each one before his eyes narrowed and he looked. "Why did you even come here?"

"I was picked by the leadership in my section as one ready for the responsibility of becoming an NCO."

"You were picked ahead of your peers?"

"Yes, Sergeant Major."

"I find that very hard to believe. I can't imagine why your unit would choose to send such a sub-standard soldier to this course. It says here in the CQ log that you were fifty-seven minutes late for last night's formation. Why were you so late?"

"Sergeant Major, I have no excuse."

"Do you have any idea how many demerits you've accumulated?"

"I was told by my platoon sergeant that it was more than 2 million."

He sat back in his chair. "You have wasted my time, your classmates' time, and ultimately the army's time by coming here and demonstrating your lack of attention to details and training schedules. I want you out of my school and on your way back to your unit. Hopefully with time and maturity, you can return and try again." He looked back down and began gathering up my counseling statements. I didn't move, because technically he hadn't dismissed me. Finally he looked back up. "NOW QUIT WASTING MY TIME AND GET OUT OF MY SIGHT!"

I lacked no small amount of motivation to do exactly as he ordered.

In the hallway outside the Commandant's office was a desk with a phone. I couldn't bear the thought of having to face everyone back in Arizona, but I knew it was time to make the call back to RLSB and break the news. My platoon sergeant, Staff Sergeant Diaz, answered.

"Sergeant Diaz, it's Specialist Jones. I just got dismissed from PLDC."

"*What?* What happened?"

"I was late for a formation."

"Oh, Brad. That's not good."

"Can I talk to Sergeant Crumling?"

Sergeant Diaz passed the phone to Jack. "Brad, what's going on?"

"I just got dismissed for being an hour late for a formation. I'm really sorry, Sergeant Crumling."

"Okay, we'll deal with that when you get back. But listen to me, Brad. I want you to get a good night's sleep before you leave El Paso, okay?"

"Yes, Sergeant."

"Brad, it's not the end of the world. Just get back here safely."

"I promise, I will." It felt like a dagger to the heart. All the trust and confidence Jack had invested in me now shattered into a million pieces. I couldn't shake the awful feeling I felt inside.

I walked over and sat down on a nearby bench. My mind was swimming in a sea of thoughts when something occurred to me, an impression that came forcefully. *I think I'm being tested. They are testing me . . . wanting to see what I'm made of . . . to see how much pressure I can take.* The impression remained, and I knew then and there, *Whatever happens, I have to hold up to anything they throw at me.*

The senior platoon sergeant instructed me to return to my room and pack up my gear. While doing so, I realized I needed to pick up some materials and my backpack from the classroom. The last thing I wanted was to face my fellow students. If it weren't for my backpack and its contents, I would have just slipped quietly away. As I approached the door, I could hear a heated argument going on inside. My classmates were having a discussion with our instructor, and I could tell that emotions were running high. I took a deep breath and opened the door. An uncomfortable silence fell over the class. They had been arguing about me and my situation. Every eye followed me as I walked around to where I had been sitting earlier that day. Nobody uttered a sound as I gathered my stuff.

When I got to the door, I turned back to face them. "I'm grateful to have met and gotten to know each one of you. Good luck and goodbye." As soon as the door closed behind me, the heated discussion erupted where it had left off. I felt grateful that they were clearly upset about what was happening to me. With my car packed, I went back to the prison to turn in my linen and meal card. My platoon sergeant came into the supply room just as I was finishing.

"The Commandant has some paperwork for you to sign before you depart."

I nodded. *Okay, one more trip into the lion's den and it will all be over.* After another three loud knocks I stood back in the sweatbox space between his desk and the door. As if I'd forgotten his words from before, he repeated himself. "I just cannot figure out why your unit sent you."

I said nothing.

He laid out my counseling statements emphasizing that each one recommended my dismissal. He then laid out several papers turning them so they were facing me. "These are your dismissal papers. Before you sign them, I need to know if you intend on filing an appeal."

"Yes, Sergeant Major, I wish to file an appeal."

He exhaled deeply. "Fine."

As soon as I indicated I wanted to appeal, suddenly he became more irritated with me. "If you're going to file an appeal, I need you to sign here in this block," he snapped, impatiently shoving the document across the desk and pulling it just as quickly away the instant I finished. "And again here." He shoved another document toward me. He seemed to want me out of there before I could finish signing.

I signed the last box and put down the pen. "Sergeant Major, how does the appeal process work? How do I file an appeal?"

He shook his head. "I have no idea. NOW GET OUT OF MY OFFICE!"

Returning to my spot on the bench, I consciously thought, *In 10 minutes this ordeal will be all but over.*

The senior platoon sergeant came out of the Commandant's office and walked to where I was sitting.

"Can you write out an appeal in five minutes?" he asked.

My jaw dropped slightly. "I believe I can, Sergeant."

From behind his back, he produced a yellow pad and pen and handed it to me. I took the pad and pen and sat back down. The first thing that came to my mind was that the original training schedule we used leading up to Saturday's twenty-four-hour pass had 1800 as the time for the return formation. When the platoon sergeants changed the time to 1700, they altered the training schedule—and one thing we were taught was that we don't alter the training schedule on the fly. I also wrote that others who had been late for formations had received more than fifty demerits, and according to my earlier encounter with Master Sergeant Ramirez, anything over fifty demerits was grounds for dismissal. Those students were allowed to do demerit details to work off some of the demerits, but they remained in the course. If they were going to dismiss me, according to my argument, they had to dismiss them also.

I wrote the appeal out in neat, legible handwriting and signed my name at the bottom before I handed the pad back to the platoon sergeant. He took it and walked back into the Commandant's office. When he came out a few minutes later, I watched his face for any expression indicating my fate.

"Only one thing left to do, Specialist Jones." Suddenly, a smile emerged and his eyes lit up. "Get your meal card and linen back. The Commandant just reinstated you."

I thought I misheard him. "I-I can stay and finish, Sergeant?"

"Yes, you can stay—if you can stay out of trouble for the next two weeks."

"That I can do, Sergeant! That I can do."

I drove back to the hangar in a daze and parked my car. I sat for a moment and stared out the windshield. The students were coming out of the building for the final formation of the day. I watched as our platoon sergeant came down the ramp from his office and walked toward the formation. That's when I got out and made my way around the back row of cars where I had parked. When he got to the formation, I was near enough that I could hear his announcement.

"Student number 071 has just been reinstated."

The entire formation erupted into cheers just as I came around the last car and into view. When they saw me approaching, the platoon sergeant sensed the moment and dismissed the formation. My classmates ran to me. I had never been mobbed before, but it was spontaneous as much as it was emotional. Several female soldiers had tears streaming down their faces. I couldn't help myself, I reached out and hugged each one. I was fighting my own set of emotions, but I wanted them all to know how truly grateful I felt for their support.

My platoon sergeant motioned for me to come over. I approached him and stood at Parade Rest. "Yes, Sergeant?"

"Jones, I want you to know that you impressed everyone by holding up under a tremendous amount of pressure. If you had broken down at any time, you would be on your way back to Arizona."

"Thank you, Sergeant."

"We've had sergeants and staff sergeants in the same situation break down emotionally. If you had not held up as you did, you would've never been offered the appeal process. You would have just been handed the dismissal papers you signed before being shown the door."

I nodded, feeling speechless.

"You do realize, though, that you accumulated a monumental amount of demerits, don't you?"

"Yes, Sergeant, somewhere in the neighborhood of 2 million."

"Plan on having demerit detail every evening from here on."

He could have said from here to eternity and I would have been grateful! "No problem, Sergeant, after what I've been through, demerit detail is the least of my worries."

From that day on, I swept, stripped, waxed, and buffed the cadre offices each night. I stripped paint off doors, counting fourteen different coats on several doors. I painted rocks and policed up areas outside the building.

I became somewhat of a celebrity for the remaining two weeks of the course. Instructors commented openly to me and others that they'd never seen someone graduate with so many demerits. Jack couldn't come, so he sent several senior NCOs from RLSB to see me graduate. Unbeknownst to me, they had approached the Commandant to tell him they were there to see me graduate. He said, "Let me tell you something about Specialist Jones. He demonstrated tremendous poise and bearing under pressure. He has great potential as a soldier and future NCO." When they returned, they shared the content of the conversation with Jack, who had them craft a sworn statement that ended up being included in the paperwork of my NCO promotion packet. As soon as I returned from PLDC with my graduation certificate in hand, I was now officially "promotable" to Sergeant (E-5).

With plenty of time to think as I drove back to Fort Huachuca, one thing occurred to me: despite the rocky road that led to graduation, in the end, I hadn't let Jack down. By some miracle, I had survived, precariously preserving Jack's trust and vision in what he saw in me. In the months that followed, I shared my unique experience with soldiers preparing to attend the course. More than a few returned—some quite a while after my class—saying they still talked about the soldier from Fort Huachuca who graduated with more than 2 million demerits.

CHAPTER 7

We Regret to Inform You

————————

It felt good to be back in Arizona, and back at work. The first thing I did was ask to see our training schedule, which I'm not sure I even knew existed before PLDC. I had a feeling our training schedule would be different, considering most soldiers in EPG were assigned to projects testing systems and equipment, unrelated to their specific MOS.

It was. Where normal units would have almost daily scheduled MOS training, our training schedule designated those hours for tests and evaluations, along with weekly classes on basic soldier tasks.

Jack saw me looking over the schedule. "What class is scheduled for Wednesday?"

"Conduct Developmental Counseling," I said.

"Guess who's going to be teaching it?" A grin broke out across his face.

I was. "Sergeant Crumling, I owe it to you—after what I put you through."

He began to laugh. "Good, because you just about gave me a heart attack."

"I know. I certainly wasn't planning on making PLDC so exciting."

"Brad, the most important thing to me is that you graduated. And I'm sure along the way you learned more than you expected."

"Well, Sergeant, I certainly know how to file an appeal. Should could come in handy for the next leadership course you send me to."

He picked up a pencil and flung it at me. "Get out of my office!"

I burst out laughing. "Right away, Sergeant!"

The morning of the class, I had all my notes and material ready to go. I felt nervous, given this was my first time to teach, but I was confident I could present the material, having the subject matter still fresh in my mind from PLDC.

About twenty minutes into the class, Jack called out to the room, "AT EASE!" Everyone jumped up to Parade Rest—I was already standing—and through the door walked Command Sergeant Major Ted Harris. "Carry on, carry on, and don't mind me," he said.

That's easy for you to say, I thought. *You're the Sergeant Major!*

Now my nerves perked up more as I continued, taking up where we left off, discussing the different types of developmental counseling, and how each one has a unique goal or desired outcome. I was relieved when I occasionally glanced over and noticed Jack and Sergeant Major Harris quietly talking near the back of the room.

When I completed the class, Staff Sergeant Diaz rose and announced, "Outstanding presentation, Specialist Jones."

I smiled in appreciation and noticed the other NCOs all nodding in agreement.

Sergeant Parson approached me and shook my hand. "Great job, Jones."

As each soldier exited the room, they shook hands with Harris. I was the last one to leave, hoping Harris departed before I finished gathering my notes. When I got to the door, I found him waiting for me just around the corner. He thrust out his hand. "Specialist Jones, I hear congratulations are in order," he said, as we shook hands.

"Thank you, Sergeant Major."

"What do say you and I have lunch tomorrow?"

"That would be great, Sergeant Major," I said, lying through my teeth. The last thing I wanted to do, after my experience in the Commandant's office, was to sit through a nerve-racking lunch with another E-9 Sergeant Major.

He smiled and nodded. "I will have my driver pick you up at noon."

"That will be fine," I said, still lying. "Thank you, Sergeant Major."

The next day, at five minutes to noon, I grabbed my hat and was leaving with just enough time to walk to the guard shack, the only entrance/exit on the secure compound where our office was located. As I passed the desk near the door, the phone rang. I reflexively picked it up.

"RLSB, this is Specialist Jones," I said. "This line is unsecure. How may I help you, sir or ma'am?"

"This is the guard shack," the male voice on the other end said. "A car and driver are here to pick up a Specialist Jones."

"I'll be right there." I walked as quickly as I could without going into a full run, not wanting to make Sergeant Major Harris, who had clearly arrived early, wait any longer for me. Sweat began to pour from my forehead and down my back.

Great. Lunch hasn't even begun, and I'm already sweating. I jumped into the air-conditioned coolness of the sedan's rear seat, removing my hat and wiping the sweat from my brow.

Sergeant Major Harris was sitting in the front passenger seat.

"Good afternoon, Sergeant Major," I said, sitting up tall and straight as an arrow.

"Jones, I've been looking forward to this lunch since I got off the phone with the Commandant at the NCO Academy at Fort Bliss two weeks ago."

I released an internal groan. *Ugh, I can't believe he knows.*

"He and I go way back," he said.

I can't believe I'm stuck in this incredibly uncomfortable position until lunch is over. Jack's probably laughing his ass off right now.

Lunch was at the base's NCO (Non-Commissioned Officers) club's restaurant. Even though the meal was delicious—I ordered the chicken fried steak—as hard as I tried, I could not relax and enjoy the experience. The conversation consisted mostly of me asking questions about Harris's career, which spanned thirty years. Finally, near the end of the meal, the subject of my cliffhanging experience came up.

"I'm glad you stood tall and graduated, Jones, because had you been dismissed, I would have driven out there with my driver and had him drive your car while you drove my car with *me* for the entire three-hundred-mile return trip. I'm glad I didn't have to do that."

I smiled, feeling awkward. "Me, too, Sergeant Major."

By the end of lunch, Harris was laughing and cracking jokes, which was nice, but still, all I wanted was for lunch to be over. When we pulled up to the Haze Hall compound, Harris surprised me by getting out of the car and shaking my hand. "Jones, let's get together for lunch again soon. I will have my driver get ahold of you."

"Sergeant Major that would be great." I hoped that was the last lie of the day. "Thank you for lunch." Even though I was uncomfortable, I was honestly grateful for his time and generosity. After that first lunch, we enjoyed a few more meals together where I was still never able to fully relax. I just couldn't figure out why he had taken an interest in me. I assumed, after talking to the school's commandant about me, he must have wanted to see for himself who this soldier was who caused such a commotion. But he never let on why he spent time with me as he did.

As winter turned to spring, in 1987, we received word that our section would be assigned several new vehicles. We had already heard rumors about these otherworldly looking vehicles from soldiers in other sections who were already using them. They were called Humvees, some type of ultimate off-road vehicles. A group of us were eager to attend a familiarization-and-licensing class taught at the Motor Pool, where we would receive classroom and hands-on instruction.

The Humvee looked like something from the future. It was wider than anything I had ever seen, with large meaty tires connected to a space-age-looking suspension system, which gave it excellent ground clearance capable of handling extreme travel conditions.

"It looks menacing," one soldier commented while we walked around the OD (olive drab) green creations parked in a line.

"Sergeant, are they new?" I asked the instructor.

"Yep, straight from the factory," he said.

They look as if they could climb trees, I thought as I looked down the row of them. *I can't wait to get behind the wheel and go off-roading.* I laughed excitedly at the thought.

We spent the first day covering vehicle familiarization and technical specs. Day two covered how to perform a proper PMCS (preventive maintenance checks and services), an important and critical requirement before operating any military vehicle. At the end of day two we were all looking forward to getting behind the wheel during the next day's practical exercise.

Near the end of class, the instructor handed me a phone message from Jack asking me to stop by the shop before heading to the barracks. As soon as I approached the front door by the office, my squad leader, Sergeant Parson, was waiting for me. By his look, I knew instantly that something was wrong.

Was there a surprise room inspection in the barracks? Did I forgot to make my bed?

"Don't worry, you're not in trouble," Tom said. He must have sensed what I was thinking. "But I have some news. Jack wanted to tell you personally, but since he had to leave earlier, he asked me to."

What can be so important that Jack wanted to tell me himself?

"We just got word this morning that Roger was killed yesterday in Manila."

Air was suddenly sucked out of the room. I bent forward, reaching out to steady myself against the building. Then I threw up in a torrent on the asphalt.

Tom put his hand on my shoulder. "You okay?"

In the deepest part of my grief, I was also mortified at what I had just done. "I'm okay. Sorry, I didn't mean for that to happen." I wiped at the corners of my mouth and blinked hard to keep from crying.

"Don't worry about me, dude, I just want to make sure you're all right."

"I will be." I stood up and tried to breathe in slowly. "What happened?"

"Yesterday, while he was riding his motorcycle into work early in the morning, he was struck broadside by another vehicle and killed instantly."

This can't be real. This has to be some mix up with another soldier. He just got there!

"What happened to the other vehicle? Who was in it?"

"Nobody knows. Apparently, it immediately fled the scene. The intersection where the accident occurred had a manned guard shack next to an entrance gate of a military compound. The military guards claimed they didn't see anything."

"I can't believe it. I can't believe he's gone." I shook my head, feeling another wave of nausea coming on. *This can't be happening,* I told myself over and over. *There must be some mistake.*

"Are you getting sick again?" Tom asked.

"I hope not," I said, forcing myself to breathe deeply.

"The whole thing is incredibly suspicious."

I stared at him in surprise. "What do you mean?"

Tom shared what little information he had. Apparently, our soldiers working with the Philippine army were being watched and followed. The assignment was supposed to be low profile, due to the threat level from guerilla elements within the country. Our soldiers were instructed not to wear army uniforms or adhere to regulation haircuts. Roger had recommended one of the Philippine soldiers for an award, and while the soldier was traveling in his dress uniform to receive it, he was assassinated by a sniper.

Roger had sent me a couple postcards, but never mentioned any of what Tom was telling me.

Tom followed me back to the barracks and sat in my room talking with me for the next couple of hours. I was in a daze, and he knew it.

Finally, I looked at the clock and realized how much time he'd spent with me. "Thanks for looking out for me. You need to get home to your wife and daughter. I'll be okay."

He rose slowly to his feet. "If you need to talk, I don't care what time it is, don't hesitate to pick up the phone."

"Thanks, Tom."

I had never had someone close to me pass away. Memories of hanging out with Roger, golfing, four wheeling, and going to Mexico flooded my mind. The magnitude of the loss I was feeling startled me.

Sleep evaded me the entire night. The next day, I had a hard time focusing during the one portion of my class I was really looking forward to, the actual Humvee driving. All I could think about was getting back to the shop and finding out if any more information had come in.

When it was my turn to drive, I followed the road that led back to the Motor Pool.

"Are you sure that's as far as you want to go?" asked the master driver, sitting next to me. "You don't want to go up into the canyon?"

Under normal circumstances, he wouldn't have had the opportunity even to ask before we would have already been there. But not today. "No thanks, I've had enough," I told him. "I'm good."

The moment class let out, I raced to the office and found Jack apparently waiting for me.

"Roger's family has requested those who were close to him serve as pallbearers at his funeral next week. I thought you might like to be included in that group."

I didn't know what to say. I had only known Roger for a little more than six months, the last several of which, he'd been gone. I felt indebted to Jack for considering how much it would mean to me to be included among others who were also close to Roger but had known him much longer.

"It would be an honor, Jack. Thanks."

"The funeral is in his hometown of Hopkins, Missouri, about one hundred miles north of Kansas City. You, John Stanley, and Vic Monaghan will be going there on orders, so you need to make sure your Class A's are ready." Going on orders meant the army was footing the bill for us to go, for which I was grateful. "In addition," Jack continued, "we got word to Duane King in Italy. He will fly into Kansas City where you guys will pick him up the day after you arrive. A color guard from Fort Leavenworth will arrive the morning of the funeral to take part, so you'll need to coordinate with them. One of you will present the flag to Roger's family after it's folded. You'll need to practice to make it look sharp."

Images of presenting the flag to Roger's grieving family forced a wave of my own grief to come to the surface. I looked down, suddenly fighting a rush of emotion.

"Brad? You okay?"

"Yeah," I said, still not looking at him. "I've just never had a close friend die."

Jack came around the desk and sat in the chair next to me. "The most important thing you will get to do in this tragedy is be part of honoring him and his service."

I swallowed hard. Jack's words brought me some comfort. "I can do that," I said.

"Good. Make us proud, Brad."

John, Vic, and I flew to Kansas City two days before the funeral. I had never been to Missouri before. The green prairies with dark and fertile-looking soil, interspersed by lush groves of trees seemed like the perfect place to be a farmer, as we passed acres and acres of farmland heading north toward Hopkins.

Roger's parents, Bill and Barbara, greeted us in the front yard as we pulled up.

Barbara had short dark hair and seemed very warm and loving. She reminded me of my grandmother on my dad's side. Bill was tall and thickly built, like Roger, having worked as an appliance service repairman. Roger looked more like Bill, but I could also see the similarities to Barbara.

Bill shook hands with John and Vic. "Welcome, welcome," he said, while Barbara hugged them. They all knew each other from having previously met in Florida. "We're so glad you could make it." Then they both turned toward the new guy.

"Hi, I'm Brad." I didn't expect they would know me.

"Brad," Barbara said and offered a warm and loving hug. "Roger told us about you while he was here on leave just before he left. Thank you for coming. It really means a lot to us, and I know it means a lot to Roger."

"Welcome to our home," Bill said as we shook hands.

"Please come in and meet Roger's brothers and their families," Barbara said, leading the way inside. They welcomed us in as though we were their own family. They invited us to sit on lawn chairs in their backyard where they were eager to hear about our families and lives in the military, including what parts of the country we came from.

Roger's mother kept looking at me. "You remind me of Roger," she said after a while. "You look like him." Her eyes filled with tears.

A heartfelt compliment from a grieving mother. I had never thought we looked similar, but I felt honored that the way I presented myself meant something to her.

"Stay for dinner," Bill told us. "It's good Kansas City-style barbecue. We're grilling steaks from local cattle. And the corn on the cob as well as the lettuce and tomatoes are from our own vegetable garden."

"Yes, please stay," Barbara said. "It would mean so much to us."

We agreed, and we ate some of the best-tasting food I had ever eaten.

During the meal their phone rang. The funeral director was calling to say Roger's body had just arrived from Dover Air Force Base, Maryland. Dover is where fallen soldiers are taken and their remains prepared before being released to their families.

As soon as they told us, we stood to leave. Roger's parents and two brothers and their wives decided to drive down to the mortuary. John, Vic, and I figured we'd leave them to have their family viewing in private, meanwhile we would make our way to the hotel and catch up with them after we picked up Duane from the airport the next day.

"No," Bill said. "We'd like you to come with us."

The invitation was unexpected, and we felt we couldn't refuse being extended such an honor.

It was dusk when our vehicles pulled into the gravel parking lot of the mortuary only a few blocks down Highway 148. I suddenly felt nervous. I had never seen a deceased person before, let alone someone with whom I had experienced so much only a few months before. The nine of us remained in the foyer while the funeral director moved the casket into position in another room.

Roger's sisters-in-law began to tear up as they hugged each other. Their husbands—Roger's older brothers, Ron and Rob—stood side by side. Bill and Barbara held hands.

I can't imagine what they must be going through. They both had the look of concerned parents as if they were waiting to see Roger in the hospital following a life-threatening accident. My heart broke for them when the double doors opened and we were ushered into the room.

Straight ahead, a lone silver casket sat unopened under overhead lights. Not really knowing how I would react to seeing Roger, I decided to stand behind John, who looked at me and gave me a reassuring nod. Somehow, it felt better to have someone between me and what would be revealed once the casket lid opened.

A mortuary employee came in from a side door and quietly and solemnly opened the casket lid. An audible gasp emanated from Roger's sisters-in-law. They both covered their mouths and began to quietly sob. Bill and Barbara, still holding hands, moved closer to the casket.

"Oh, Roger, my poor boy," Barbara said.

Roger's brothers enveloped both Bill and Barbara, clutching them from both sides.

John, Vic, and I remained toward the back not wanting to infringe on the family's profoundly personal moment with their son and brother. We waited for several long minutes before the three of us slowly moved forward.

I peered down on my friend. Roger's arms were folded across his chest with white gloves covering both hands. He was wearing his army-green

Class-A uniform, complete with rank and medals. The right side of Roger's face looked peaceful and serene, as if he were only sleeping. I couldn't seem to grasp that here lay the close friend I had high-fived on the golf course after a great shot.

I finally steeled myself to take a closer look. The injuries to the left side of his head and face revealed the unmistakable severity of the collision. His helmet was no match for the force of the impact. The level of reconstructive work made me grateful for the dedicated efforts of the men and women who worked on Roger at the Dover mortuary. I walked over and stood next to Barbara putting my arm around her. It was spontaneous and natural. She looked up at me, tears streaming down both our cheeks, neither of us speaking. I didn't want to clutter the sacred spirit that permeated the room where a dearly departed son, brother, and friend's spirit felt close by, offering comfort and assurance that one day, we would see him again.

The next morning, we departed Hopkins heading south to meet Duane's flight from New York into Kansas City. After showering him with handshakes, hugs, and "It's good to see you again. How's army life in Italy?" we caught Duane up on everything that happened the day before, including the surprise invitation from Roger's parents to accompany them to the viewing. Duane wasn't sure he wanted to see Roger, preferring to remember him from the many memories they shared. I couldn't blame him. *Knowing what I know now, I would have rather not seen him in that condition.*

But Duane was eager to see Roger's parents. He was the one most acquainted with Bill and Barbara, having spent time with them when they traveled to Florida to see Roger. They were extremely grateful Duane could make the trip after arriving to his new duty assignment a short time before.

Bill and Barbara invited us to stay for dinner again. I did not want to infringe on their energy and resources, but I'm not stupid. I couldn't bring myself to decline their offer of another wonderful meal. I wasn't disappointed. It was an exceptional feast of barbecued pork loin, corn on the cob, and salad. Afterward, the four of us remained seated around the kitchen table talking with Bill and Barbara about their son.

Up to that point, with so many extended family in town for the funeral, none of us really had the opportunity to discuss our feelings about Roger. I felt hesitant to share my own feelings, not knowing if that would only add to their grief. But having Duane there seemed to break the ice. Duane, John, and Vic shared some humorous experiences they enjoyed with Roger during their months together while working in Florida. Bill and Barbara shared stories from Roger's childhood. Of the three boys, Roger was clearly the free spirit, wanting to go out and see the world, unlike his brothers who had both settled down, gotten married, and were raising families in small farming communities nearby.

I mostly sat and listened, but when it felt right, I offered my own testimony. "I haven't known Roger as long as Duane, or Vic, or John, but from the moment he returned from Florida, he unselfishly took me under his wing and showed me the ropes of a completely different job from the one I'd signed up for. From day one, he was like the best big brother anyone could ask for. I'm still amazed at the impact he had on me in such a short time. I'm grateful that I was able to have that time with him."

Bill excused himself and disappeared momentarily down a stairwell. When he returned, he carried a clear glass gallon jug by the handle, which contained only a small amount of red liquid. "This is what's left of a batch of fruit wine Roger made while home on leave a few years ago. We would be honored if you'd share a glass with us." After Bill poured a small amount into glasses Barbara set on the table, he raised his glass. "We couldn't be more grateful to enjoy something Roger made with his own two hands . . . to share something with you, his close friends—the ones he talked about and cherished while he was away from us. To Roger."

Through tear-streaked cheeks, we followed in unison. "To Roger."

During the early morning hours of the next day, Thursday, May 14, 1987, we walked in silence, not wanting to interrupt the peace that prevailed along the quiet streets of Hopkins. Military funeral honors involve time-honored elements intended to express deep gratitude for those who have served our nation. With the funeral service scheduled for 2:00 p.m., we needed to look over the cemetery's graveside layout for any obstacles we would have to navigate while moving the casket. One soldier, placed at the corner of the casket, issues clear but quiet commands. It takes practice to make the marching maneuvers look professional.

Once the casket is set, as pallbearers, we lift and secure the flag above the casket, holding it in place. At this point, the honor guard's seven-person rifle team initiates three rifle volleys for the twenty-one-gun salute. A lone bugler plays "Taps," which is the National Song of Military Remembrance. The final note of Taps is our signal to begin folding the flag.

Correctly folding the American flag, and making it look good, takes practice. The flag is folded in half lengthwise, then again in half lengthwise with the stars pointing upward. Then it is folded starting from the opposite end from the stars thirteen times in a triangular fashion. On the thirteenth fold, a flap remains open where three shell casings are inserted before being folded in. The triangular shape symbolizes the hats colonial soldiers wore during the Revolutionary War. It would be my privilege to place the three spent shell casings—representing duty, honor, and country—into the flag, after retrieving them from a member of the rifle team.

Using a practice flag we brought from Arizona, Duane, the senior ranking member, led the four of us during walk-throughs of each segment. The moment we began, I had that same impression come over me that I had in those early mornings on Barton Parade Field at Fort Gordon. I could tell the others felt something similar as the friendly banter between us suddenly stopped the moment we began. This was sacred. Holy.

We remained quiet as we traveled back to the hotel where we pressed our Class-A shirts and pants and spit shined our shoes. After donning our uniforms, we checked one another for proper alignment of awards (medals), nametags, and branch insignias. We each unwrapped a brand-new pair of white gloves, putting them in our jacket pockets.

"Everybody ready?" Duane asked.

We nodded.

"Let's honor our friend," Vic said.

Looking into each other's eyes, we simultaneously said, "Let's."

The procession of cars turning off Highway 148 from both directions onto East Barnard and Thompson streets were immediately faced with bumper-to-bumper cars already parked on the blocks surrounding Wray Memorial United Methodist Church. The entire town of Hopkins, population approximately six hundred—and then some—seemed to be in attendance. The chapel was filled to overflowing. We made our way up the aisle of pews to a spot close to the entire Melvin family.

Promptly at 2:00 p.m., Rev. Mark Hibbard began the service by welcoming everyone and offering an opening prayer. A chorister led the congregation in singing "The Lord's Prayer," followed by Rev. John Shipley's eulogy of Roger's life and military service. He then added his own personal comments regarding the tremendous loss he felt knowing how much Bill and Barbara loved and nurtured their boys over the years. Rev. Hibbard rose to the podium and delivered a poignant and comforting message about how those we are blessed to have in our lives leave a lasting mark, and once departed, continually remind us of the glorious reunion ahead. The congregation joined in singing the final hymn, "How Great Thou Art."

The four of us gathered around and began to slowly move the casket down the aisle with Roger's family close behind. We deliberately and slowly maneuvered the casket into the hearse. Roger's family began loading into several dark sedans while we hurried to the cemetery. On the way, I didn't see a single moving vehicle. The streets were deserted. At the graveside we positioned ourselves and waited for the hearse. The location of the cemetery provided an elevated view of Highway 148. Finally, the hearse turned onto the road. The procession that followed seemed endless. When everyone got in place, we slowly slid Roger's casket from the hearse, lifting it as it fully emerged. I was chosen to give marching commands since I needed to move from my corner spot to receive the casings after completing the first couple folds of the flag.

The silence, as all eyes were now on us, was only broken by the sound of a gentle breeze coming through the trees. I took a deep breath and issued the first audibly low command. "Forward, March. . . . Left . . . your left . . . your left right . . . left." The commands kept us in step with one another.

Once we reached the grass, we made a slight left turn and marched directly onto the platform. "Mark time . . . march . . ." brought us to a stop with our feet still marching in place. "Ready . . . halt." We gently lowered the casket and returned to the position of Attention. "Center . . . face." We executed a facing movement turning toward the flag. Slowly we reached down with our gloved hands, we secured the flag, and pulled it taught and flat just above the casket.

The honor guard captain called the firing party to Attention. On the command of "Ready," in unison, each one raised their rifle up to about waist height. "Aim." They raised their rifles to their shoulders. "Fire." The crack of the first volley made some in the large group flinch. After firing, they returned their rifles to the ready position. On the subsequent command of "Ready," the firing party pulled the charging handle—sending the spent casing flying—and released it, seating the second round. "Aim. . . . Fire." The crack echoed in the distance. "Ready. . . . Aim. . . . Fire." *Crack*, the final volley sounded.

The bugler began to play "Taps." The moving and powerful notes, a call to remember those who gave their lives in the service of their country, seemed to pierce each of us to the core. I could hear many in the large congregation surrounding us, sobbing. Looking up at John and Vic, we made eye contact several times while holding the flag. We were each fighting valiantly to hold it together.

When the final note of "Taps" trailed off, we began to fold the flag. Following the first two diagonal folds, I stepped a few paces to my right to receive the three casings from an alternate rifle squad member who marched over and placed them into my hands. I marched to the other end of the casket where Vic and John held the flag with the final fold open. I gently slid the rounds beneath the top fold. Vic and John neatly folded the final flap in before spinning the flag so the long end was toward me. I took it and ran my hands slowly along each side, ensuring each corner was crisp and straight with no visible red showing.

Duane, a few paces to my left, where he waited to receive the flag. I folded the flag, apex up, against my chest, and pivoted to face Duane. As soon as we locked eyes, I could see through my own tears that he was fighting mightily, as his eyes welled up with tears. I folded the flag down from my chest and spun it until the long side faced Duane. He looked down at it, gently reaching up with both hands and received it from me. I slowly saluted the flag. Duane stepped to Roger's mom who sat wiping tears from her eyes. Spinning the flag, he knelt directly in front of her. With one hand resting on top and the other hand supporting from below, he extended the flag and rested it on her knees. He paused, taking a deep breath, before he began.

"On behalf of the president of the United States, the United States Army, and a grateful nation, please accept this flag as a symbol of our appreciation for your loved one's honorable and faithful service."

Barbara seemed to realize how hard Duane was fighting to maintain his composure. She gently patted his arm. "Thank you, Duane."

Duane stood and took one step back, then slowly raised his right arm to offer one final salute, before turning to march to where we stood off to the side. Silent tears fell from my eyes as I watched his every move. As Duane approached, he could no longer hold back the tide, dipping his face into his hands and sobbing next to us. The four of us gathered around in a circle of brotherhood, arms entwined in a private moment of unity and support.

"All right, you guys," Duane said, as he finally pulled himself together and wiped tears from his face. "Knock it off." We chuckled at the irony of his statement.

We decided to remain in our dress uniforms for the gathering back at Bill and Barbara's home following the funeral. As afternoon turned to evening, we bid Roger's family goodbye and God bless, with hugs and handshakes and more tears. Saying goodbye to Bill and Barbara was especially hard. It had been a sacred and singularly unforgettable privilege to honor the service and sacrifice of their son, and our friend, Roger Dean Melvin.

Before dawn the next morning, we loaded up and headed for the airport in Kansas City. We sat in silence through most of the drive, absorbed in our own thoughts and memories of Roger and the things we had just experienced.

It was not easy saying goodbye to Duane, knowing he was off to Italy for the next several years. In the military, it's those unspoken words when saying goodbye. They communicate the reality—that chances are, we'll probably never see each other again. One more loss to grieve.

CHAPTER 8

In View of These Qualities

———————

After Roger's funeral, to keep me busy and help me decompress from the whole emotional experience, I looked forward to working on a major new project with several upcoming multiple-month trips scheduled. The TDY (Temporary Duty) trips were to attend operations and maintenance classes contractors taught on their portion of the equipment in the new system, and they would keep me traveling through summer and fall of 1987.

Also, it didn't hurt that most contracting companies requested military personnel not wear uniforms while attending training courses. A request we were more than happy to comply with, along with the added bonus of relaxed haircut standards, depending on who was in the class, what rank they had, and whether or not they chose to enforce those standards while in a travel status. Our project supervisor was a civilian, Steve Dodson, who already shared his laidback opinion when it came to things like maintaining military dress and grooming standards. Steve was more concerned that we conduct ourselves professionally than whether or not our hair touched our ears.

Steve introduced me to Specialist Emmett Terry, a new soldier to our section. Emmett, a large-statured country boy, who grew up in the hills surrounding White Sulphur Springs, West Virginia, would be my coworker on the project. With Roger gone, Emmett quickly became one of my closest friends. He had just returned from a tour in Korea, returning stateside with his beautiful Korean wife, Soonja.

The Enhanced Position Location Reporting System (EPLRS), had similar characteristics to JTIDS—the project my coworkers/friends were currently testing while "living the dream" in condos on the sandy white beaches of Florida. One similarity with the system was the setup of a wide communication network over a large area. The EPLRS system was designed to establish a secure computer-controlled communications network, managed centrally via a large Network Control Station (NCS) for data distribution and position location reporting. Previously, the army relied on individual radio sets to report friendly and enemy positions, using maps dependent on terrain association provided by soldiers on the ground. With GPS-based systems like EPLRS, battlefield commanders could make better decisions based on increased and accurate positioning—greater situational awareness—of friendly and enemy combatants.

With one main-frame, and three mini-mainframe computers, the NCS acted as the main communications hub for each individual "man-pack" unit that individual soldiers carried. The man-pack came mounted in a custom-made backpack, with an attached handheld device for communicating the soldier's current position with the NCS, and provided users the ability to communicate over non-voice radio with other users in the net.

The twelve-week operations and maintenance course for the computers in the NCS would be the first class I would take, taught at Sperry/Unisys in Minneapolis. After that class, I was scheduled to take a sixteen-week class, which covered all other associated equipment within the NCS—including man-packs and test-sets—at Hughes Aircraft Company in Fullerton, California. An earlier version (PLRS) of the EPLRS system had already been fielded to the Marine Corps, which meant operations and maintenance manuals already existed and were available. In weeks leading up to that first class in Minnesota, we studied the operations and maintenance manuals, which the navy shipped to us. Among the three of us in the section on the project, not one of us had any knowledge or experience with microprocessor fundamentals or programming.

We located an instructor who taught computer theory only a few blocks away at another facility on base. He agreed to teach us a highly condensed crash-course in microprocessor fundamentals. He turned out to be extremely knowledgeable and did his best to teach us everything he felt we needed. Despite some days feeling as though I was getting blasted by a firehose of information, I came away knowing a lot more about processors than I ever imagined.

About this time, several large boxes came to the section containing the first desktop processors any of us had ever seen. I helped unpack each one—including large monitors—and turn them on. Most of us had no clue about their capabilities or use in an office environment. I was not the least bit interested in trying to figure them out, but several soldiers already owned, or had experience with, the first available personal computers, such as Commodore 64s, and they may have known then what the rest of us would later find out: computers were well on their way to becoming the single most influential factor in emerging technology.

The week before Emmett and I left for Minneapolis, we headed to the finance office. With our travel paperwork in hand, we were there to sign for travel money. A nicely dressed middle-aged gal on the other side of the thick glass pane watched us momentarily before she spoke up. "Can I help you?"

"Uh . . . yes, ma'am, we were told to report here with our travel paperwork," I said.

"Can I see your paperwork?" she said. "Just slide it under the glass."

We both did as she asked, giving her all the paperwork we had been given, hoping she could find the one she needed.

She scanned through each pile. "Looks like you are both here to pick up a travel advance for your upcoming TDY trip, beginning this Sunday."

"Yes, ma'am," Emmett and I said in unison.

"You'll need to sign some paperwork, and I need to see your military IDs."

We pulled out our green ID cards and slid them under the glass. TDY trips used government per diem (daily) calculations based on locale and duration of days to determine the amount an individual would receive. Prior to the evolution and ease of credit cards—for official government travel—Emmett and I were receiving travelers' checks.

"Okay, if you'll just sign here, you will each receive a little more than twelve thousand in American Express traveler's checks."

My jaw dropped. I had to stop myself from blurting out, "*Twelve thousand dollars?*" Instead I looked at Emmett, whose eyes were as big as mine.

As soon as she stepped away to get our money, I turned full-on to Emmett. "Dude, twelve thousand dollars? I've never even *seen* that amount before, have you?"

"Not on my watch," Emmett said, starting to laugh. His laugh, which was a huge source of entertainment to me and anyone else who heard it, sounded like *The Flintstones'* Barney Ruble with a bunch of hilarious high-pitched wheezing and snorting thrown in for good measure. When he laughed, it never failed to crack everyone up.

The finance lady returned with two equally thick stacks of traveler's checks booklets, sliding each stack under the glass. She made a valiant attempt, but ultimately gave up trying to maintain her serious demeanor. Once she heard Emmett laughing, she could no longer contain herself and burst out laughing hysterically. "That has to be the funniest laugh I've ever heard," she finally managed to say.

"Yeah, tell me about it," I said. "I actually have to work closely with this guy for the next six months." We cracked up all over again.

After finally catching our breath, Emmett and I picked up our stacks and began thumbing through the pile of booklets, containing hundreds, fifties, twenties, and tens.

After signing each one—we had to sign when we received them and again when we spent them—we walked out of the finance office feeling self-conscious, and maybe a bit paranoid, with our pockets bulging with more money than either of us had ever dreamed of.

I ate my final breakfast—for the next three months—in the chow hall early Sunday morning, June 7, just prior to Steve (our boss) picking up Emmett and me in a rental car for the trip to the airport and our nonstop flight from Tucson to Minneapolis. Going from Arizona to Minnesota was like going back home for me. The state's many lakes (almost twelve thousand of them) surrounded by lush green deciduous forests and 70 percent relative humidity made my continually dry skin feel as if it could finally breath again.

We had prearranged individual lodging for the entire summer at a condominium complex not far from the airport, south of I-494, in the suburb of Bloomington.

From day one, the material and pace of the course were intense. The first computer was a standard thirty-two-bit processor that weighed several hundred pounds, and supported three other smaller processors. There were four of us from Fort Huachuca, Emmett and me, who were E-4s, and two civilians, Steve and Frank, along with five higher-ranking (E-6 or above) soldiers from Fort Gordon. Those soldiers were there to take the course, and after returning to Fort Gordon, create the lesson plans for future MOS training classes. The difference between us and them was Emmett and I were both part of aviation branch—him as an avionics guy and me as a radar repairman. On the other hand, they had all been trained as computer operators/programmers in their MOS training. When we traced different command executions through the various sections of the processor, they understood what was going on, whereas the rest of us were fighting to keep our heads above water.

The four of us from Arizona met and studied together nearly every evening during the first few weeks. And in order to remain physically fit, Emmett and I began working out together as soon as we found a health club that allowed us join for the time we'd be there. Emmett towered over me at 6'5". And weighing nearly a hundred pounds more, he was the ideal lifting partner in the weight room. Even though he could bench press—with one arm—the weight I was pressing, he always encouraged me.

"C'mon, you got one more left in you," he'd say. "You can do it, you got this." Working out with Emmett not only helped me deal with the stress from class, it helped me bulk up beyond what I had attained during basic.

During the week, we spent extra hours studying together, but on the weekends, we had the time of our lives. Minnesota is known for its extremely cold winters, and apparently after being cooped up indoors, residents take full advantage of the outdoors and the beautiful weather during the summer. In July, the twin cities hosted Riverfest, a giant out-door craft festival, with nightly live concerts by top-named acts, such as Whitney Houston and Heart. We rafted just across the Wisconsin state line down the Apple River, and we took in Minnesota Twins baseball games in the brand-new Metrodome in downtown Minneapolis.

Most of all, my favorite thing was to have a barbecue at one of the nearby lakes and just hang out by the water. Relaxing on the shores of Bush Lake gave us the place and time to get to know the other members in our class, who were also scheduled to attend the system level training classes that fall in southern California.

The remaining days passed much quicker when the course material shifted from programming to processor maintenance. Finally, I felt like I was in my element; troubleshooting and maintenance were where I learned the most about the processors. One of our final days in class, an instructor commented on the outside temperature, which was just over 70 degrees that day. "From here on, it will not get any hotter than it is today, and it will just get colder." It made me glad I was heading back to the warm and dry weather of the southwest.

Initially, we were scheduled to go directly to California from Minneapolis, but word came from the office that our class had been delayed two weeks. I looked forward to California, but it would be good to return to Arizona and see Jack and everyone in the shop before heading out again.

Prior to flying back to Arizona, I spoke with Jack on the phone. "I hope you were smart with your TDY funds, Brad," Jack told me. "The day after you arrive, the finance office will be expecting you and Emmett to turn in the unused funds they gave you."

I was glad to inform him, "Jack, that won't be a problem. I still have that entire California portion . . . old man." I couldn't get through the sentence without laughing.

"You little punk, if you were closer, I'd lodge my boot firmly in your backside."

"That's impossible, Jack, you never wear your boots."

He couldn't help laughing at the comment. "We'll take this up when you're back in the office."

It was good to hear his voice and hear him laugh. Three months had already passed since I had seen him nearly every day, and I realized just how much I missed him.

The two weeks back in Arizona were a nice break before heading out again on the next leg of our training. It felt good to get behind the wheel of my GTI and see everyone back in the office.

Soon enough, Emmett and I were back in the finance office signing another mountainous pile of traveler's checks, followed by one of the shortest flights I'd ever taken, landing at John Wayne Airport in Orange County.

During the 1980s, southern California was considered a Mecca for defense contracting. Hughes Aircraft, McDonnell Douglas, and Lockheed Martin were just a few of the companies with large operations in and around Los Angeles and San Diego. Hughes Aircraft had large facilities in separate locations around Orange and LA counties, known as Missile, Satellite, and Ground Systems Groups, each one employing thousands.

The Hughes Aircraft Ground Systems Group in the foothills of Fullerton was where the entire EPLRS system was located in a huge secure lab, with lecture classrooms nearby. Following the operations and maintenance courses, the system was tentatively scheduled for Operational

Testing (OT) in a real-world environment back at Fort Huachuca later in 1988.

Shortly after arriving, we received a baptism-by-fire of sorts. While sitting in our rental car waiting for a light at the intersection of Beach Boulevard and La Palma, a late seventies-model VW Bug with half a dozen Anaheim police vehicles shot past us and the bus next to us. Luckily, the bus was stopped next to the curb, creating just enough space for the fleeing Bug to pass between us without sideswiping us or the bus. The five or six vehicles in front of us were not as lucky, as the Bug sideswiped cars on both sides, slowing him down as its four-wheel wells sent up a high-pitched screech, leaving deep gouges down the entire length of each car.

I couldn't believe the driver forced his way through such a narrow gap, leaving a trail of debris as he shot into the path of cross traffic on La Palma. The chase almost ended there when the driver gunned it across the intersection into the path of two oncoming cars. As luck would have it, both drivers reacted quickly, power sliding as they swerved dramatically, tires screaming as they slid around both sides of the Bug, only narrowly avoiding T-boning the assailant.

We were close enough to see the terrified expressions on the unsuspecting drivers as they slid nearly the entire length of the intersection before regaining control. No cars were coming from the left, giving the Bug, now dragging four dangling fender wells, a clear path ahead on Beach Boulevard.

Nobody had ever witnessed a high-speed chase, let alone nearly been involved in a hit-and-run from a fleeing vehicle. In California, high-speed chases were becoming a new spectator sport, delivered directly to living room televisions by news helicopters flying high above the unfolding action.

"Follow them!" we yelled at Kevin, our boss, when the stoplight turned green. We could easily see flashing lights ahead as more police cruisers and California highway patrol (CHIPS) motorcycles continued the pursuit, but before long, they disappeared in the distance.

Hoping to catch the outcome later on the nightly news, we turned right on Ball Road. With only a few blocks remaining to our destination, and much to our delight, we came upon the smashed remains of the VW Bug, surrounded by a dozen law enforcement vehicles. The light ahead turned red, temporarily allowing us a front-row seat to the final moments of freedom the driver would enjoy. Apparently, he ran when his Bug came to a violent stop after it smashed head-on into a larger and heavier vehicle at the intersection. At first, we couldn't see any cops. Then a large group of officers emerged from the neighborhood with a sweat-soaked and strung-out-looking dude in handcuffs.

He looks just like Slash from Guns N' Roses, I thought when I saw his huge head of hair. He was wearing only jeans, no shirt, and no shoes. Watching the whole scene unfold, we looked at each other in utter amazement. I finally spoke up, saying what we were probably all thinking, "Man, life in California is rad!"

Roughly one month after arriving, on Thursday, October 1, I met Emmett and Steve down by the rental car around 7:15. After traveling north on Beach Boulevard, we took a right on Malvern Avenue just after 7:40. We were listening to the radio when the song suddenly stopped in the middle. The disc jockey's voice pierced the silence: "Dude, look at the walls moving."

Emmett and I looked at each other. "Earthquake?" I asked.

"Must be on the other side of town," Emmett said. We shrugged it off as something that didn't affect us—until we pulled up to Hughes Aircraft and saw a huge crowd standing in the parking lot.

"Maybe there was an earthquake, and it was big enough that everyone around here felt it?" Emmett said.

We waded through the crowd until we found Ralph, our instructor. He seemed calm, even though he and everyone else raced toward the exits as soon as the shaking started.

"Where were you when it hit?" I asked him.

"In the classroom, getting things set up for the day. I knew by the way the building was swaying that it was a big one, and I needed to get out quick. Did you feel anything?"

"Not a thing," Emmett said. "We were going about forty-five miles an hour. The only way we knew something happened was the song on the radio suddenly quit in the middle, and the DJ said something about the walls swaying."

Ralph shook his head in disbelief. "I can't believe you didn't feel anything while driving down the road. Your rental car must have good suspension."

Word finally came that structural engineers had checked the building and declared it habitable and sound. Managers allowed their employees to enter when they felt comfortable. We made our way to the classroom right behind Ralph. During the second hour of instruction another earthquake hit. It was the weirdest, most unsettling thing to feel and hear the building flex as a whole. It was as if I could hear and feel the steel beams, holding the building together, groan under the force. Emmett and I simultaneously reached laterally across the table and grabbed the edges of the desk with our hands. Ralph figured now was a good time to inform us about the nature of earthquakes. "Aftershocks are normal after a big quake. But don't worry, this building is brand new and was built on rollers for this very purpose."

That's good to know, I thought. But rollers or not, that was the eeriest thing I'd ever felt *and* heard *ever.*

The next day, when word somehow reached the office back in Arizona, the phone rang in the classroom. I picked up and heard Jack on the other end. He was calling to instruct us to stock up on water and nonperishable food, and if and when the big one hit, we were to make our way and report to El Toro Marine Corps base in uniform.

"Oh yeah, and one more thing," he said. "Sergeant Major Harris is coming out there in two weeks for a site visit. He specifically asked that you pick him up from the airport and be his driver while he is there. So have fun with that. . . . And make sure you and Emmett get good haircuts before he gets there."

I could tell he really enjoyed imparting that last piece of info. "I'm so glad you called, Jack. I thought maybe you forgot about us," I said and chuckled. "Not to worry, we will be standing tall and looking good when he gets here."

The day before Harris's arrival, Emmett and I reluctantly went into a barbershop and hacked off all the wonderful hair we had grown since arriving. I starched and pressed my uniform and spit shined my boots. My spine stiffened the moment he walked off the plane.

"Jones, how are you?" he asked.

"Great, Sergeant Major. Welcome to California."

We drove straight to Hughes Aircraft where Emmett and I gave him a tour of the huge lab, which contained the three mockup NCS's, each with four Unisys computers inside, and the room where we were currently learning how to repair the individual man-pack units using a test set. We then showed him into our classroom where we introduced him to our instructors and fellow class members.

Even in this environment, in the presence of our classmates who had been with us in Minnesota and the EPG and Hughes civilian contractors, his mere presence commanded respect. Our classmates from Fort Gordon, who outranked Emmett and me by at least two grades, were impressed by him.

"Where has your career taken you thus far?" he asked each one.

As each one explained the different units and places they'd served, invariably he personally knew a senior leader they had served with. It was uncanny how he knew someone from pretty much every unit and/or place they had served.

His conversations with our classmates continued during lunch in the large Hughes cafeteria. Following lunch, Harris pulled out a copy of the latest *Army Times* containing the promotion point totals for all MOS. "This may be of interest to some of you," he said.

Up to that point, I had accumulated 550 promotion points from, among other things, completing PLDC, scoring well on my PT test, and completing several correspondence courses. Emmett had already shared with me his frustration about his MOS—also in aviation—and how the cutoff score for him to get promoted to Sergeant E-5 had been at 998 points, for as long as he could remember. Emmet was on his second four-year enlistment, yet we were both E-4s. As far as time served, he was going on six years, while I was somewhere in my third.

Like Emmett's, more than a few MOS's had cutoff scores that continually remained at 998 points, which meant soldiers had to go way above and beyond, doing extra things, like completing correspondence and/or college courses, to accumulate more points for promotion in their field. Fair or unfair, for some, the effort took years.

When I opened that *Army Times*, I quickly found 93D—my MOS—and scanned across the column. In the column under E-5, I saw a number I thought couldn't be right. The printed number in the column read 495.

No way could that be the correct point total. That's got to be a misprint, or the point total for MOS 93C or 93E. I scanned back to the MOS column and started over. I read the number again: 495 points for promotion to E-5.

Suddenly I wasn't sure I wanted to say anything to everyone in the room for fear that I could be mistaken. Emmett must have seen the look on my face. He came around the desk and looked over my shoulder,

"You're a 93D, right?" he asked, scanning the page. "Well, I'll be a monkey's uncle. Bradley Jones, you just got promoted."

Suddenly everyone in the classroom erupted at the same time. "What?" they said, excitedly. "Are you serious?"

"Serious as a heart attack," Emmett shot back to everyone in the room.

"Let me see that," Sergeant Major Harris said. "Hmm . . . 93D . . . yep, looks official to me."

Everyone gathered around the table. "Congratulations, Sergeant Jones." I shook hands with everyone, feeling slightly dazed.

I can't believe I'm getting promoted to Sergeant E-5.

Harris immediately got on the phone and called Fort Huachuca. He had EPG's admin section put together a promotion packet to send in the mail. I wasn't due to return to Arizona for two more months, and he didn't want me waiting that long to officially be promoted.

The following week, the package arrived containing my promotion orders and several sets of rank for my uniforms. A lieutenant colonel visiting from another base happened to be touring the Hughes facilities the day the package arrived. He readily accepted the offer to come to our classroom and perform my promotion ceremony in front of everyone associated with our class. The only thing missing was Jack and Tom. I just wish they could have been there. And Roger. Boy, he would have been proud to see his protégé.

CHAPTER 9

King Rat 3

———

A few weeks after our teams returned from southern California, CSM Harris unceremoniously announced his retirement (for health reasons) in front of a large gathering of NCOs from EPG.

"I know some of you do not like me or my leadership style. To those of you who feel that way, I want you to know, I will be in the area for a few weeks following my final day in uniform. If you see me, and have the guts, I suggest you come tell me to my face what it is you don't like about me. Then I will gladly show you a thing or two."

I wasn't sure if he was joking or not, but nobody laughed and a tense hush fell over the auditorium. Harris was dead serious.

I was not the only one in the theater that day who was equally impressed, *and* blown away, by those comments. He faced his critics square on and stood up for his leadership. On the way out after the meeting, I overheard a number of soldiers comment, "Wow, I can't believe he threw down the gauntlet like that. That took guts."

Harris was a soldier's soldier, continually advocating for troops to train and be proficient in basic combat skills, or "field-craft," as it's known in the army. Harris was of the mindset: when all else fails, everyone in

uniform is ultimately an infantryman, and picking up a weapon and joining the fight should be second nature, no matter what. Also, he was not
a fan of soldiers coming straight to EPG from AIT (Advanced Individual
Training), as I had.

EPG's unique mission—coupled with extended travel to contracting
companies all over the States and with demanding test schedules involved
in developing and testing emerging technologies—left very little time,
if any, for training even in the very basic skills. This placed tremendous
pressure on senior NCOs in EPG. For some leaders, it didn't sit well, and
inevitably their feelings and comments made their way back to Harris. His
direct way of openly calling out his critics and addressing them head on,
left no doubt that this guy was a man of his word.

Sweat soaked and working under a blazing sun one afternoon a few
weeks later on a remote corner of Huachuca, a group of us were unpacking containers full of EPLRS equipment outside the facility that would
serve as the center of operations for testing—a hangar called Black Tower.
It was called that after the air traffic tower—painted black—that stood
several stories above, and in contrast to, the large white hangar.

I had just set some equipment down when I turned around and found
myself face to face with a smiling Harris. Startled, I went to Parade Rest.

"Sergeant Major. . . . What brings you out to Black Tower?" I inquired.

"Doing one final tour of each facility, saying goodbye to the fine soldiers here at EPG," he said. "How's the set up for testing going?"

"Fine, Sergeant Major."

"Tell me something, Sergeant Jones," he said, appraising my appearance. "When are you going to get a haircut?"

"Today, Sergeant Major!" Even in his final moments, he couldn't resist
commenting on the fact that my hair was getting dangerously close to my
ears.

He motioned for me to follow him as we walked off to a more private
distance from the facility. "On Friday evening, I'm going to celebrate my
last day in uniform at a dinner. My sisters will be there. They are flying in
from Ohio, and . . . I'd like you to come along."

The impact of his invitation pierced me to the core. *I can't believe he just asked me to spend the evening celebrating his final day in uniform.* Deeply moved, I nodded. "Sergeant Major, I would be honored to celebrate with you and your family."

"Great, here's my address." He slipped me a piece of paper as we shook hands. "We'll meet at my house at 1800 before we go out. I'll look forward to seeing you Friday."

"Looking forward to it, Sergeant Major." I watched as he turned and walked toward his vehicle and driver waiting close by.

Of all the people in EPG—of everyone in the military he had served with—whom he could have invited to dinner, he asked . . . me. I felt humbled and honored . . . and amazed.

Three days later, I parked in front of the beige one-story rambler on Meadowlark Drive. A large Arizona walnut tree stood in the front yard, offering shade to the front half of the house.

Despite his new status as a civilian, I still felt nervous walking up to the door. I took a deep breath and rang the doorbell.

"Joooones!" Harris said, opening the door. "Look at you with a fine haircut!" He pulled me inside with his outstretched hand.

"Thanks, Sergeant Major. Somehow, I knew you would like it."

To my right, I couldn't help noticing the hallway. Both walls were covered with several rows of frames and plaques, all neatly and meticulously hung, forming a wide swath that ran down the hall and around the corner.

They look like they're in formation. Dress right dress, I thought. It was the largest collection of accolades I had ever seen.

"Ah yes, there's nothing like a good haircut," he said and then introduced me to his two younger sisters, Hazel and Edna. "This is Sergeant Jones," he told them. "He's one of my favorite young soldiers, but you can call him Brad."

"Nice to meet you both," I said as I shook hands with each of them.

"Thank you for coming to celebrate with us," Edna said.

They were both warm, huggable, large-busted middle-age gals, with bright eyes and spunky personalities to match. I was in my early twenties and Harris had to be in his early fifties, so that meant Hazel and Edna were probably in their mid-forties, as far as I could tell. I instantly felt comfortable with both of them. They were quick to smile and laugh with each other and their brother, and looking at both of them, I could see the resemblance to Harris in their smiles and the shape of their eyes.

"Brad, tell us where you're from and what you do in the army," Hazel said.

They both listened intently as we talked about where I grew up and what I trained for—compared to what I was now doing. More than anything, I was dying to look at Harris's military history displayed on the walls that I'd noticed when I first walked in. Jack had a few plaques on the wall behind his desk, but I'd never seen this many in one place. The chance to look at an entire career from private to command sergeant major was a once-in-a-lifetime opportunity, and fearing I'd miss my only chance, I couldn't wait any longer. "Mind if I walk down memory lane, Sergeant Major?" I asked, pointing toward the hallway.

"By all means," he said.

I started with the first plaques—service recognitions from his tours in Vietnam. Each had accompanying photos showing a very young Ted Harris as an MP working in a Vietcong POW camp. I slowly worked my way down the hall, looking at similar plaques and photos from later tours in Korea and Germany, which showed Harris starting to rise up the ranks.

He looks so young. Like so many always say about me. I wonder if back then he had any clue he would ascend to the very top enlisted rank.

By the time I rounded the bend in the hallway and came back up the opposite wall, I had seen literally dozens of framed awards alongside plaques that said things like "For distinguished and dedicated service" and "For exemplary leadership."

This man has done it all, I thought, looking over his graduation certificate from the United States Army Sergeants Major Academy at Fort Bliss, Texas, the place where I already had some "fond" memories of my own—what with being nearly kicked out and all.

I was still soaking up, and in, his remarkable and distinguished thirty-year career when his familiar voice snapped me out of transfixion.

"C'mon, Jones, time to go," he said, calling to me now from the front door he was holding open for Hazel and Edna.

Dinner was at the Mesquite Tree restaurant. We dined outside under lights strung from the low-hanging branches of the restaurant's namesake—a giant mesquite tree—with spectacular views of nearby Carr Peak, one of the highest crests in the Huachuca Mountains. The restaurant dates back approximately 115 years, originally serving cowboys as a gambling hall and saloon.

As we ate and conversed, it was easy to see that Edna and Hazel adored their older brother and were proud of his career full of accomplishments. I thoroughly enjoyed their sibling banter during dinner, as Edna and Hazel lovingly teased their older brother.

It was as revealing as it was humorous to see Harris verbally outgunned by his sisters. I was grateful to see this side of him—a side, I'm sure, not many got to see. I felt as though I was looking through a window into the wellspring and family dynamic that surely helped to mold his character. He seemed truly happy, and as the banter continued during dinner, I could tell he was loving every minute of it.

After saying goodbye to both Edna and Hazel back at his house, it was finally time to say goodbye to "the man" himself. I put out my hand to shake his, and while shaking hands, he pulled me close and threw his arms around me in a bear hug. I was completely caught off guard by the unexpected display of affection. I returned the hug.

"Thank you for taking the time to show me what a great leader is," I told him. "And for kicking my butt when I needed it."

"I'm proud of you, Jones," he told me. "You keep pressing forward and taking care of soldiers, and good things will come."

"Thank you, Sergeant Major. I will always remember you and your example to me."

"I hope so. Don't make me come back here and kick your butt." He smiled.

"I won't," I said, surprised that we were both wiping tears from our eyes. "I promise."

As I thought about him and what he meant to me personally, it occurred to me, *There's no one I'd rather follow into combat than CSM Harris*, and that's the highest compliment for any military leader.

I was surprised at my feelings over losing CSM Harris. Not having lunch with him anymore. Not having him harass me about needing a haircut. Even though he wasn't going to be around the military any longer, I had no doubt that his legacy would live on and would stay with me for a very long time.

At least I still have Jack around to harass me, I told myself for comfort. So when I heard a nasty rumor a few weeks later that Jack was leaving, I was at his doorstep in a flash.

He was surprised to see me at his home. "Boy. You think you can just drop by whenever you darn well please?" But I noticed as he said those words, he had a twinkle in his eyes.

"Yeah, well, I came by because I heard a nasty rumor that you might be leaving us, and I figured you could probably use some instruction on how to spit shine your boots since you haven't worn them in ages." My attempt at humor was only to mask what I dreaded. I needed to hear him tell me what I'd heard was just that—a rumor.

The pained look on his face, though, confirmed the truth. "Get in here," he said. He sat on his recliner and I sat on his couch across from him. We looked at each other for a moment.

I broke the silence. "So it's true you have orders for an overseas tour?"

"Yep. Germany."

"Are you going?" I asked, hoping he would say no.

"One more overseas tour, then I'm done."

"Why not just stay here and retire?"

He nodded sadly. "I could do that, but it's one last chance to see Europe and I don't want to pass that up."

I felt as though I'd just been punched in the stomach. I was losing everyone I looked up to—Roger, CSM Harris, and now my closest mentor and friend.

"When do you leave?" I hoped that he'd say next year or in six months—something to give me time to mentally prepare and grieve.

"I have to report-in to the unit by mid-September, but I will be taking thirty-days' leave to visit family and friends back home in Pennsylvania before shipping out."

That gave me a month and a half to prepare myself for him leaving.

Jack had been the closest thing to a father figure to me. My own father rarely communicated with me of his own accord. In the years since I'd left the northwest, I had received exactly one letter from him, and that was during basic. Jack somehow, for whatever reason, consciously or unconsciously, sensed that void and graciously stepped in to fill it. Before coming to Arizona, I felt rudderless. But more than anyone or anything else, Jack helped me find my bearings, and the thought of him not being there with and for me conjured up an image of being alone and adrift on the open sea.

I hoped the very busy upcoming EPLRS testing schedule would help me deal with losing an important father figure and friend. But deep down, I knew that no distraction would cover the deep sense of loss I was already feeling.

The following week, I was grateful when numerous semi-trucks arrived carrying large black equipment containers that we offloaded and unpacked inside the hangar at Black Tower. Parked outside our shop, on the hangar's north side next to the tower, three large five-ton trucks were parked, each with an NCS (Net Control Station) trailer in the truck's bed. Each NCS came with its own sixty-kilowatt generator that provided power. Once the EPLRS equipment was deployed, meaning man-pack units spread out to the far reaches of the base and the NCS up and running, the actual testing criteria required a connection between all man-pack units leading all the way back to the NCS. Once the net was established, the system would undergo testing to reliably, and securely, pass message traffic between everyone in the net.

As the maintenance team, our job was to provide support services (repair) for the NCS and all man-pack units and their associated laptops used to record message traffic. So not only was this test necessary for the teams to make sure they could all communicate well, but also for our team to weed out any problem areas.

With more than a hundred man-pack units alone, EPLRS testing employed many civilians in the area that summer. They were divided into groups of five to seven with a soldier from EPG as their team lead.

Team leads were assigned multi-channel two-way radios for communication. The test director, who was a huge fan of James Clavell's Shogun novels—which center on Europeans in Asia, exploring the cultural impact of East meets West—came up with call signs based on them. As maintainers, our call sign was King Rat.

The section functioning as the overall test operations center used Tai-Pan Base as their call sign. The NCS operators used Noble House. And the soldiers serving as team leads for all the man-pack carriers were given Shogun Warriors as their call sign.

With Steve as the civilian lead, and Sergeant First Class Kevin Watson as NCOIC (NCO In Charge) of maintenance, they were King Rats 1 and 2, which made me King Rat 3.

In the first few weeks, after familiarizing the civilians with how to operate the man-packs, team leads—Shoguns—drove their teams and equipment out to predesignated sights where they set up their equipment, turning it on and making sure it was fully operational. They were more or less practice-runs for when testing would eventually take place. Some had to travel by dirt road to the farthest reaches of the base, so getting out there and getting set up took several hours. While this was occurring, the Noble House soldiers drove an NCS to a hill—not far from Black Tower—and set up the NCS for operations. Once the NCS was up, the individual man-packs were supposed to see the signal from the NCS, and through a secure exchange, receive permission to join the communication net.

It was hot and late in the afternoon the day of our first attempt to establish net communications between the NCS and roughly eighty-to-

one-hundred man-pack units. I grabbed a radio—we called them bricks—
and drove up the road to where the NCS was already set up and running.
Specialist Sara Adams, the NCS operator, was nervous to make that first
call over the radio.

"You can make the first call," she said to me, holding out her radio.

But I felt just as nervous. "I would," I said, trying to break the tension
with humor, "but you know . . . ladies first."

She inhaled deeply and shrugged. "Okay, here goes." She pressed the
button and began to speak into the radio. "Tai-Pan base, this is Noble
House 1," she said.

As soon as I could catch her eye, I gave her an encouraging nod and
thumbs up.

"Noble House 1, this is Tai-Pan base, go ahead," came the voice on
the other end.

"Base, the NCS is up and operational, ready for net-communications
with Shogun man-pack units."

"Good copy, Noble House 1. . . . Break, break. . . . Shogun warriors,
be advised, your man-pack units can now be powered on."

A flurry of radio traffic started as leads instructed their team members
to power on their units and report back. I looked at Adams and Rick
Posey, a Hughes contractor, and held up my hand with fingers crossed.

The first report came in. "Tai-Pan base, this is Shogun 12. All of my
team members are reporting no net-comms with the NCS." The other
fifteen Shogun teams reported in one after another, all reporting the same
thing—no one was communicating with the NCS.

My stomach lurched. *This is not how the system worked in the test lab
at Hughes back in California. This isn't good. With no net, nobody communi-
cates. Now what do we do?*

Suddenly Rick grabbed my arm. "You need to jump on that radio and
tell everyone to enter the digits X dot I and push send."

"You want me to do what?" I said incredulously. I had never heard of
that command, let alone used it.

"Grab that brick and make a net call and tell them to enter X dot I, then send. If you don't do it, this whole day will be wasted. You have to do this. After each update, this command executes the update, and it would be better coming from someone in maintenance than a contractor like me."

The last thing I wanted to do was put myself out there in such a huge way—especially on the first day.

"Dude, you have to trust me," Rick said.

If nobody knows who King Rat 3 is, they will undoubtedly know who I am after this. I inhaled deeply. *Okay, here goes . . .* "Tai-Pan base, this is King Rat 3." I waited for a response.

"King Rat 3, this is base. Go ahead."

"Base, permission to make a net call to see if we can fix the man-pack net issue?"

A good few second pause followed. *I'm sure those in base-ops are asking each other, "Who is King Rat 3?"*

Base finally came back. "King Rat 3, good copy. Proceed with net call."

"Break, break. . . . This is King Rat 3 with a net call for all Shogun teams. Be advised, each team member needs to enter X dot I, then press send, on their man-pack units. . . . How copy, over?"

"King Rat 3, this is Shogun 1. Good copy, over." Each of the remaining Shogun team leads reported the same. There was another long pause, and then suddenly the radio chatter went into overdrive as radio traffic overflowed with each team reporting in. "Shogun 1 reports all team members have entered the net." And so on down the line as each team and its member saw their net-connectivity indicator light up for the first time.

I tilted my head back and momentarily felt a wave of relief wash over me—until the voice from base-ops snapped me back into the moment. "King Rat 3, this is Tai-Pan base."

Now they know who I am. . . . I hope that's a good thing. "Tai-Pan base, this is King Rat 3. Go ahead."

"King Rat 3, many thanks for helping us get over that hurdle. . . . Please stop by base-ops as soon as you can. We would like to meet you and say thanks."

"Tai-Pan base, this is King Rat 3. Good copy. Glad to be of service. King Rat 3 is out." I looked at Rick, who was smiling and nodding.

"You thought I was going to lead you astray," he said, with a twinkle in his eye. "But ole Rick saved the day. And I'm pretty sure I just made you look like a superstar, didn't I?"

Adams and I both chuckled.

"You absolutely did, Rick. Thanks."

That one incident continued to pay huge dividends to me and my reputation during the succeeding months as testing continued. I realized that others—both military and civilian—looked at me as someone who knew what he was doing and could get things done. And that made me feel good.

After that initial technical hiccup, the whole process of getting teams and their equipment set up across the desert and ready to test became routine.

As contractor-trained maintainers, our daily routine consisted of troubleshooting and fixing broken or inoperable man-pack units in preparation for the following day's testing. We quickly realized that having a mobile maintenance team out on the test range with certain capabilities and quick-change parts made sense. That way team members didn't have to sit all day with a broken man-pack unit, which, with more than a hundred units deploying out across the desert every day, became fairly common.

On one particular Friday afternoon, I was riding shotgun in a pickup that our maintenance shop supervisor, with SFC Watson driving. We were on our way to a site following a tremendous rainstorm, frequent during the rainy monsoons of August, to check on some equipment.

We could see a long straight section of dirt road ahead with a fresh mud puddle that ran for at least the length of a football field. The moment

the puddle came into view, I looked at Kevin and recognized a smile forming. He stomped on the accelerator.

We hit the mud puddle going more than sixty miles per hour. The wall
of water that flew up around the truck completely enveloped us, shroud-
ing the outside world. We could feel the truck hydroplane as we skated to
the other end. We were both laughing hysterically as the pickup emerged
from the shroud of muddy water.

"Let's do it again!" I blurted out.

Good thing Kevin was an avid outdoorsman, having grown up
four-wheeling and hiking in the mountains of Colorado. He immediately
turned the truck around, only this time he got more of a running start.
The truck hydroplaned even more this time. Laughing, we turned the
truck around for a third and final pass before we continued on to our
destination.

By the time we arrived back to Black Tower, the afternoon sun had
dried and baked a nice mud coating that completely covered the outside
of the truck. I used a brush and high-pressure hose to thoroughly wash the
truck before leaving for the weekend.

On Monday morning, I grabbed the logbook and drove the truck over
to the motor pool. Every Monday, all sections in EPG were required to
"dispatch" their assigned vehicles at the battalion motor pool.

The military's PMCS (Preventive Maintenance Checks and Services)
program is a proven and vital method of centrally tracking and providing
preventive vehicle maintenance and services, ensuring that the large and
varied fleet of vehicles in each unit remain in good working order in the
event they are needed in time of war.

I pulled the truck into one of the open bays that morning and began
closing out the paperwork as several mechanics began the PMCS process.

"What have you been doing with this truck?" one of the mechanics
said loudly as soon as he lifted the hood.

I came around to the front to see what he was talking about. "Sergeant, I don't know. . . . I wasn't the last . . ." I began to say.

There in the engine compartment was the unmistakable results of our vehicle desert marine flotation test. The entire compartment and engine were covered in a thick chocolate brown layer of dried mud. The layer was so thick, I couldn't make out some of the engine components. Several technicians gathered around and began poking it with screwdrivers, breaking off chunks as they attempted to see how far they could push their tools into the layer of mud.

Oh no, I thought, now busted. It never occurred to me to clean under the hood! The mechanic with the logbook scanned the paperwork to see who drove the truck last. With a sheepish look, I said truthfully, "I wasn't the last person to drive the truck." I knew full well that Kevin had signed the dispatch log on Friday—and at that time, passengers were not listed on the dispatch paperwork.

Technically, I was off the hook. Notwithstanding, the supervising mechanic, a staff sergeant who outranked me, said, "You get this truck over to the wash rack right now and thoroughly wash this thing until it shines!"

"Right away, Sergeant!" I answered back, looking forward to a job that, for some reason, I have always loved doing—blasting a muddy vehicle with a high-pressure hose.

I felt pure delight as I watched fist-sized mud chunks explode off the engine under the high-pressure jet stream. I pulled the squeaky clean truck back in the bay so the mechanics could complete their inspections. As they were doing that, I returned to the wash rack and finished having fun as I blasted all the mud chunks into a nearby drain.

Several weeks later, following the regular Monday morning vehicle routine, I grabbed the logbook to dispatch one of the new five-tons myself, since I was one of only a few licensed drivers. The truck was already hooked up to the generator trailer, so I jumped in and fired it up for the journey from Black Tower to the other end of the base where our motor pool was located.

On the way over, I didn't notice anything unusual until I slowly pulled into the motor pool. At first, I noticed several soldiers who stopped what they were doing and turned to watch me. I thought they were looking in my direction because I was driving one of the new five-tons. As soon as I stopped and put the truck in park, I spotted a large slow-moving bank of white clouds drifting forward until it enveloped the cab where I sat in all my glory. I didn't know what had caused the show, but I knew whatever it was, it wasn't good. I had to talk myself into exiting the cab. When I finally stepped out, I looked back as the growing cloud bank continued to gush from the trailer's axle like a giant waterfall.

I walked back to the trailer, hoping the cloud bank would obscure my identity, at least until my four-year enlistment was up. Back down the street from where I'd come, rising above the trees, was a long trail of clouds extending down the road as far as I could see.

I quickly located the cause: I had neglected to release the very visible—and handy—emergency trailer brake, per the instructions for a thorough PMCS, before I began my journey across the entire base.

Surely some wondered, *Who's the idiot driving that truck with the giant white cloud coming from the trailer?* Looking at the motor-pool mechanics, each one standing motionless and staring open mouthed intently in my direction, I knew if I could have, I would have crawled under the nearest rock rather than face everyone.

Suddenly, the front door of the motor pool office swung open, and out came the Officer in Charge (OIC), a Captain. He paused, scanning the scene with a quizzical, perplexed look on his face. Finally, after a moment, his gaze landed on me. Then he looked down, slowly shaking his head, as if to say, *No, this cannot be happening.*

After another long pause our eyes met.

Oh man, hang on, because here it comes!

"Sergeant Jones. Can I safely assume you did not perform a proper PMCS on that trailer before towing it here?" His voice was surprisingly controlled and measured.

With all eyes on me, I looked down and offered a thoroughly embarrassed, "Yes, Sir."

He paused again.

Okay, now here comes the storm!

"All right, pull it into one of the bays so we can get to work on it."

I blinked hard to hide my surprise. Fortunately, I had the good sense to walk back to the trailer and release the emergency brake before backing the trailer into a bay. Even then, smoke still billowed from the trailer axle.

The mechanics were quick and efficient as they jacked up the trailer and removed the tires. The brake pads were red hot and about to burst into flames. I was lucky I had not driven farther and started the trailer on fire, surely destroying a rather expensive and brand-new piece of equipment.

The captain came back out and put his arm around me. "This should cure you of ever getting in too much of a hurry, possibly skipping a step as you perform a thorough PMCS, don't you think?"

Again, I looked down to hide my embarrassment. "Yes, Sir, I won't forget this anytime soon."

I have never forgotten the way he handled himself, despite having every reason to come down on me for all the extra work I created for his mechanics, not to mention the cost of the parts to fix the trailer. I felt as though he could see that I was already feeling a tremendous and acute amount of personal embarrassment. If he had unleashed his anger on me, I would have stood there silently taking it, because that's what soldiers sometimes face as a result of their action or inaction. But this exceptional leader taught me that surveying the person and scene before reacting is as revealing and important, as the overarching impression one leaves on (young) soldiers by how we treat them when things go south, as they inevitably do.

By the end of August 1988, we had enough reliability/maintainability data on the EPLRS system to complete that first field (OT-1) Operational-Test. With OT-1 in the books, we said goodbye to many of the civilians who had helped us gather the data during the process. Most would soon return to their studies at their respective colleges or universities, having played a part in the technological advancements to keep our military one step ahead.

For most, the process of compiling test data became the focus for the next several weeks, while Emmett and I performed a logistical (spare parts) evaluation on the computers and peripheral equipment inside the NCS (Net Control Station). In addition, Steve asked me to attend weekly meetings where the team discussed deduction and processing of test data. The Friday afternoon meetings were a high-level "who's who" of the project, which included managers from Hughes Aircraft and Unisys, and test officers from EPG.

During one Friday afternoon meeting, I was sitting next to SFC Watson, when he told me to take care of the NCS for the weekend. During the week, we kept the NCS parked behind our office building, but on Fridays, we parked it on a nearby compound with twenty-four-hour security.

"No problem," I told him. As I climbed up into the cab, my mind drifted to the activities I had planned for that weekend. I pressed the start button and the 240-horsepower Cummins engine came to life. I had to turn the truck in a wide arc away from our office building, before turning back and traveling down the narrow alley next to the building. Everything felt normal as I put it in drive and pulled away from the building. I did not get far before I felt the five-ton suddenly jerk. And feeling a large and powerful vehicle, such as five-ton, jerk is never a good feeling. Suddenly, like a bolt of lightning, what I had neglected to do flashed into my mind.

I had forgotten to unplug the two large power cables—each cable had a large coupler about as big as a large bottle of Coke, which attached to the connectors on the outside of the NCS. The other end of the power cables connected to a junction box attached to a telephone pole, which stood just outside the windows of the room where the meeting continued.

The brackets used to attach the junction box to the telephone pole were no match for the force of the five-ton. The junction box violently ripped away with a loud steel-on-steel screeching sound. Everyone in the room jumped at the sound, bringing the meeting to an immediate, and abrupt, end. Everyone in the room ran to the bank of windows to see what would suddenly, and violently, rip the junction box completely from the telephone pole. What everyone at the windows witnessed was the five-ton pulling away from the building with about fifty feet of power cable still attached to the junction box being dragged along behind.

As soon as I stopped the truck and put it into park, I jumped down to the ground and stood beside the cab not wanting to believe I had done something *again* involving a vehicle.

The back door suddenly burst open, and out poured a stream of people with shocked looks on their faces.

"Are you all right?" Watson asked me.

I nodded. "Yeah, I'm okay."

The disfigured junction box wasn't though. It was still connected to the NCS power cables and the power lines that were once attached to the telephone pole.

Kevin asked someone to call the base corps of engineers. They immediately dispatched a truck and crew. The truck pulled up, and two engineers got out and began surveying the damage.

"How did this happen?" one engineer asked after looking things over.

Watson saved me the embarrassment. "Well, one of our high-speed soldiers, in a rush to get the five-ton over to the secure compound, drove away without unhooking the power cables that led to the junction box."

The engineers looked at Watson, then each other for a split second, then as if on cue, they both roared with laughter. "Where is this hero?"

Watson pointed at me standing there looking down and shaking my head.

Still laughing, one climbed in the bucket and the other operated the controls extending it up the pole to the power lines. He used a large pair of heavy-duty bolt cutters to sever the line, lowering everything to the ground. While the bucket was still fully extended, a leak suddenly erupted from the hydraulic line about halfway up the extended crane arm. I had never seen a high-pressure hydraulic leak before. I stood mesmerized as the huge arcing vapor cloud spewed out as the bucket slowly sank to the ground.

"Well, I think we can start our weekend now," the guy operating the bucket said. "We'll come back on Monday and finish the job."

"Will I have to pay for a replacement junction box?" I asked nervously.

"No, you're in luck," the engineer at the controls said, still clearly amused. "We are in the process of replacing every junction box on the base, and we have yet to get to the ones in this area. But if this had been a new one, yeah, you would probably be paying for it to be replaced."

A week later, I received an invitation to a dinner party at the Mesquite Tree restaurant by the Hughes Aircraft and Sperry/Unisys field technicians. During dinner, the Hughes techs were commenting about having to repair the cable connectors I had damaged. They marveled at the force required to pull each phase connection apart. After listening to them, I realized they didn't know who damaged the connectors.

Finally, one of the contractors asked, "Did anyone ever find out who did it?"

Already having had a few drinks, they screamed when I finally spoke up and admitted that I was the one responsible.

They couldn't wait to hear how it happened. When I explained, the entire party roared with laughter. I have to admit, I had it coming.

I couldn't help but think about CMS Harris. *Man, if Harris had been there to see me destroy that cable and junction box . . .* With all these contractors laughing hysterically at my expense, I would almost rather have had Harris chewing on my butt for my blatant lack of attention to detail. In my head I could hear Harris telling me, *"Attention to detail, Jones. Attention to detail."*

When their laughter finally subsided, I reacted the same way I had that day, standing there, acutely embarrassed, beside that idling five-ton. I looked down, shook my head, and shrugged my shoulders. *Well, at least I didn't drive the five-ton—with the power cables dragging behind—all the way across the base to the motor pool.*

CHAPTER 10

Course Shift

———————

I stepped into the narrow room that ran the length of the hangar and wiped the layer of sweat from my forehead, then looked at my watch. *If I hurry, I can still make it to the chow hall,* I thought. I grabbed my hat and walked into the hangar, passing about two dozen large, pre-staged plastic containers for packing up man-packs and other equipment starting first thing the following morning.

I looked ahead through the open hangar, which seemed to act as a frame, encompassing the giant stacked boulders of the Dragoon Mountain range thirty miles to the northeast. As I walked around to the front of my car, parked outside, I recognized Jack's sedan pulling into the large gravel lot. I waved, and he nodded as he pulled up beside me and shut off the engine.

Jack was in the process of out-processing, or "clearing," from the base, prior to departing for the east coast to visit family in route to Germany. Despite working a demanding test schedule—seven days a week, twelve-to-fourteen hours a day—I was aware, and internally dreading, his fast-approaching departure date. Still, I felt awful that I had been so busy on my project that I had hardly seen, let alone, spent any time with him during his final weeks and days.

The week before, Jack brought his replacement out to Black Tower to meet the team. My brief first impression of Master Sergeant Conner was, for the most part, positive. He was returning to Huachuca, having previously served in EPG, and was in the process of moving into a house he owned, and rented out, during his overseas tour.

Working long hours every day served as a reprieve for the simple fact that I didn't even want to think about Jack no longer being there. When I did think about it, I felt a sinking feeling in the pit of my stomach. The previous Saturday, I stopped by the office to grab something on my way out to Black Tower. As I was leaving, something told me to look inside Jack's darkened office. I opened the door and turned on the light. The sign on the desk and the plaques on the wall had already been removed and packed up for some office space five thousand miles away.

I stood there, momentarily immersed in the memories: that nervous kid asking to talk to Jack that first day; Jack coming around the desk to sit beside that same kid, distraught and in shock, after finding out about Roger. Those memories sustained me like a warm blanket, which was suddenly about to be stripped away. It was the first time in my young military career that I consciously thought, *This is the end of an era.*

Jack got out of his car and looked around for a moment. I thought maybe he came out looking for someone else on some work-related matter. Then as if satisfied with what he saw, he put his hands into the pockets of his dress green slacks and slowly walked around his car, taking exaggerated and elongated steps, flinging his feet in front of him with each step. It reminded me of a slow carefree walk someone might take strolling down the sidewalk and whistling along the way. That's when it hit me. *He came all the way out here to see me.*

"Boy . . . take two minutes and tell me everything you know." He said as he leaned against his car.

"Ah Jack, the things I have archived up here—" I said, pointing to my head, "would make your head explode." The comment made us both chuckle. "What brings you all the way out here?"

"Well, I came out here to see how you're doing . . . and to see if you wanted to grab a bite to eat."

"And miss the delicious meal the army has already provided for me at one of two chow halls available to me if I break every speed limit between here and main post?"

"And who says I don't take care of my troops—keeping them from getting arrested and thrown in jail by the MPs for driving like a maniac?" He smiled.

"Thanks, Jack, for saving me from myself."

Over dinner we talked about what he had learned from Master Sergeant Conner about his new assignment in Germany.

"You mean to tell me you two are literally switching places?" I asked, still trying to wrap my mind around how the army could be so large and yet so small.

"Yep, and I have more time in grade"—more time as an E-8—"than the guy that Conner served under, so I will have the pleasure of letting him know I will be taking over as the section NCOIC as soon as I get settled there."

"Did Conner say how this guy will take the news?"

"Conner said he's not going to like it one bit, but it will be a much-needed change—for the better—to the poor leadership atmosphere this guy has established and maintained as the section NCOIC."

"Lucky for them they will be getting you and the type of leadership I've benefitted from."

"Thanks, Brad." He smiled with a hint of sadness. "By the way, your paperwork with your reenlistment options recently came across my desk. Have you given any thought to your reenlistment options? With your training and experience, you have several unique opportunities available to you."

A parade of thoughts went through my mind regarding something I'd held close to the vest and had yet to share with anyone about what I had been seriously contemplating since earlier that year. But now his question caught me off guard. While considering my response, I realized this conversation would probably be my only opportunity to explain my thoughts and feelings that led up to what I was considering.

Since my early teens, one question that seemed to plague me was, *If I was born to a different set of parents, would I still be me?* In my search, I had attended many different churches and could never seem to find a satisfactory answer.

From the time I shipped to basic until my first few months in EPG, my brother, Mark, had been serving in New England as a missionary for the church he joined, due in large part to his relationship with his high-school sweetheart. Mark recognized and acknowledged an inner desire to develop spiritually, and since embracing things that helped jumpstart his spirituality, he now had renewed focus and drive for, and in, his life. I was impressed, and admired him, for the many positive changes he made leading up to, and since, returning from missionary service.

After spending time with Mark over the holidays the previous Christmas, I embarked on my own journey of spiritual self-discovery, and through much prayer and self-reflection, I had experienced a spiritual awakening. For the first time, I felt that many of my questions, including the one about being born to different parents, had finally been answered. Suddenly, I found myself contemplating a new path for my life—a path beyond the army and the job I had grown into.

I had kept these deeply poignant thoughts to myself. The only other person I'd told was Emmett, whom I'd invited to the private service where I was baptized by immersion. The reality was, I was seriously considering following in Mark's footsteps and serving a mission. I remembered how Jack had always trusted me with important errands, and with that thought, I decided to extend that same trust to him by telling him the truth. *I'd rather he hear it directly from me than from someone else.*

I took in a deep breath and let it out. "I've pretty much decided to leave active service at the end of the year."

"Oh?" His face registered genuine surprise. "Are you going to take that position with Sperry/Unisys I heard their field-tech Larry offered you?"

"Not exactly. I'm contemplating going in a different direction." Everything, I knew, hinged on my next sentence. *I hope what I'm about to tell him doesn't upset him, especially after all he graciously invested in me as a soldier.*

"I think I'm going to serve a mission like my brother did." The subject of my brother's missionary service had come up a time or two over the previous two years when Jack and I would talk.

"If I don't go now, I'll miss the opportunity to do something that had a huge impact on his direction in life." I paused. "I hope you're not upset with me."

"First of all, I admire someone who's willing to sacrifice for their convictions, whether they're spiritual, or political, or what have you. You go and follow your dreams. I'm fully confident you'll be successful whatever you choose to do."

"The only reason I can go forward and be successful is because of you and the interest you took in a punk kid from Oregon who could never seem to get a proper haircut."

I didn't expect to get choked up, but I could feel it coming on, and I had to keep swallowing it back, so I could say what I felt. Through welling pools of tears in my eyes, I forged ahead. "I can never thank you enough, Jack, for taking such good care of me, and for teaching me what a true leader does for those he leads."

Jack smiled. He didn't appear emotional, but I could tell by the expression that came over his face, which I can only describe as fatherly, that my compliment struck a chord.

"Well, boy, I ain't done with you yet! I'm not leaving for a couple more days, so I can certainly cram some room inspections in before I go!"

"You could do that, but I may be forced to file an appeal. And you know I won the last appeal I filed!" I said, breaking up the emotional moment and cracking us both up.

"Yes, you did," he said.

I picked up the check to pay when Jack snatched it out of my hand. "C'mon, boy, let's get out of here. This one's on me."

"I won't argue with the boss."

It was dusk when we exited the restaurant. We both looked to the west as yellow-shaded clouds melted into orange and then red, stretching all the way to the horizon.

"Ah, I'm going to miss seeing that," Jack said, motioning with his head toward the sky.

"They are nothing short of amazing," I said. "Let me know how things go in Germany."

"Will do. And good luck with your plans. I hope things work out for you."

"Thanks, Jack. For everything."

"It's been my pleasure." We shook hands for what I knew would be the last time. I stood by my car in that parking lot and watched as he waved one more time as he drove away. As much as I didn't want to face it, I also knew that was probably the last time I would see Jack. That empty feeling, the one I'd felt to some degree before, that routine part of serving in the military, returned. Only this time, it felt like it might never go away.

The following week I stopped by the office to pick up the reenlistment paperwork Jack had mentioned. I was tempted to reenlist and remain at the base, and in the job I was confident doing. But each time I thought about it, I experienced an unsettled feeling mixed with confusion, which I didn't experience when I contemplated following in my brother's footsteps. In fact it was quite the opposite. When I thought about serving a mission, I felt calm and peaceful. I took that as a personal sign that the major course change I was about to implement was the right thing to do for me.

Ever since arriving at Huachuca, I had grown close to the soldiers and their families in our section. I can say unequivocally that I loved and admired them all, each in their own separate ways. But at the same time, I recognized some things that I knew deep down I wanted to avoid as a future husband and father. One of the things I mentally noted was the toll drinking can exact on not only the person but the whole family.

I was all for enjoying myself during down time or on weekends, and many of the soldiers I served with chose to drink responsibly with little to no adverse consequences during those times. The thing that got me thinking differently were those who made it a regular, almost nightly, habit. Over the years, as we kept in contact, the vast majority of them had to sacrifice tremendously to overcome their drinking habit. Like most, many started drinking in moderation, and then it ultimately progressed to the point that alcohol became a much larger crutch than they'd ever initially intended.

"At that point," one admitted to me, "I couldn't imagine doing anything without alcohol being involved. That's when I realized I had a problem." The sad reality was, nearly everyone I've ever known who started out enjoying something to drink as a way to relax and enjoy themselves, further down the road ended up realizing that the very vehicle that once offered them a way to blow off steam and decompress eventually turned into an unmanageable beast and a demanding task master.

In early October, I was only a week away from starting to out-process from active duty when I received unexpected news. I was being awarded an Army Commendation Medal, or ARCOM, for short. Steve and Kevin were the first persons to see the paperwork before I did.

"I've never seen a soldier get an ARCOM on their first try," Kevin said to me. "In my career, the award always gets downgraded to an AAM"—Army Achievement Medal—if it's the soldier's first time being recommended."

"I didn't even know somebody recommended me for an award, let alone an ARCOM," I said.

"Well, it's pretty clear from the paperwork who recommended you," Kevin said, handing me the DA 638 form. I scanned down the page and couldn't believe it. Jack submitted the paperwork without ever saying anything to me about it.

"Even though he recommended you, the award still needed approval from above Jack," Kevin told me. "You must've impressed somebody up the chain of command."

"It probably had something to do with how well I field tested that trailer's emergency brake system. Or maybe it was based on my results from the telephone-pole, junction-box, mounting-bracket, stress-test that made me infamous throughout EPG."

"Probably that last one," Kevin said, chuckling and shaking his head.

Monday, October 24, 1988, dawned cool, but quickly warmed as the sun bathed the grassy field behind the EPG barracks. Colonel Downey, the EPG Commander, pinned my first major award, the Commendation Medal, to my uniform.

"Thanks for all your hard work while serving here at EPG, Sergeant Jones," he said. "This award is well deserved, and we're sad to see you go."

I had only briefly met him a time or two before, and was surprised that he knew me enough to know that I was leaving the service. "My pleasure, Sir. I will miss all the great people I've had the privilege to serve with over the last three years. It's been the opportunity of a lifetime. Thank you again, Sir."

"Don't be a stranger, keep in touch. And let us know how you're doing. Good luck in the next chapter. Make it a good one."

"I'll do my best, Sir."

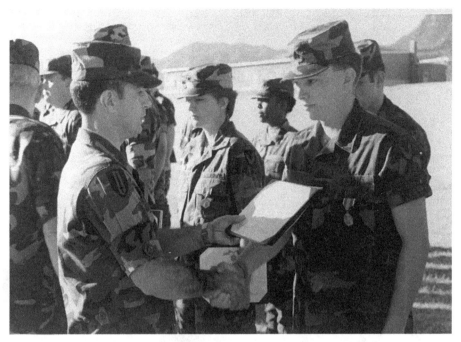

My final formation at Fort Huachuca receiving an Army Commendation medal
from EPG Commander Col Downey Oct 1989

The next night, I walked down to the CQ desk just after midnight and officially signed out of EPG . . . and the Army. It suddenly hit me how much the Army had provided me since I stepped on that plane in early December 1984. I knew some, and maybe even many, lamented their decision to raise their right hand and serve, but that was not my experience by a long shot.

I barely slept for the next five-to-six hours, waking up numerous times to look at the clock. Finally, as night gave way to the light of day, I arose and took one last shower in my bathroom. I grabbed my comforter, sheets, and pillow, and stood by the window looking up at the Huachuca Mountains and the canyon that was responsible for helping me wear-out several pairs of running shoes, as I tried to work out numerous personal issues through the sweat of mile after mile. Huachuca canyon, for me, had become a personal place of worship, a temple of sorts, with trees leading to spired peaks of personal inspiration.

Where will the next canyon of spiritual and physical solace and inspiration be for me? I wondered.

I stopped by the CQ desk and handed my room key to the groggy sergeant sitting behind the desk.

"You out of here?"

"Yep, I'm gone."

"Good luck, and drive safe," he said, putting out his hand to shake mine. "Only five more years and I'll be doing the same thing."

"I'm sure that twenty-year, monthly retirement check will make the transition much easier than mine."

"I imagine it will." He smiled. "So long, Jones. Be good."

"I will do my best." I turned and walked toward the door and the parking lot where my GTI sat already packed with all my gear. I stepped through the door and out of the red brick building that had been my home for the last three years and took one final long look out across the sunlit desert that had grown on me. I would miss being able to see the mountain vistas in the distance, and the way the desert would light up for a split second when lightning struck during a monsoon thunderstorm, and most of all I would miss the incredible sunsets that occurred regularly.

While looking over the desert expanse, all at once, I suddenly felt a flood of emotion. I was proud that I did not succumb to the temptation I'd seen with other soldiers departing the military. Among some, it seemed to be a scorched-earth type attitude, leading some to feel the need to trash and burn everything that represented the military to them, including what may have been an otherwise decent reputation. I was grateful to leave the military on my own, good terms, with no regrets to haunt my conscience later on.

I also felt a measure of excitement and anticipation for what Colonel Downey called the "next chapter." After four years of military service, I had grown as a person. I felt confident that I could survive on the outside, and with enough hard work and determination, possibly even prosper.

CHAPTER 11

The Paris of South America

My four years of training and field maintenance helped me quickly land a job fixing photocopy machines in the greater Portland area. I worked with several experienced techs who were both excellent at cleaning, diagnosing, and fixing copiers. After a month, I was out on my own servicing machines all over the city where I had grown up. I ran into more than a few people I went to school with, though most didn't immediately recognize me. I got a big kick out of the looks on their faces as they mentally compared the memory of what I used to look like—the long hair and punk attitude—with the crewcut and more adult version now standing before them.

After working and saving for half a year, I submitted the paperwork declaring my intention for missionary service. Three weeks later, I received a thick envelope in the mail calling me to serve for two years in the Argentina—Buenos Aires North Mission. I was going to South America, of all places, and I barely spoke a word of Spanish. My education would come by a two-month crash course and then immersing myself into the culture. Sort of like basic training all over again—but without the constantly yelling and demanding drill sergeants.

I departed Portland for the training center on a warm, rainy day in mid-July 1989. I drove through the rain for the next four hours, until finally, west of Boise, Idaho, the rain and clouds gave way to blue sky and clear sailing ahead.

The rocky and jagged mountains of Utah reminded me of the Huachuca mountain range back in Arizona. I felt remarkably at home in the high desert of Utah. I made my way to Provo, where I checked in at the MTC (Missionary Training Center).

I was assigned to a class of missionaries, like me, learning Spanish for service in Argentina. Previously having experienced four years of institutionalization, army style, I knew I was well prepared for the regimented schedule of the MTC. Some had a hard time adjusting to the atmosphere, but for me, it felt familiar and even second nature. Spanish classes during the morning and afternoon, followed by further study in the evening. The rapid pace had us hearing lessons and speaking to each other, all in Spanish, in a matter of days. One day, while walking through the main building with several other missionaries, I noticed a group of army officers touring the facility.

"Excuse me, Major," I asked as I approached the group. "Mind if I ask what the army is doing here?"

He seemed startled by the question, but quickly recovered. "We're here to tour the facility and its successful language-teaching methods, which we intend to duplicate at DLI in Monterey, California. You ever heard of DLI?"

"Yes, Sir, it stands for Defense Language Institute. I've been to the base."

He raised his eyebrows in admiration. "You ever served in uniform?"

"I just recently ETS'd from the active-duty Army after serving four years." I extended my hand to shake his. "Sergeant Bradley Jones."

He turned to the other officers. "Gentlemen, we have a missionary here who just left active-duty having made Sergeant during his four-year enlistment."

I noted everyone's rank as they gathered around.

"Colonel, nice to meet you. . . . Lieutenant Colonel . . . Captain . . . Major," I said, shaking each hand.

"What did you do for the army?" the colonel asked.

"I was originally trained as a radar repairman, but I ended up working in Test and Evaluation's Command at the Electronic Proving Ground at Fort Huachuca, Arizona."

"I think that's the way to go," the colonel interjected. "Do four years of active-duty and then serve a mission. Being here is probably a walk in the park for you?"

"Yes, Sir, absolutely. And contrary to what some missionaries may say, the food here is way better than chow-hall food." The comment made everyone laugh.

"Where are you going?" the major asked.

"I'm going to Argentina."

"Ah, Spanish speaking then?" the colonel asked.

"Yes, Sir."

"Well, when you get back, you come see us," he said, handing me his card. "We'll be happy to put you in a Spanish-speaking linguist position and send you back to Fort Huachuca for 'Intel' [army intelligence] training."

"Thank you, Sir," I said, shaking their hands once again before they moved on.

Two months of memorizing vocabulary—on a daily basis—and speaking Spanish almost exclusively with our classmates and others, along with studying Scriptures, in the context of sharing our beliefs and doctrine, all in a foreign language. Even though I felt semi-confident, I could say whatever I was feeling and/or thinking. I had to laboriously translate in my mind what I wanted to say into Spanish, which took time and effort, but the more I did it, the easier it became.

Our mid-September departure had us on a flight to Miami where we had a long layover before our nonstop flight to Buenos Aires. Our group, which consisted of a dozen missionaries, sat in a restaurant in the terminal for our last meal for a very long time on American soil. I looked around and noticed uneasy expressions throughout most of our group. Then it hit me when everyone ate in silence. *I wonder if anyone here has ever been outside the States?*

About midway through my hamburger basket, I spoke up. "Has anyone ever traveled outside the States?"

The question was met with mostly blank stares, followed by quick glances at one another to see who was willing to answer first.

"I don't know about anyone else here," one finally said, "but I've never even traveled outside of Utah."

Slowly everyone shook their heads, not one had traveled outside the country. I vividly remembered my feelings moving to another continent and when I left for basic, knowing I would be gone four years. As I thought about those experiences, I realized they had prepared me for this moment, this experience. Going to South America felt like a giant adventure to me, and deep down I knew we'd be okay. When I shared this with the group, it seemed to resonate with them.

We boarded our flight around midnight and tried our best to get some sleep. I dozed here and there, but was awake enough to see the first light of day out my window seat. On final approach, the landscape on the outskirts of Buenos Aires looked like parceled farmland. The grass surrounded occasional patches of trees that were a deep green as far as I could see.

After we landed, walking up the jet-bridge, I could feel and smell the humid air outside. It reminded me of how Georgia smelled. Kind of a damp foliage aroma.

I was the first one through the doorway after passing through customs. Ahead of me stood a couple I recognized from a picture I'd seen— our mission president, Gustavo Berta, and his wife, Mirta. Her eyes lit up and she smiled as I approached. Gustavo, also smiling, stood next to her. He was young looking—actually, they both looked young. They both put out their hands. "Mucho gusto," they said at exactly the same time, then looked at each other and chuckled.

I could hear other missionaries coming up behind me, so I shook their hands and stepped aside as the rest of our group approached with the same bewildered expression I'm sure I wore. Several other missionaries introduced themselves and guided us with our luggage to vehicles waiting in the passenger pickup area. I could hear everyone around me speaking Spanish, and I could not understand one word. To me, everyone spoke a million miles an hour, with each word melting into the next.

Once settled into our vehicle, the passenger missionary upfront turned and said in English, "Welcome to Bwhenose Eye-rays." His pronunciation seemed almost exotic.

Oh, that's how they say Buenos Aires.

The drive from the airport was a visual onslaught. The green grass and trees whizzing by out the window looked lush, bathed in the bright morning sunlight. We saw many types of trees, including pine, flowering jacaranda, and palm trees, among others, all a different shade of green. The neighborhoods and homes were mostly off-white concrete, or redbrick, with orange-clay tiled roofs similar to the Spanish-styled roofs on many homes in the southwest, except they all had unique and different shapes. No two houses looked the same. Some homes were large and spacious with much smaller basic homes sitting right next door. There seemed to be no lines delineating the rich and poor.

We took a side ramp and merged onto another two-lane freeway. "This is Avenida General Paz," the missionary riding shotgun said. "It separates 'Capital'—the very large downtown or city part on the inside—from the 'Provincia,' or suburban provincial section on the outside. The mixture of homes and giant apartment complexes, with modern metal and glass buildings, interspersed with older drab-looking buildings, was a stark contrast unlike anything I had ever seen.

We got off the freeway and drove through San Isidro, an upscale area where the mission office and the Berta family lived. We pulled into the driveway of a nice redbrick home, with an orange-tiled roof, surrounded by a large rod-iron fence.

Mirta offered two upstairs guestrooms with bunk beds for anyone needing to sleep. President Berta wanted to interview each of us separately.

While I waited my turn, I made my way through the kitchen and into the backyard.

I looked around, and there in the grass by the pool was a lawn chair with comfortable-looking cushions. I sat down and leaned back, stretching my legs out, and instantly felt the warmth radiating up from the cushions. I took out my wayfarer sunglasses and put them on. I tilted my head back and promptly fell into a deep sleep. I'm not sure how long I was out, but it felt like only a minute had passed before a missionary gently shook my shoulder.

"It's your turn to be interviewed," he said with a smile.

I immediately shot up out of the chair. "How long have I been asleep?"

"You've been out for a while," he said.

"Man, I feel much better," I said as we walked into the house.

President Berta's office had a desk on one side of the room and two comfortable chairs with a small table in between. He invited me to take a seat in the chair next to him, then he asked me to say a prayer before we began the interview. I said a simple prayer in my broken Spanish. I thought of the airport and how I couldn't seem to understand any conversations going on around me. However, in this moment, sitting next to this formerly successful businessman, now turned spiritual leader for more than 150 missionaries and an entire mission covering one of the most densely populated cities on the planet, I suddenly felt a spiritual enlightenment that opened the way for me to understand nearly every word of our conversation.

He held my paperwork. "It says here that you served four years in the United States Army before coming here?"

"Si, Presidente."

"What did you do in the army?"

I couldn't think of the word for *maintenance*, so I improvised, combining English and Spanish. "Maintenance de radar y computador."

He nodded, indicating he understood. "Si, mantenimiento de radar y computadores."

To which I nodded in return.

"How do you feel about serving here in Argentina?"

"Presidente, I feel a lot of love right now in my heart *and* in this room. And I'm here to share that love with the people of Argentina."

He leaned forward in his chair. "Thank you for coming here."

"I'm happy to be here," I said.

The interview ended with him offering a prayer that sounded both spiritually uplifting and eloquent, even though I didn't understand all of it. We hugged, and he opened his office door to see me out. I couldn't get over how miraculous it was that I could understand him. I thought of some of the commanders I'd served under during my time in uniform. The truly exceptional ones went the extra mile to bridge the gap and get to know their soldiers. President Berta reminded me of the very best among those leaders.

He spent the next hour conferring privately with his two assistants (APs) regarding who they felt would be good "trainers" for each of us new missionaries, based on their good qualities and work ethic. Each piece of paper had the training missionary's name and location where they were currently serving. President Berta laid those pieces of paper on his desk and, after interviewing each one of us and calling on inspiration, the three discussed possible companionships until each of us was matched with a trainer everyone felt good about.

By the time identifying each companionship was complete, it was early evening and we were ready to dine on our first Argentine meal. Mirta had busily spent all afternoon preparing a meal of *lengua de vaca*. Cow tongue.

I was famished, but not so sure about this meal. *Cow tongue? Really? Our very first meal, and we're already experimenting with our stomachs?*

President Berta asked me to offer a prayer over the food. My prayer was short and sweet, giving thanks for the meal and asking that it bless our body with health and strength, especially emphasizing the strength, as I silently added, *to get the lengua down and keep it down.* I couldn't help thinking and visualizing, *I could use a good burger or some pizza right now.*

The first course was a green salad with a vinaigrette dressing, which wasn't too bad. Just as I was finishing my salad, one of the APs tapped me on the shoulder and motioned for me to follow him into the kitchen.

"Hey, sorry to interrupt your meal, but you and two other missionaries are going out to a zone in Mendoza. We have to take you to the bus station right now."

I was so relieved my stomach would not have to undergo experimental treatment that it was easy to ignore it groaning with hunger. We threw our suitcases into the van and roared off.

The driver and passenger upfront were the two missionaries who had driven us from the airport. "Better fasten your seat belts," the one in the passenger seat told us. "This is going to be close."

We traversed the cobblestone streets of San Isidro before turning south onto an onramp to the Pan American Highway, called the "Pan-Americana." The driver stomped on the gas, and about the time we merged onto the concrete highway, we were screaming along at sixty to seventy miles per hour. By the sound of the engine, the van couldn't go any faster. We weaved our way toward "Retiro," the main bus station. At one point the passenger missionary suddenly turned and as he laughed, he yelled, "Hang on!" The van suddenly launched into the air, all four tires off the ground, after hitting a spot where two concrete slabs had buckled upward, forming a ramp. Everyone launched up off their seats, straining our seat belts until they pulled us back down. The van landed with a loud *Pahrump!* sound as the shock absorbers bottomed out, then back into the air again before finally settling for a solid four-point landing.

I couldn't help myself as I yelled, "Yeeeeeaaaah! Let's do that again!" Everybody cracked up.

What a ride, I thought, *I could get behind this kind of driving.* There didn't seem to be any rules for driving, or if there were, they were not enforced like back home. It was a free-for-all unlike anything I'd experienced. After getting off the freeway, we turned onto a giant boulevard, weaving in and out as we raced past other cars. Finally the driver pointed toward a large building that looked like an airport terminal, only for touring buses. I could see buses everywhere, probably between fifty and a hundred, parked and moving around the enormous terminal.

We rushed to grab our gear and find our particular bus, arriving just as the driver was starting to shut the outside luggage doors below the passenger windows. One of the office missionaries handed each of us a ticket, while the other helped the driver load our suitcases. They both exhaled a giant simultaneous sigh of relief. "Made it!"

"How long will it take to get to Mendoza?" I asked.

"It's about a fourteen-hour trip," another missionary said. "You better hurry and jump on."

On the outside, the bus was nicely painted and sleek looking. Inside it had plush seats with foot-rests and plenty of leg room. Custom televisions came out of the roof just off the aisle, so each seat had one nearby for viewing. The view from the passenger windows was much higher than any bus I'd ever traveled on. I'd been in transit for more than forty-eight hours . . . and now I was sitting on a bus for another fourteen-hour trip. *At least I hope we get a great view of the city and the countryside between here and Mendoza.*

And what a view it was. We crossed from the east side of Buenos Aires to the west. The architectural panorama was mesmerizing. Houses and neighborhoods interspersed with tall buildings in close proximity to large shantytowns called "villas." The homes in the villas were constructed of pretty much whatever people could get their hands on. Before leaving the MTC, we had an instructor from Argentina come talk to our class. He warned us about going into the villas, that muggings were common, and with our white shirts, ties, and western look, we would be looked upon as wealthy foreign targets.

He talked about the nationwide custom of drinking *mate*, pronounced "mah-tay," a customary drink of hot water poured over a small container of herbs—or yerba—with sweetener, that's drunk through a metal straw with a built-in filter called a bombilla.

"Everyone drinks maté," he said, "so expect an invitation in pretty much every home. Also, when contacting people in their homes, you do not knock on their door. You stand out in front of their yard, or gate, and clap."

Buenos Aires, and its surrounding suburbs—a city the size of Los Angeles—seemed to go on endlessly, and I was transfixed by what I saw.

It reminded me of crossing America on that bus from South Carolina to Oregon for Christmas during basic training, and how much that ignited and inspired my love for my country. I couldn't think of a better way to see what would be my home, and the people I would live among, for the next two years.

CHAPTER 12

Shadow of the Andes

The sun began to set as the luxury bus neared the outskirts of Buenos Aires.

I fell asleep until around midnight when the bus pulled off the highway and onto a dirt parking lot. The three of us—Brower, McKean, and I—were thirsty so we exited the bus and walked into a dimly lit structure that looked like a cross between a barn and a bar.

The inside of the building looked like something out of the wild, Wild West. We ordered sodas, which came in weathered glass bottles that looked as if they'd been used and re-used many times.

By midmorning we crossed into the Mendoza Province, which butts up against Chile, on our way to San Rafael, a city with a population just under a hundred thousand. Mendoza looks like the American southwest with the green oasis of San Rafael from all the trees that lined the streets. When the bus pulled into the station, all three of us got off, expecting that this was our stop. One of the missionaries waiting at the terminal informed us that McKean was the only one staying. Brower and I had another three-hour ride farther north to the town of Tunuyán. I was hungry and asked one of the experienced missionaries for a recommendation for something to eat.

"Have you tried choripan?" he asked.

"Nope, we've only been in the country for just a little more than twenty-four hours," I said.

"Oh man, you gotta try some choripan," he said. "Come with me."

We followed him into the terminal, where he helped us navigate our first food purchase. I couldn't understand a word he said to the lady behind the counter, but I was grateful when she handed me what looked like a small sub sandwich with a thick, deep-reddish-looking chorizo sausage, cut in half lengthwise, and covered with lettuce and tomatoes.

"That sausage-looking thing is called chorizo," said the missionary, who looked young, but handled himself like a much older young man. He also spoke so rapidly I could hardly understand anything he said.

"You need to put some chimichurri on it before you take a bite," he said.

"Chimi . . . what?"

"Trust me you'll love it." He grabbed a nearby dish and spoon and began to spread some on. The chimichurri looked like a thick oil-and-vinegar mixture with a whole bunch of ingredients that looked like spices. I closed the sandwich up and took a bite. The richness and depth of flavors that exploded in my mouth were pure delight. The chorizo didn't taste anything like what I expected. It was spicy, but not too spicy, like Italian sausage, and the chimichurri added a fantastic salsa flavor all its own. I had found the first food after arriving that I could sink my teeth into again just as soon as I could. I gobbled down the sandwich and promptly ordered another.

I turned to the missionary. "That was *awesome*."

He smiled. "Before you get back on the bus, you need one final thing."

"What's that?" I asked.

"An alfahor," he said.

"An alfa . . . what?"

"C'mon, I'll show you."

We headed to a tiny walk-up store with a window. I followed his lead and watched as he spoke fluently to the guy in the window. Again, not understanding a word.

"This is an alfahor," he said, handing it to me.

I opened it, and inside was a single flat-and-round-looking something or other, covered in chocolate. I took a bite. Under the chocolate were two cookies, and sandwiched between them was a layer of chocolate mousse, something like what's between an Oreo cookie, but chocolate flavored.

"Well, what do you think?"

"Two things," I said. "First, this is absolutely delicious. And second, I need a few more for the road."

We both laughed, and he ordered more for me.

Three hours later, when we pulled into the bus station, Brower and I climbed down onto the platform and shook hands with Russ Crockett.

"Is this our final destination?" I asked.

"For you it is," he said. "We need to take Brower out to his area, which is about an hour from here."

Okay, one more bus ride. This makes three whole days in transit. Then I remembered something. *Just like when I crossed America by bus. I saw places and things I never thought I'd see. Now I've crossed Argentina. What a way to start this adventure.*

That night, after returning, I took my first shower in three days. Next to the toilet there was the first bidet I had ever seen.

"The bidet. Do you ever use it?" I asked Crockett, while I unpacked.

"Absolutely. You sit down, turn on the warm water first, and then turn the center knob to control the upward flow. If water starts coming out of your ears, you have the pressure turned up too high." He laughed.

Crockett couldn't have been more right.

As missionaries, the schedule we maintained was straightforward. Rise at 6:30. From 6:30 to 8:30 we spent personal time shaving, showering, eating, and studying on our own. Four years in the Army made for a seamless morning routine for me. I began my mornings by exercising from 6:00 to 6:30, then fell into the regular schedule. At 8:30 we studied a missionary manual as a companionship, and then went over our schedule for that day and that week.

The majority of towns in Argentina have a plaza located at the center, with statues of historical figures, celebrated among Argentinians. There was a general excitement among the members in Tunuyán for the upcoming groundbreaking and construction of a new chapel. Most people in town seemed to know about the construction project, which was set to take place on a vacant lot near the center of town.

Our function as missionaries was to serve and support individuals and families within and without the local congregation. For those with whom we came into contact, there were some with no particular religious beliefs, or possibly they were members of an organized religion, but maybe not generally familiar with the tenets of that religion. However, the one common thread was that each one was searching for answers to what many consider life's perplexing questions regarding our purpose. I felt a connection with the people who were searching for answers, given that I had spent years searching and asking for myself.

As I met and talked with people, I quickly picked up those who were contemplating the very questions I had contemplated. If God really exists, what is His role in this life, and how can we know for sure? Back then, I was scared to death of nuclear war, and wondered what was to stop everyone from annihilating one another. The question that came to me repeatedly was if God does exist, would He stop us from destroying one another through global thermonuclear war? To those with similar questions, our message was pure and simple: Yes, God exists, and He cares about His children (mankind), and is aware of each and every one of us.

With them, we shared the power of personal prayer and how to recognize when God answers prayers and speaks to us individually. At the conclusion of our message, we left the ball in their court. We then invited them to turn to their own personal prayers about the truthfulness of our message.

An asado (bbq) Argentina 1990

In January, after being there four months, I received word from the mission offices that I was being transferred back to Buenos Aires. I didn't want to leave Mendoza and the people I'd grown to love and admire for their kindness and hardworking ways. But I was grateful I'd gotten to spend time with them.

I began the return trip in the afternoon and ended about midday after another panoramic crossing through Buenos Aires, a city with a vibe and pulse all its own. Four missionaries were waiting for me at Retiro, including my new companion, Marcelo Gervanth, who grew up in the city of Mendoza, just north of Tunuyán. A beautiful city of plazas and tree-lined streets I visited a number of times.

My new area, called Pontevedra, was situated on the far outskirts of Buenos Aires. To get there, we caught a bus from Retiro to Once (pronounced Own-say) train station—my first ride on the greater Buenos Aires' metro rail system, the second most extensive commuter rail system in the Americas, after New York. From the outside, the stone facade of the

Once railway station looked old and gothic, like a building you might see in Paris.

After purchasing tickets on the Sarmiento line, we didn't have to wait long for the next train.

When it stopped, the doors opened and we quickly found a seat.

"How long till we get to our station?" I asked Marcelo, as soon as we sat down.

"We pass about ten stations before we reach the Morón station. This line passes through the heart of Capital [downtown] Federal."

The train line traversed a tightly compacted alley of tall and taller apartment buildings on both sides. Signs and concrete walls along the way were covered with spray-painted graffiti, all written in Spanish slang, which made absolutely no sense to me. We stopped at major train stations, including Caballito, Floresta, and Liniers, where more and more people crowded on. As we passed major boulevards, it was like looking down a long canyon carved between buildings on both sides. At stops, people fought to get off, while others pushed like linebackers to get on. I'd never seen anything like it. Soon, we crossed over the line from Capital to the suburbs of Ramos Mejia and Haedo.

At the Haedo stop Marcelo motioned to get ready. "Ours is the next stop."

We shouldered our backpacks and grabbed my suitcases, then bulldozed our way toward the door. "Permiso. Lo siento. Permiso," we said apologetically as we pushed passed other passengers.

Marcelo looked back at me. "When that door opens, stay right behind me and keep moving forward."

"Bueno," I said.

The train pulled into the Morón station where we could see a horde of people waiting on the platform. I felt like I was back in basic, moving under fire with my squad. As soon as the train stopped and the doors opened, we hit that wall of people like a freight train, slicing right through the crowd.

"Wow, this is way different from Mendoza," I said, laughing at the absurdity of the moment.

We hopped on an ornately decorated, colorful bus, called a *colectivo*, for a forty-minute ride, getting to know each other along the way.

Pontevedra had a small centrally located plaza, with numerous neighborhoods stretching off down dirt roads, from the only paved main road running down the center of town. "We have a brand-new chapel," Marcelo said. "Our place is just a couple blocks from there." The small house where we lived sat on the corner of Capital Giachino and la Calle de los Italianos.

The house had a water tank on the roof, as did most homes in Argentina. Our shower was a five-gallon tank mounted on the wall in the bathroom. Inside the tank, an actual element, like a burner on a stove, heated the water for a hot shower. The shower knob opened the flow up to a plastic showerhead that gravity fed the water from tank. We had to time when we turned on the heating element because if we left it on for too long, it would bring the water to a boil. There was no actual shower portion in the bathroom, the floor and walls were completely covered with black-and-white tile, with a drain in the middle of the floor.

The climate in Buenos Aires was much more humid, with warm muggy days, and plenty of rain.

After serving in Pontevedra for a month, I was called to be a leader over the district we were in, which included missionaries serving in several nearby areas. I was surprised by this "promotion" but grateful for the opportunity. The Army had taught me how to lead well, and I looked forward to putting those principles and practices into work here. My role as a district leader, or DL, was to hold weekly meetings with those in the district, teach missionary principles, gather weekly stats, and hand out much anticipated mail.

I became aware that a couple missionaries in the district expressed frustration that I was made their DL when they had been in country much longer and had a better grasp of the language. The reality was, I sympathized with their feelings. I was as shocked as they were when the call came. As I began leading weekly district meetings I thought about and drew upon leadership principles I had studied and used while in uniform. In particular, I remembered two important leadership principles I'd learned: Set an example, and know your people and look out for their welfare. During that initial period, I visited each area and worked with each individual missionary for a day. I just focused on getting to know that missionary. "Where are you from? What were you doing before? What will you do after?" I found those questions helped to break the ice. I could tell that using the principles was working when each one began to open up to me at some point during the day. They all wanted to know about my experience in the military, which I was more than willing to share. A couple even commented that when they found out I had already served four years in the Army, they were sure I was going to treat them like a sergeant treats a private. I was glad to prove them wrong.

After several months serving as a DL, I received a letter from President Berta informing me that I was being transferred to Merlo, a nearby city, to serve as a zone leader (ZL) over that zone. Zones were comprised of three to five districts, generally covering several cities with substantial populations. Once again I was stunned by the call.

Merlo had a vibrant downtown next to the train station with many shops and storefronts.

My new area, called Merlo Heights, was only a short bus ride from the paved streets and neighborhoods in Merlo proper. It was reminiscent of Pontevedra, where the pavement ended and the dirt roads began. The small congregation met in converted space above a large corner lot pharmacy. They were tight-knit, faithful people, willing to help and serve one another.

The Merlo zone covered the city of Merlo with a population just less than four hundred thousand, plus a number of smaller outlying suburbs down the Sarmiento train line. With an upcoming zone conference only a week away, I would have the chance to meet everyone in the zone. President Berta and his wife would be there to each deliver an inspirational message and enjoy a meal together with the entire zone. My new companion, Brett Bringhurst, an excellent and experienced ZL.

As a ZL, Bringhurst and I rotated visiting each area and companionship in the zone. I employed the leadership principles I'd used as a DL, just on a larger scale. I felt content in my role as a ZL in Merlo.

After two months, Bringhurst went home and my new companion was Miguel Romero from Cordoba. I learned a lot from Miguel about how to work, not just hard but smart. His knowledge of the Bible was impressive, which made him an effective missionary.

After one month together, while going through the mail for the zone, I came across a letter from the mission offices with my name on it. I opened it and began scanning the page. I had to read through it a second time before I looked up at Romero.

"You're not going to believe this," I said in shock.

"What? What does it say?" he asked.

"I just got called to serve as one of President Berta's assistants."

"No way! That's a huge accomplishment and honor."

"I know!" I couldn't believe it.

Each mission has two or more missionaries—known as APs or assistants to the president—who serve as personal assistants helping the president run the day-to-day operation of the mission.

Most APs are called during the last months of their mission, I thought. *I'm going into this position after only eleven months in the country.* I knew this was a possibility, but I figured it would follow the previous pattern, and *if* the call came, it would be after I'd served as a ZL for a while, maybe even in another zone—not after only three months as a ZL. I knew my name was getting around as the convert missionary who had already served four years in the military. I had already been approached by a few missionaries whom I barely knew who announced, "I heard you're going to be an AP."

Word got around quickly.

I always answered with, "Not unless I get my act together."

What I really wanted to say was, "Dude, shut up. That's the last thing I want to be thinking about." The truth was, I didn't want these upward movements to go to my head. I was in this country to serve. Nothing else.

The mission office was located ten minutes away in the affluent and residential city of San Isidro.

In my first few days as an AP, I focused on adapting to the pace and flow of working in an office environment where things moved rapidly. It reminded me of working on a project back in Arizona when testing was underway. Taking an interest and focusing on getting to know the missionaries in Pontevedra and Merlo became a microcosm for adapting the same principle to more than two hundred missionaries spread out over twelve zones.

I thought back to when I was promoted to sergeant, and the effect it had on lower enlisted soldiers when I helped them with assigned tasks. It was important to me to show them I wouldn't ask them to do something I wouldn't do myself. In the offices, there were missionaries serving as financer, secretary, and supply, along with others who dealt with housing for the hundred or so properties where missionaries lived. If someone needed help, my motto was, *Who cares whose job it is, lend a hand.*

As APs our job was to prepare a monthly training message that President Berta would deliver to each zone during that zone's conference. Following roughly eleven zone conferences, we prepared the mission board for monthly transfers—when missionaries were in an area for four to six months, it was usually time to transfer them to another area.

Each month, missionaries were going home, and their spots had to be filled by incoming missionaries.

The routine schedule in the offices took a little more than three weeks each month, leaving a little less than a week for the thing I looked forward to most: picking an area of the mission and going there to get to know and work with the missionaries serving in that particular area. I packed my backpack with a few days' worth of clean clothes and hopped a train, followed by a bus to get to some of the outlying areas. It was during these visits that I got to know some of the great missionaries, who like me, were fighting battles within and without, to teach by example how love conquers and connects us all in the universal brotherhood and sisterhood of man.

Working closely with President Berta left an indelible mark on me as a leader and a person. He showed me that engaging other leaders in all areas of the mission on a regular basis was an important key to success. He led by example in many ways, admonishing us to push ourselves, as he applied the same principle in his own life. He was also fun, never hesitating to pick up a guitar and sing a song, or to let others experience his singular brand of humor. He was young compared to the other mission presidents, only thirteen to fourteen years older than I was. In the months I had the privilege to work with him, I realized he was an excellent mixture of Jack and Sergeant Major Harris, both leaders I respected tremendously and tried to emulate.

By April 1991, I had been an AP for six months and was itching to spend my final months back out in the field. One evening, following a meeting with the entire staff, President Berta asked me to remain while the others left his private office. Mounted on the wall to the left of his desk was a giant cabinet made of wood, with large front panels on hinges that swung out to reveal photos of every missionary arranged in zones, districts, and areas. He walked to the cabinet and swung open the front panels, then turned to me and spread his arms out wide.

"Where do you want to go? I will send you any place you want."

Man, I love this guy.

In our travels to different parts of the mission, for some reason, one small town, Salto, about 120 miles to the northwest, had stuck in my mind since my first visit.

"How about sending me out to Salto?" I asked.

"Done."

The chapel in Salto was a large converted storefront with giant windows that faced the street in the heart of downtown. Offices toward the back and on the second floor served as classrooms. My companion, Allen Barney, and I lived farther toward the rear in two converted rooms, one a bedroom and the other a kitchen. The congregation was small, and struggling with inexperienced leaders, but to me it was heaven.

My final weeks and days passed much too rapidly, and before I knew it, I was back in President Berta's office for my final interview. I couldn't help thinking back on saying goodbye to Jack and Harris. How do you adequately convey how much that person has touched your life? Especially when the majority of those realizations come after you or they have departed. I could see in his eyes that he cared deeply about me. I know he felt like a father to all his missionaries. I felt it when he leaned forward and with emotion said, "I want you to know from the moment you got off the plane, and from our first chance to talk, I knew you would be someone I could count on to lead others."

"I know my personal convictions about this work have been a major driving force, but I also know that my four years in the Army played a huge part as well."

"Thank you for choosing to come here and serve the people of Argentina. They will not forget, nor will I forget your service to them and to me and my family." He smiled. "I look forward to staying in contact and watching how things turn out in your future."

"I look forward to that too," I said, feeling my own emotions beginning to swell. "President, it's been the greatest privilege of my life to come here and get to know you and your family, and to be touched by so many people, including all the missionaries I've been blessed to meet and get to know. I feel like I can only express a fraction of what I feel." To keep from completely losing my emotions, I looked out the window. "I'm going to miss that lawn chair out back," referring to where I fell asleep that first day in the country. "It was always calling to me."

He laughed and we both stood. After he offered a poignant prayer calling on the powers of heaven on my behalf, he embraced me in a hardy Argentine *abrazo* (hug).

The next morning, I looked around the inside of the airport, remembering my first impression had been something like, *What a dump.* At the foot of the escalator, I turned and gave the Bertas one final hug, not wanting it to end.

President and Sis Berta with Jason Pratt and me 1991

They both said "*Te quiero mucho,*" they both said with tears in their eyes. *I love you very much.*

"*Yo tambien te quiero mucho. Gracias por todo lo que me han hecho,*" I said, the words flowing swiftly and easily off my tongue. *Thanks for all you've done for me.* I wiped my cheeks and stepped on the escalator.

I glanced around one final time as the escalator carried me up, giving me a view from above. *This place isn't so bad. I don't know why I thought it was such a dump two years ago.*" That's how much my perspective had shifted.

CHAPTER 13

Shadow of the Rockies

―――――――

Within two weeks of arriving back home and spending time with my family, I had arranged a spot in a Provo apartment complex with several other missionaries who also returned from Argentina that July of 1991. I had a letter from Brigham Young University waiting for me when I got home, thanking me for my recent application, but politely declining. At age twenty-six, I enrolled at the nearby community college, which in no way affected my excitement to finally be living the college life I had heard so many missionaries talk about. I loved the atmosphere of the nearby campus and the myriad of outdoor activities to choose from. The abundance of world-class hiking in nearby canyons was reminiscent of the canyons I ran and hiked in Arizona.

About a week after moving into my apartment, I needed to call home. Since our phone wasn't working, I headed across the complex to see if Angela, my roommate Dan's girlfriend, would let me use hers.

"Come in," she said. "Hey, everyone, this is Brad. He served with Dan in Argentina and now they're roommates. Brad, this is Kirsti . . . Angie . . . Jenne . . . and Randi."

"Hello," I said, awkwardly waving my hand in their direction. I picked up the receiver off the wall phone and dialed the number. As I talked on the phone, I glanced around and watched as the girls discussed their different classes. Randi in particular had a light-hearted laugh and easygoing personality.

She was tall, at five-foot-ten inches, with brown curly hair, sun-kissed with highlights. She was strikingly unique looking, like a movie star from Hollywood's golden era of the 1940s and '50s, bearing a stunning resemblance to a young Judy Garland.

I would love to get to know her.

My opportunity came the next week, when my friend Brian, with whom I'd served in Argentina, invited me to go on a group date with his roommates that Friday.

"Got someone to invite?" he asked.

"I'll figure it out," I said.

The week flew by, keeping me inundated with classes, part-time work, and homework, and by Friday afternoon after my last class, I realized I needed to do some quick inviting. I called apartment 220 and nervously asked for Randi.

"Hi, Randi. Uh, it's Brad. . . . I hope you remember me. I'm the one who used your phone the other night?"

"Oh, you mean the guy who *hijacked* our phone for almost two hours for his personal use?"

"Yeah, that one."

We chatted a little and then I knew it was now or never. "Would you go out with me tonight? Maybe see a movie and get some ice cream?" I asked, then held my breath.

"Sure, I'd love to."

I couldn't help notice that our date felt different. Right away, I felt totally relaxed around her, feeling like I could just be myself.

For days after, my thoughts kept going back to Randi and how I felt with her that night. But I knew she would be heading to her eighteen-month missionary service after fall semester ended. I had just returned from that life-changing experience, and I didn't want to interfere with hers. But I also really liked her and wanted to go out with her more seriously. It left me in a precarious spot.

By the next Friday, I knew I wanted to see her again, so I called and asked her out on a second date. Over dinner at a local restaurant, we talked about our shared love of modern music. Like most of my friends, she could not believe I had already spent four years in the Army. As I walked her to her apartment door at the end of the date, I wanted to kiss her. I sensed (hoped!) that she felt the same. We lingered for a moment before I finally leaned in and met her leaning toward me.

She met me halfway! I thought, as sparks flew (for me) when our lips met for the first time. \

Randi Wells Fall of 1991

We dated for the rest of the semester. I loved every moment I got to spend with her, though in the back of my mind, I felt the time pressure. She would be leaving for home at Christmas break, and not returning for a year-and-a-half. She was called to serve in the Argentina—Mendoza mission, where I had spent my first five months serving. Despite knowing where she would be, I realized that deep down I didn't want her to go. The closer we got to the end of the semester, the more I had this sinking feeling when I thought of returning for spring semester knowing she wouldn't be there. I finally concluded that I should at least share how I was feeling before she left.

Our last date was the final day of exams before we were both scheduled to depart the next day, and I was nervous. All through dinner and dessert at her favorite ice-cream parlor, I tried to figure out a way to bring it up. Finally, toward the end of the evening, I took a deep breath. "I feel so conflicted right now. Part of me doesn't want you to go, and the other part doesn't want to interfere with the life-changing experiences waiting for you as a missionary." I began to tear up and saw that she was doing the same. "I'm willing to wait for you over the next eighteen months, to see if we still feel the same when you return." I pulled out a gold bracelet, a gift I had received when I departed Argentina, and gave it to her.

"I will miss you terribly while I'm gone." We hugged, mixing our tears as our cheeks touched. I walked her back to her apartment and gave her one final kiss. "I love you, and I'll be waiting here for you when you get back."

Randi reached up and ran her hand along my tear-soaked cheek.

"Okay," she said. "And I love you too." She covered her mouth to keep from sobbing and quickly stepped inside the apartment and closed the door behind her.

I stood there for a moment. *I can't let her go.*

I was in a deep sleep when one of my roommates, Kyle, grabbed my shoulder and shook me awake. "Randi's on the phone for you."

"What time is it?" I asked, still groggy.

"It's just after 6:00 a.m."

I pulled on my sweatpants and sweatshirt and walked into the kitchen and picked up the phone. "Randi?"

"I need to talk to you."

"Okay, can you come over? It's quiet here. Everyone's still asleep."

She agreed.

I unlocked the front door and sat down on the couch, rubbing the sleep from my eyes as I waited. Soon the door opened and Randi walked in. Her hair was pulled back in a ponytail and she was wearing blue sweatpants and an off-white pullover. She came to the couch and sat beside me. For a moment we just stared out the sliding-glass door to the snow-covered ground.

Finally she looked at me. "I've been awake all night praying. And I feel without a shadow of a doubt that I should delay going to Argentina."

Suddenly, I was no longer groggy. "Are you sure about this?"

"Absolutely."

My heart leapt with excitement. The dread I'd felt about coming back the next semester vanished.

"Okay, how do you think your parents will handle the news?"

"I'm not sure. I hope they won't be upset. It's not as if I haven't told them about you."

"Oh yeah? What did they say when you told them you were dating some older guy who already spent four years in the Army?"

"Well, ever since I mentioned you to my mom, she's reminded me several times not to let you distract me from going to Argentina."

I put my arm around her and pulled her close. "And how has that worked out for you?"

"I told her not to worry about it, but I think she's on to me." She leaned in and kissed me.

Her parents were both shocked at the sudden change in her life's direction, but they could not argue when Randi told them, "I didn't make this decision lightly. I spent an entire night on my knees in prayer before feeling a deep and profound sense of peace that my decision to stay home and pursue my relationship with Brad is the right thing to do."

The next few months were a whirlwind of spending as much time together while balancing part-time work, class, and studying. She was the one for me. And I was ready to make that commitment. Randi and I picked out a diamond engagement ring. And when it was sized, I placed it on her finger that very night while sitting on the couch in my apartment.

She smiled as she stretched out her hand to admire it. "I love it," she said.

We set a wedding date of May 2, 1992, a week after finals.

Since Randi was from Southern California, we planned to have the wedding ceremony at the Los Angeles LDS temple with a reception to follow at a chapel back in her hometown of Yorba Linda. As the day approached, we never anticipated that we would have our celebration in the height of the smoke and fire of the Rodney King riots.

Randi looked radiant in her long flowing sequined gown with her shoulder-length hair pulled up on the sides. The reception her parents arranged and funded was way more extravagant than I expected, and when all the tables were pushed to the side and the deejay kicked off the music, we all had the time of our lives dancing through the rest of the evening.

They say the initial period in any marriage is an adjustment for both parties. Ours was no different. We came from very different backgrounds and had to figure out how to meld and solve issues, hopefully with love and unselfishness, as a newly married couple.

Randi was extremely kind-hearted toward others, almost to a fault. She could not stand by and watch others suffer without reaching out. As the middle child she was usually in the role of counselor to her family members. I wanted to support her, but I could also see the toll it was taking on her. It seemed from the moment our life together began, the cracks in her parents' marriage began to show. Despite a valiant struggle to emotionally hold herself together as her parents' thirty-three-year marriage faltered, then eventually failed, it only seemed to compound her own feelings of insecurity and self-doubt.

Following a particularly emotionally challenging trip back to Yorba Linda where her parents had retreated to different parts of the home she grew up in, her world seemed to come crashing down—something I was not prepared to handle. Being there for Randi and her fragile emotional state became the new reality for me—an anxious and bewildered new husband. Fortunately, we had the good sense to move forward together.

Despite the emotional upheaval going on, we were extremely blessed to welcome a healthy baby boy into our small family. Matt was born in April 1993, and we were absolutely smitten with him.

While Matt was still an infant, I was working a part-time job for a pipe manufacturer between classes when a full-time employee learned that I had spent four years on active duty. He asked me about it. I told him about my unique experience training as a radar repairman and then later working in test and evaluations instead of fixing radars.

"Did you ever serve on active duty?" I asked him.

"No, my entire career has been with a bridge-building unit in the National Guard."

He shared several experiences from his years of service that seemed to speak to me about my connection to my previous service that never really left me. I realized how much I missed being in the military. *What if I signed up again?* I wondered what Randi would think. Her brother-in-law Jeff was already serving in the guard, so I hoped she'd be okay with it.

Finally one evening after Matt was asleep, I shared the coworker's story with Randi. "Well, anyway, I'm thinking about joining up again."

"You should, definitely! If that's what you want to do, go for it."

Within days I walked into a recruiting station and asked about serving once again. The recruiter suggested a personal tour later in the week to visit several nearby units. He informed me that the first unit we would visit that day was an aviation unit comprised of AH-64 Apache attack helicopters. I told him there was no need to look beyond the Apache battalion.

After visiting the Army Aviation Support Facility (AASF), I raised my right hand once again and enlisted in the Utah National Guard. I enlisted as a regular guard member—one weekend a month and two weeks in the summers—while I attended college full-time. Within a few months of enlisting, I put college on hold to attend six months of 68X Apache Armament MOS training at Fort Eustis, Virginia, taking Randi and Matt along with me.

We drove cross-country from Utah to Virginia in our little blue Geo Metro packed to the brim with our personal things. We stopped at Fort

Huachuca and Fort Gordon, Georgia, along the way. I was able to show Randi where I lived and worked in both locations.

"Wow, it's so weird to see where all the stories you've told me actually took place," she said.

"I know. It's even weirder to be back. I never thought I'd see these places again."

After arriving in Newport News, we drove to Fort Eustis and followed the directions to the barracks and unit to which I was assigned. I walked in to the building and found the CQ desk along the main hallway near the center.

The sergeant at the CQ desk watched me approach. "Signing in or signing out?"

"Signing in, Sergeant," I answered, handing him a copy of my orders.

"Do you need a room here in the barracks, Sergeant Jones?"

"No, I'm here with my wife and son. I need to find accommodations for the three of us."

"You need to go over to the housing office. If they don't have a place for you and your family, they will give you a statement of non-availability, so you can get reimbursed for renting a place off-post. You need to report back here tomorrow morning at 0630 to begin in-processing. Understand?"

"Yes, Sergeant," I said, as a sudden realization hit me like a hammer. I had just signed back into the regular Army and that meant I was no longer in charge of my own time. That night at a nearby hotel, I tossed and turned throughout the night, looking at the clock numerous times, fearing I was going to sleep through the alarm. Finally, around 5:00 a.m., I willed myself out of bed and quietly shaved and showered. I put on a clean uniform and looked at my reflection in the mirror. It had been more than four years since I wore the uniform on a daily basis.

I looked at Randi and Matt, both sleeping peacefully, unaware of the mixed emotions I had been feeling since signing in the previous night.

I was relieved when I was given the next few days to find a place to rent and get my family situated.

Our class consisted of seven "prior-service" soldiers, with a few of us being sergeants (E-5) and the rest specialists (E-4), along with about a dozen private's fresh from basic training. It was a completely new world for them. They had just come from the gauntlet of basic, and I could tell from the looks on their faces they wondered what it was going to be like to attend class with us.

They were good soldiers starting a new phase of their lives, and I identified with their nervous feelings at being in the same class with somewhat experienced prior-service soldiers. When I went through my first MOS school, I was only with classmates fresh out of basic.

Right away, I noticed that two sergeants delighted in the fact that they had tremendous amount of power over the new soldiers, who responded as they had been trained: answering, "Yes, Sergeant," or "No, Sergeant," and standing respectfully at Parade Rest when being spoken to.

I hoped they could tell that I was not going to treat them the same way. I never liked when I was treated that way, and I certainly was not going to take part in what was quickly becoming a toxic environment.

MOS training can be a demanding, high-stress environment, adding to the workload of classes and tests while trying to learn a new job.

Most new soldiers handle the combined stress fine, but I could see a few of them were rethinking their decision to join the military altogether.

I remembered back to my own early active-duty days. A few of my classmates during radar school simply had had enough and began purposefully failing exams in order to get discharged. Our instructors, who treated us fairly well, repeatedly assured us, "This is not the Army, you will not be treated this way when you get to your unit and start doing your job."

One day during a class break, I pulled a few of the new soldiers aside and reassured them that I could see what they were being put through. I let them know that they could come to me when or if they felt the need, but that as long as I was around, I would not let things get out of hand.

"Trust me, when you get to your permanent duty station, it will not be like what you're experiencing here." It was not so much what they were being put through, but the *way* they were being treated. The two sergeants delighted in sadistically exercising authority over them during class each day.

"Hey, Private, what's this on the floor? I thought I told you to sweep, not swing the broom back and forth like you did back home," they'd say. "Don't make me keep you here all night. Do it again. These floors better shine, or you're mine."

I could tell the soldiers were relieved to see that not all sergeants were power-hungry tyrants. One new soldier, Private Buck, who wore glasses and looked like a bookworm type, was struggling more than the rest. Word came up to all of us in the class that he could not pass the run portion on the Army Physical Fitness Test (APFT).

Typically, we all did daily PT at the same time in two separate groups—the prior-service soldiers led by a platoon sergeant, and the new soldiers led by their drill sergeants. The two toxic sergeants in our class made comments about Buck in front of the whole class for failing to pass the run portion of the test.

Shortly thereafter, we found ourselves finishing a PT session on the same field where the new soldiers were taking a PT test. I went over and asked Buck if he had passed the push-ups and sit-ups portion, which he had. The large group began the run portion with all of us fellow classmates standing along the track, and the two toxic sergeants screaming at Buck each time as he passed by.

I'd had enough of their leadership style, so when Buck ran past again, I joined him running around the track. I talked to him about his breathing, to pull from the bottom of his lungs by flexing—it feels like pushing out—his stomach, in order to completely fill his lungs with air. As we ran, I told him to focus on this deep-breathing technique and nothing else. As we passed the graders and were given the run time, I knew that if Buck did not speed up, he was going to fail the run.

So I instructed him to now focus on lengthening out his stride a little bit at a time, telling him just to keep up with me. He did exactly that, and on the last lap, we began to pour on the coals, coming around the last bend where a huge crowd stood screaming encouragement at the top of their lungs. We crossed the finish line with a few seconds to spare, his drill sergeant loudly announcing Buck's time and that he had passed. The crowd of soldiers erupted in cheers. I put my arm around Buck's shoulder. "See? You can do this!"

The six months passed quickly and with graduation in sight, Randi and I looked forward to returning to Utah. But I noticed she'd begun to complain of constantly feeling fatigued. Matt had just started walking, so I assumed trying to keep up with him was the cause.

"It's like trying to harness lightning," I told her.

"That's probably it," she said and smiled.

But more symptoms began to appear. When they felt like severe flu-like symptoms, she said she thought she should go to the ER at the hospital on base.

"Any chance you might be pregnant?" the ER doctor said, as he looked up from her paperwork.

Randi and I just looked at each other. "I don't think so," Randi said.

"Why don't we just play it safe and find out for sure?" He examined her briefly and left while a nurse had her take the pregnancy test.

"There's no way I'm pregnant," Randi said. "I'm still nursing our ten month old."

"Well, we'll find out for sure in a few minutes," was all I could think to say.

The door opened and in walked the doctor. "Congratulations, Mrs. Jones, you are pregnant."

You could've knocked me over with a puff of air.

So it was with Matt in his car seat, and Randi a few months pregnant, we drove from Virginia back to Utah and I resumed college while working part-time.

Randi's health remained unpredictable, but we chalked it up to her being pregnant again. In September 1994, Adara came into our lives. If Matt was a bolt of lightning, Adara was pure sunshine. She was such a happy and healthy baby, with big eyes and wispy blond hair. She was the kind of baby that makes people want to have another.

We were certain that now that Randi was no longer pregnant, her health issues would clear up. But they only got progressively worse. She suffered near constant low energy, and regularly felt achy flu-like symptoms, especially in her neck and back.

We sought the help of numerous medical professionals and therapists who diagnosed her with everything from depression to Epstein Barr syndrome, chronic fatigue, and hyperthyroidism, to name a few. But their prescriptions never seemed to make her symptoms ease up or go away altogether. Getting an exact diagnosis seemed to elude us for the next few years.

Both Matt and Adara provided us with joyful moments as they became aware of things like Christmas and their birthdays. Randi insisted on taking both of them to Disneyland as soon as each one turned three. While still taking a full load of courses, I applied for a full-time job at my guard unit's aviation hangar, where around eighty full-time federal employees worked to maintain the Apaches. The job came with excellent benefits, including health insurance, which was a motivating factor for me. I interviewed, along with several others, and was tremendously relieved when I was offered the position.

I was surprised at how easily I transitioned from college student and part-time employee back into wearing an Army uniform every day, while getting to work on aircraft valued at 15 million dollars apiece. Matt and Adara loved coming to the hangar, and with my help, climbing in and around the helicopters.

And Randi and I found a piece of property in a new housing development, and watched as our first home was built. Despite our struggles it was a magical time.

I was not prepared one evening, after crawling into bed and despite her health struggles, when Randi confided in me that she wanted to try for one more baby.

"Are you sure?" I asked.

"Yes, I'm sure," she answered.

"How can you be sure?"

"Because I just feel it."

"I don't know. I'm going to have to think about it."

Even though I was afraid that another pregnancy might make her health worse, after a few more late-night conversations, we decided to act in faith and try for one more child, knowing at least now, we had good health insurance.

I was grateful that during that third pregnancy, though Randi's health still remained a concern, it never seemed to worsen. And in July 1998, McCandliss, a healthy baby girl, came into our lives. She had wispy blond hair like her sister. And Matt and Adara, now old and autonomous enough, were both fascinated with her. Randi seemed like a pro taking care of Mimi, a nickname Randi came up with right away.

In the months that followed, my concern for Randi's health never strayed far from my mind. Though this third and last pregnancy had been healthy, it seemed only to prolong an accurate diagnosis that we could then properly treat.

Between her emotional and physical challenges, I honestly never knew, definitively, where one ended and the other began. One doctor diagnosed her with severe gallstones, and a surgeon subsequently removed eight large gallstones from her gallbladder. Following the surgery, the surgeon told me he'd never seen that many, that large, in all the gallstone surgeries he'd ever performed.

After the surgery, we felt optimistic that her health might improve, but again, her symptoms returned, and whichever treatment or procedure we tried, over time, never proved effective. Our efforts on the path to some semblance of health proved to be a constantly moving target that stretched my ability and stamina to the breaking point.

Why is this happening? What did I do to deserve this?" Those self-centered thoughts at times, plagued me. I knew Randi couldn't help how she was feeling; she was just as frustrated about it as I was. Maybe more so. I wasn't sure how to deal with these challenges. In the Army, if something broke, we fixed it. But this wasn't the Army, and Randi wasn't a machine.

Slowly, almost unperceptively, I began to recognize within me the intuitive makings of an equilibrium of sorts. Inner feelings of peace frequently helped to offset the heightened level of concern and anxiety I experienced when I contemplated Randi's prospects of ever improving her quality of life. Somewhere in the ditch digging and soul searching, a profound truth distilled upon me drop by drop. A truth that could only come from God: that in this life, I am not expected or required to fix all the challenges brought on by our trials. In some cases, I am called only to endure them. At excruciating moments, I was permitted to tap into what felt like an altogether ethereal reservoir, allowing me to listen, *just* listen, to Randi's deeply personal and painful feelings, which she shared only with me.

Many nights I would hold her while she cried and lamented that she was failing as a wife and mother were excruciating at times. I wanted more than anything to see her eventually overcome her emotional and physical challenges that seemed to weigh her down, at times, into deep despair. When it came to the kids and me, she wanted nothing more than to take care of us the same way she saw other wives and mothers taking care of their loved ones.

The kids and I were the beneficiaries of a never-ending wellspring of care and concern that lived within her heart. I had to be particularly careful when commenting on things that I liked or wanted. One afternoon I returned with the kids from a nearby pet store, telling Randi about a guy who had brought in an Australian Shepherd puppy to sell on consignment. I asked the guy what breed it was, and he kindly gave me a crash-course in the breed and the dog's family friendly temperament.

Returning home, I shared my experience at the pet store with Randi. Within two weeks I came home to an early birthday present, a tri-mix Australian Shepherd puppy we named Sarah.

To help manage my stress level, I poured myself into fixing and maintaining the Apache helicopters. The work couldn't have been more therapeutic for all my worry and concern for Randi's physical and emotional health. Tearing apart, cleaning, and servicing a 30 MM chain gun, just one of the weapons systems on the Apache, seemed like an odd way to handle the stress, but it worked for me.

CHAPTER 14

The Arabian Peninsula

D espite our struggles with Randi's health, we continued to enjoy our new home and family life. In addition, I was grateful to have a job that allowed us an hour each day to work out and maintain a level of physical fitness. Regularly running and working out in the weight room were both instrumental in my ability to navigate work and home life. Each month, during drill weekends, I served as a squad leader to approximately a dozen part-time soldiers, some with much more experience on the helicopters than I had. Even if I outranked them as their squad leader, I determined that I could learn from their level of expertise.

The weapons systems on the Apache are amazing, especially the M230, 30-millimeter chain gun. The impact of a ten- or twenty-round burst from the gun is lethal. Each round is its own separate grenade. The 30MM rounds are fed into the gun by a hydraulically driven feed chain that could easily be described as complex. The feed chain runs from the ammo box, turning several corners and changing angles to eventually descend from above into the gun. A ten-round burst takes mere seconds, so the timing of the gun and the feed system is critical. It was my favorite thing to work on.

Robert Warren, Ken Giles and me loading a real Hellfire missile
for Apache gunnery operations

I found nothing more satisfying than dismantling and servicing a gun, or troubleshooting a finicky feed system prior to exercising the system during our yearly two-week training exercise.

One day during test firing, an aircraft returned early to the landing pad reporting that the gun had malfunctioned. When I climbed under, I saw what the pilot was referring to. When a gun malfunctions on an Apache, it typically results in the ammo chain being balled up in a giant knot by virtue of the sheer speed and force of the hydraulically driven motorized feed system. In simple terms, it's a colossal mess, which takes time and effort to untangle.

After returning to the hangar later that day, we hoisted the one-hundred-thirty-pound gun onto the bench in the shop. I began cutting safety wire and loosening bolts that held the guns' different sections together. As I manually operated the bolt into the barrel breach, I could see where the bolt was catching ever so slightly as it exited the breach.

I scratched my head—we all did, as none of us had ever seen this issue before. What's more, my father had come to work with me that day and was watching all of us try to figure out what happened and how to fix it. That night I could not stop thinking about what would cause the bolt to ever-so-minutely contact the breach. Suddenly, while helping the kids with their prayers before bed, it came to me. I walked out and said to my dad, "I'm pretty sure I know what happened."

"Yeah? What do you think it is?" he asked.

"Well, we just had a team here earlier to overhaul each gun, and one of the things they did was remove the breach, which is secured by metal pins that have to be inserted correctly. I think they inserted one, or maybe both, backwards, minutely pushing the breach out of position."

Dad pursed his lips and nodded.

I couldn't wait to get to the hangar the next morning and see if my hunch was correct. I pulled the set screws holding the breach pins in, and just as I thought, one had been incorrectly inserted. By mid-morning, I had already replaced the broken bolt pieces and was in the process of reassembling the gun.

The following year, in early 2000, we began to hear about an upcoming six-month deployment providing aerial security for Operation Southern Watch, in support of the no-fly zone over Iraq. We would run aviation operations from Camp Doha, a base on the outskirts of Kuwait City. With medical bills piling up, the extra money during a deployment would certainly help out. Randi and I had long conversations about the workload on her with me gone, and its effect on her health and the kids. Despite the challenges, Randi encouraged me to volunteer to go.

Saying goodbye to her and the kids on the large concrete flight line next to the hangar was one of the most gut-wrenching moments of my life. When the bus pulled away, I watched them fade in the distance, tears streaming down my cheeks.

From nearby Hill Air Force base (AFB), we took off in an Air Force C-5 Galaxy. Two Apaches were anchored in the belly, along with containers carrying enough tools and spare parts to get the aircraft up and running as soon as we landed in Kuwait. From Dover AFB, Delaware, we flew nonstop to a base in Rota, Spain. After overnighting in Rota, we began the last leg of our journey toward the Persian Gulf, landing at Kuwaiti International Airport (KIA) sometime after midnight that first week of July 2001.

When we exited the plane, I looked around and couldn't understand why they parked the door of our plane directly in the jet wash—the exhaust—of a nearby plane. When I got close to the other plane's engines, I suddenly realized that the engines were silent and the wall of exhaust I thought I was feeling was the normal heat rolling across the tarmac.

The desert heat was unlike anything I had ever experienced, even during my three years in Arizona where I spent plenty of days in the 115-to-118 degrees normal for Tucson and Phoenix. I couldn't help but feel as though I'd stepped into a blast furnace, instantly, beads of sweat began to roll down my face, back and arms. I don't remember ever sweating that heavily before.

We loaded onto a waiting bus for the trip from the airport to Camp Doha.

Even though darkness obscured the surrounding landscape along the route, the freeway was modern and well-lit. As we approached an off-ramp, I could see movement just off the roadway.

"Look, they're playing soccer under the lights of the off-ramp," a fellow soldier said.

And they were dressed in white Arabic robes with headdresses.

"It's got to be a hundred degrees outside, even though it's after 1:00 a.m.," I said in amazement.

Camp Doha sat directly adjacent to the waters of the Persian Gulf. Not only did we have to deal with daily temperatures of 125 to 128 degrees Fahrenheit, the air coming off the ocean was *beyond* humid, making the heat of the air feel even heavier. It was, quite literally, stifling.

We had to wear gloves when working on the aircraft, since surface temperatures were hot enough to cause serious burns if we touched anything with our bare hands. It was a monumental adjustment working on equipment in that kind of heat—sweat towels around our necks became a regular part of our uniforms to keep the profuse amounts from dripping onto the instruments inside the aircraft. Everyone wore hydration back-packs throughout the days and nights.

The base was a converted shipping port, with enormous parking lots and approximately twenty warehouses. Our living quarters were located in one of the warehouses, with two-person rooms each, furnished with two army beds, two army wall lockers, a television, and a refrigerator. We had to shower in nearby trailers. The warehouse next door had a large gym with a full-length basketball court, boxing ring, and a gigantic weight room, with plenty of free weights and machines to choose from.

The first couple days we attended in-processing briefings about the base and the surrounding city, people, and culture. One briefing was about a nearby suburb named Al Jahra. Apparently, the town's citizens were hostile to the Kuwaiti government over not being descended from a particular bloodline found in the rest of the population, who were considered full-blooded Kuwaiti citizens. We were informed that Al Jahra was strictly off-limits to US military. I could not help but think about our Native American tribes, consigned to reservations as part of our country's history.

Ali Al Salem Air Base, located west of Camp Doha, was home to US and British Air Forces, and was the location from where we would execute numerous flight operations. As soon as we finished unpacking, we prepared for our first convoy to Ali Al Salem for gunnery operations, when pilots practice shooting 2.75-inch rockets, 30MM rounds, and Hellfire missiles in the Kuwaiti desert. Armament section responsibilities included functional weapons systems tests and loading each aircraft with ammo. The temperature was already climbing above 120 when our convoy assembled at the airfield. A dozen vehicles, including Humvees, fuel tankers, and several Jeep Cherokees loaded with our equipment. I was chosen to be the trail vehicle in one of the Jeeps.

Riding shotgun with me was former Marine Mike Azarow originally from New Jersey. Everyone liked Mike and his sense of humor, despite his continual use of Marine Corps lingo and his fanatical devotion to the Pittsburgh Steelers that bordered on psychosis.

Gunnery operations Ali Al Salem Air Base

This would be the first operation testing our ability to perform in the oppressive heat and humidity. The convoy exited the main gate and headed south on Doha Road, turning right on Highway 6. I marveled at the tan desert landscape as far as I could see. Once on Ali Al Salem Airbase, we slowly made our way passed a combination of newer modular structures alongside older concrete buildings that appeared to be barracks and offices.

"Look at that," Mike said, as we drew closer to the airfield. "Left over battle damage from Desert Storm."

Sure enough, just off the runway sat several enormously thick concrete hangars with gigantic holes blown through the roofs. Inside each looked like a scene out of an apocalyptic movie. Long strands of rebar hung straight down from each gaping hole nearly reaching the ground. It looked like spaghetti hanging down from the ceiling, and from the distance, we could see how thick the rebar was, indicative of the enormous force of the blast. One hangar looked as if Godzilla had stomped on it.

"I remember hearing about this," Mike said.

"Where was your Marine unit when all this went down?" I asked.

"Saudi," he said without looking over. "We were at an airfield in the Saudi desert."

Farther down the flight line was the open area where the fuel tankers had parked and were unrolling fuel lines next to four large concrete landing pads. It was 53 to 55 degrees Celsius when we began to unload our gear and set up for the first wave of Apaches. By the time the first wave departed, we were pouring liter bottles of water down our fronts and backs. The aircraft rotor wash surrounded us with a cloud of sand and grit that permeated our clothing and mixed with our sweat. Soon we got into a grove and did our best to not focus on how hot and uncomfortable we all were.

Late that afternoon, we cleared the last Apache for the short flight back to Camp Doha. Despite our sandy, gritty, sweat-soaked uniforms, we couldn't help smiling and high-fiving each other for surviving the brutal elements. Mike and I again followed behind the convoy as the trail vehicle on the return trip back to Doha.

No more than a few miles down the freeway, I felt the steering wheel suddenly begin to shudder, and I recognized the familiar feeling of a blow out in one of the tires.

"I thought you PMCS'd this thing?" I said, referring to "Preventative Maintenance Checks and Services." I looked at Mike, and we both laughed nervously.

"I did, I did, Sergeant Jones," Mike shot back as I hit the brakes and pulled over to the shoulder, just as the shuddering became increasingly violent.

"You think they'll send someone back to rescue us?" I asked as we both watched the convoy disappear in the distance.

This was before cell phones, so we had no way to communicate with anyone from the convoy. Furthermore, I realized that I had been so busy looking around on the way there, that I had not paid attention to the route. Nor did I have a strip map of the route, a requirement for each and every vehicle in a military convoy.

Mike and I got out and looked at the right front tire, shredded from the heat and the distance we traveled from the moment the steering wheel began to shake. I looked around. *I'm in a foreign country, it is hotter than hell, and I am now faced with the prospect of finding our way back to base, in an area unfamiliar to the both of us. Great.*

The fact that we were in uniform at the very least made us stand out from the clothing commonly worn by the local Arab population. To say I was nervous would be putting it mildly.

Fortunately, each Jeep had the familiar spare tire attached to the spar on the back of the vehicle. Despite the Jeep's white color, we were still shocked by how hot the exterior surfaces were as we searched for the tire jack. We put on gloves to keep from burning our hands.

It did not make matters any less stressful that nearly every vehicle that whizzed by honked for some odd reason.

"Why does everyone keep honking?" Mike asked.

"Don't know. I hope it's just something cultural and not for some other reason."

Finding the jack turned into quite the ordeal.

We completely unloaded our equipment from the cargo area, thinking the jack would be located somewhere in the rear.

We were now sweating profusely—again—and we were wrong; the jack was nowhere to be found in the back. We looked under the hood in the engine compartment. No luck. "I thought you said you PMCS'd this thing. I'm wondering what part of the procedure instructed you to hide the jack," I said, trying to inject some humor into our situation. I hoped one or more of the vehicles from our convoy would double back when they realized we were no longer there.

Finally, we pulled up the second-row bench seat, and there underneath was the jack and lug wrench!

"Uh, Sergeant Jones, I think I've located the jack," Mike said, as we both stood sweating and staring.

"Oh, that's where you hid it. Nice going, Mike!"

We used every towel we'd brought with us to wipe away the river of sweat that dripped from our heads and faces. With the spare installed and the equipment again reloaded into the back, we made our way down the freeway, hoping to recognize something familiar.

At last, we could see the two smoke stacks that sat adjacent to Camp Doha way off in the distance. "Keep those stacks in sight," I told Mike, as we headed in their general direction. Paying attention to those stacks, I was surprised when the freeway came to an end, emptying onto a large boulevard.

Oh no. We're driving right through the center of Al Jahra.

I must have missed some sort of freeway interchange we were supposed to take. At each stop light, we could see that all eyes were on us—two incredibly nervous and lost GIs. At one intersection we pulled up alongside a pickup truck with a camel laying down in the back, similar to how people have dogs riding in the bed of a truck back home.

I seriously considered pulling the camera out of my backpack sitting close by, but quickly dismissed the idea. I had to keep telling myself to "just keep moving" toward the smoke stacks that were looming larger and larger above Al Jahra's city structures.

"That looks familiar," Mike said, pointing toward a freeway entrance. It was the freeway that skirted Al Jahra leading toward Kuwait City. Within a few minutes, we found the road heading north to the main gate of Camp Doha. After passing through a security check at the main gate, we made our way over to the fuel point, finding the last of the vehicles from our convoy getting fuel.

"What took so long at the main gate?" the soldiers from the other vehicles asked, clueless that we had been left behind shortly after leaving Ali Al Salem!

Mike and I looked at each other and shook our heads. Neither one of us recounted what we had just been through, but afterward, as a leader,

I made sure *each* vehicle in a convoy had a strip map and was thoroughly briefed on the route and need to maintain vehicle accountability within the convoy.

The armament section was divided into two teams, one for day shift and the other for night. Another staff sergeant (SSG) named Allen Foote was the overall section supervisor along with supervising the day shift, while I supervised the night shift. Foote was an excellent mentor leading up to the deployment. More than anybody, he was responsible for my proficiency as a maintainer, generously sharing from his own wealth of knowledge and experience.

Just prior to departing Utah, a soldier joined the section who out-ranked both Foote and me. He was a Sergeant First Class (SFC/E-7)—one stripe above SSG/E-6—who was experienced on the Apache airframe, but had little-to-no experience on the armament systems. About two months into the deployment, the phone in my room rang. It was First Sergeant (1SG) Byron Hobbs. Throughout the Army, first sergeants are referred to as "Top" in reference to their senior or "top" position in the unit. 1SG Hobbs—Top—called to tell me that Foote needed to go home on emergency leave, due to a death in his family. He then informed me that the SFC/E-7 was now in charge.

Regardless of this guy's higher rank, I'm the one with the knowledge and experience to effectively run the section, I thought after I hung up. I immediately picked up the phone and called Top back.

"Top, I know he outranks me, but I have way more experience than he does. I'm in charge of the armament section."

A long pause followed while he absorbed what I said. "You know what?" he finally said. "You're right. You're in charge."

Most of the Armament section from L to R Curtis Fowden, Mike Felter, me,
Tim Winters, Robert Davis, Mike Azarow, Mike Zesiger, Chris Banks

After we hung up, I knew I'd done the right thing. I felt absolutely compelled to step up in that moment. I arrived at the point in my career where I possessed the confidence in my own experiences and knowledge to lead others. From that day on, I supervised the day-to-day maintenance in the armament section for the remainder of the deployment.

We became familiar with the civilian contractors who provided security on Camp Doha, based on their tan uniforms, which were slightly different from the patterned camouflage versions we wore. Late in the afternoon of Tuesday, September 11, I was out on the flight line with several other soldiers working on an aircraft. We noticed multiple base security vehicles race past the airfield toward the nearby towers located at the corners along the wall surrounding that side of the base. When they reached the towers, they jumped out and quickly climbed the stairs taking positions along the perimeter with their weapons at the ready.

We all stopped what they were doing and watched to see what would happen next. I could see them scanning the area beyond the perimeter with binoculars.

"Maybe it's an exercise or something," I said. "You guys keep working, while I head over to flight ops to see if they know what's going on." I walked to the other end of the large airfield—referred to as "the ramp"—and entered the flight-ops office. As soon as my eyes adjusted to the light level, I knew something was seriously wrong.

Scanning the room, I looked at the three flight-ops soldiers sitting at their desks staring straight ahead. A radio, tuned to the Armed Forces Network (AFN), sitting on a cabinet played loudly enough for me to hear. The reporter's panicked voice immediately caught my attention.

"What's going on?" I asked.

A soldier sitting nearest to me turned his head slowly, still trying not to miss a word coming from the radio. "A passenger jet crashed into one of the World Trade Towers about an hour ago, and a second plane just crashed into the other tower."

An incredible sinking feeling came over me. I knew things were about to change. I remained in the office for a few more minutes in stunned silence as the reports continued to come in from a scene of unparalleled fear and chaos back in our homeland. Finally, I raced back to my team, who was just finishing up.

"You guys are not going to believe this," I began. My tone was serious enough that everyone stopped what they were doing and looked at me. "Two airliners just crashed into the World Trade Towers in New York about an hour apart. Both buildings are totally in flames."

Everyone's faces gave away the shock and the realization of what this meant. We cleaned up, put away our tools, and closed out the logbook in silence. The loud, sometimes irreverent banter, common among us was absent. We loaded into a Jeep and drove to the chow hall where we could watch the latest news reports on the numerous big screens playing the twenty-four-hour news cycle we had become accustomed to.

The normal level of chatter inside the chow hall was uncharacteristically absent, as each of us tried to absorb the enormity of the moment. Soldiers whispered if they needed to communicate. The expression on everyone's faces was unmistakable. It was a look of resolve. Most encounters in a chow hall were brief, with little or no eye contact. Suddenly things were different, each one of us—mostly strangers to one another—now looked each other in the eye and nodded, an acknowledgment of our solidarity and commitment to our duty.

Our lives were now different. Our careers were now different. It was as if a sleeping giant had suddenly been awakened. Things turned deadly serious. I had never been issued live ammo before, or given much thought to the possibility of one of my soldiers losing their life. That thought weighed heavily on me in the following days, as operations continued, but now those operations took on a level of realism unfamiliar before. The level of uncertainty—bordering on fear—in our now-post-9/11 world was deep and unmistakable.

Our task force commander spoke to us in blunt, direct terms. As one of the most forward deployed combat units, Army planners were weighing options to possibly forward deploy us into the austere terrain and environment of Afghanistan. Our personal and combined unit-readiness was paramount.

"Be ready." The commander used sobering words. "Be ready."

I felt confident in my soldiers and our ability to execute our mission. The thing that kept me up at night was the need for strict silence when it came to communicating with our families. When and if the call came, that communication would suddenly go dark, and no one knew when it would resume. I certainly didn't want to put Randi and the kids through that kind of trouble, but the reality was we were now at war, and for us things could change very quickly.

Initially we remained confined to the base. All travel, except for increased security flight missions flown by our Apaches, was restricted, which meant no more trips into Kuwait City. The Kuwaiti citizens had always treated us with kindness and respect as we wandered through the gold souks and other shopping areas we frequented. In fact, it wasn't uncommon for Kuwaiti women to approach us on the streets and in broken English say how much they loved America.

After several tense and uncertain weeks, word came that a scheduled convoy from Camp Doha to Ali Al Salem Air Base for another gunnery operation would be executed. Before departing Camp Doha, the convoy assembled on the flight line. For the first time we were issued thirty round clips with our M-16s. Except for a weapons qualification range, I'd never been issued live rounds before. I looked down at my weapon. *We aren't playing around. This is serious.* I looked at the others and realized I wasn't alone in feeling the gravity of the situation.

From our vantage point on the tarmac, we watched as the massive military might of the United States was unleashed. Overnight, nearby giant parking lots, normally empty, would suddenly fill with new and different armored weapon systems, then following an inventory and inspection, the soldiers and equipment would disappear just as quickly.

Word finally trickled down that our task force needed to extend beyond the original six-month deployment time frame, providing security for the incoming military units using Camp Doha, and nearby Ali Al Salem, as jump-off points for combat operations in Afghanistan. I could tell Randi was relieved when I could finally share that news, but also unhappy with the uncertainty of how long we would be extended. I could tell she was losing steam and needed me at home.

In early January 2002, we received news that another Apache battalion would replace us in the next month or two. Many of us were looking forward to attending events for the winter Olympics being hosted in Salt Lake that February. We resigned ourselves to watching Olympic coverage from Kuwait, which was tempered by the fact that nearly every soldier in Utah had been called to active duty to prevent another attack many felt was imminent.

In February, the Olympics began, just as we finished up cleaning and packing our equipment. Members from the replacement Apache battalion trickled in, with the main body arriving by mid-month. A number of us were up late watching the Olympics in the day room, when our Commander appeared in the doorway. "Wake everyone up, we're going home."

High on adrenaline, we went from room to room flipping on the lights and sharing the exciting news with our fellow soldiers.

Within two hours we were on buses headed for KIA and a flight home. Nobody could sleep. Nicely dressed and pretty flight attendants greeted us as we entered the large jumbo jet. We quickly found seats, and as the plane taxied and lifted off, our entire task force erupted into deafening cheers. We were on our way. We made stops in Italy, Germany, and Bangor, Maine, before landing at McCord Air Force Base, Washington, for the demobilization process, which includes medical screening and turning equipment and uniforms.

When we landed at Salt Lake International Airport, the scene was different from what we'd anticipated. With new security restrictions in place, family members waited in the baggage claim area. When the first group of us appeared at the top of the escalator, the crowd went nuts. I spotted Randi and the kids as soon as I stepped on the escalator. As the kids ran toward me, I scooped them up into my arms and kissed each one repeatedly. Randi poked her head in between the kids, and again she met me halfway. It felt good to be home—even if I wasn't sure for how long or what would happen next.

CHAPTER 15

A Defining Moment

In those first few days of my being home, I could sense Randi physically release the pressures from all she'd handled while I was gone. She slept like she hadn't slept in years. I didn't mind, since it gave me one on one time with the kids.

About a month after arriving home, many of us returned to our jobs. It was great to be back in the shop, working on the aircraft and equipment that weathered the sand and grit of the Kuwaiti desert. Back in the armament shop, we were all more or less equal; the only thing separating us was our level of experience. I was happy to be back with coworkers, though I soon realized that I missed being part of a team and taking care of my soldiers.

When an opportunity arose for me to take one of the few remaining slots in an upcoming two-week resident advanced NCO leadership course—Advanced Non-Commissioned Officer Course (ANCOC)—taking place at the nearby National Guard base, only ten minutes from my home, I jumped at it. Though I was required to spend nights on the base, at least I was close enough to go home and check on Randi and the kids each day.

The week after graduating from the course in the spring of 2002, I went to see SFC Myron Skousen, our full-time training NCO. Myron and I had been roommates our final few months in Kuwait.

"How quickly can I get a slot in the final ANCOC class I need?" I asked.

"Funny you should bring that up at this time," Myron said. "We just got word that the Army is going to revamp the entire NCO academy program, including the number of classes for both the basic and advanced course requirements."

"What does that mean for me?"

"It means that had you not taken and graduated from the first phase of ANCOC last week, you would be required to go back and complete two new courses at the basic level, followed by upcoming new classes at the advanced level."

"So, in this case, it was good that I was Johnny-on-the-spot?" I asked with a grin.

"Absolutely. You are the only one I know of here in the aviation community who will get grandfathered through because you acted quickly and accepted a shortfall slot on such short notice."

"When can I get a slot in phase two?" I asked. "And where is it taught?"

"We have quotas for classes this coming summer. It's at WAATS"— the Western Army Aviation Training Site—"in Marana, Arizona. Shall I get you a slot?"

"Do it," I said, without a moment's hesitation. "I don't want to give the Army any reason to rescind grandfathering me through."

"A wise choice," Myron offered, and grinned.

That fall I accepted a position with the Federal Aviation Administration (FAA) at the Salt Lake Air Traffic Control Center. I felt torn about leaving my full-time job working on helicopters, but I couldn't refuse the better pay and opportunity for much greater upward mobility. Plus, it continued my federal service, which, by then, had grown to more than a decade.

To celebrate my new position, and increased salary, I did what any red-blooded American would do—I purchased a used, and very clean, red 1998 Jeep Wrangler, which I picked up from the dealer a few days before departing for Marana, Arizona, in June 2003.

I had never traveled down through that stretch of Utah and Arizona. The highway through the red-rock formations of Moab and the cathedral-like spires of Monument Valley was breathtaking. Flagstaff reminded me of the ski trips I took to Sunrise ski resort on the Fort Apache Reservation while stationed Arizona.

The course offered an advanced leadership curriculum with instructor-led lectures in an open-discussion format, covering the importance of leading soldiers, especially in the current combat-deployment cycle. The experience level in the class was evident from day one. Each of us had previously led a squad or section—some during perilous combat operations. The relaxed atmosphere allowed us to express and share our experiences with one another.

Like most Army leadership courses, our class bonded immediately, spending our free time taking in the natural wonders of Arizona.

By the end of the course, I knew I had been among greatness—blessed to hear, feel, and learn from true heroes who inspired me tremendously. The stories and experiences we shared during the two weeks about the sacrifices everyone so willingly gave felt as though we were on sacred ground among my classmates.

Following class graduation on Friday, June 27, I drove north through Flagstaff toward the Arizona-Utah border, stopping at Glen Canyon Dam where I called home.

"You're coming home tonight?" Randi asked.

"Yeah, I want to surprise the kids by being there when they wake up in the morning, so don't say anything to them."

"Okay, they'll be so excited to see you. I told them you wouldn't be home until tomorrow night. They're pulling out sleeping bags and making popcorn for a movie night in the family room, so you'll have to sneak around them when you get here. Oh, I'm so excited, I can't wait to see you!"

"Me too, babe."

"I love you. And please drive carefully."

"I love you too. I will."

"See you in the morning, Bradley Paul," she said.

I fully expected to stop at some point and sleep, so I was surprised that throughout the southern part of Utah I felt awake and alert. Morning's first light silhouetted the outline of the Wasatch Mountains when I pulled into the driveway around 5:00 a.m.

Quietly entering through the garage, I paused in the family room and looked down where Matt and Adara were sleeping peacefully on the floor. Making my way down the hall to our bedroom, I found Mimi cuddled up next to Randi.

I paused at the foot of the bed and noticed that Randi was sleeping with her hair covering her face. *That's odd. She never sleeps like that.* After a decade of marriage, I knew how she always had her hair pulled back in a ponytail when she slept.

I went around to the side of the bed and placed my hand on her hip. She was ice-cold. I took hold of her forearm and tried to pull her over from her right side. Her whole body retained the same position as I lifted her.

A sudden pulse ran through my entire body like a thunderous surge of electricity. *No. This cannot be happening.* My mind refused to accept the reality of what my eyes were seeing. *She's only thirty-three. I just spoke to her on the phone.* I started hyperventilating. *This has got to be a horrible dream. She can't leave us . . . not now, not like this.*

Scenes from our life together erupted in my mind's eye. *Traveling on LA's freeways on our wedding day amid the destruction and riots following the Rodney King verdict. Being by her side at the births of our three children. Seeing her joy spending the day at Disneyland and Newport Beach with the kids, where she never tired of body surfing and boogie boarding.*

As I replayed these scenes, I suddenly felt a distinct and powerful peace wash over me. It was as if she were standing next to me, whispering, "Everything is going to be okay. I'm fine and I'm no longer suffering physically and emotionally."

I'm not sure how long I stood there, trying desperately to grasp and process everything. Looking at Mimi, peacefully sleeping and unaware, I came around the bed and gently picked her up and cradled her in my arms. *How am I ever going to tell her that her mother is gone?* I wondered, looking at her innocent chubby little face. *She's her mother's little sidekick.* My mind went to Adara—*always her mother's little helper. And Matt, her firstborn, the apple of her eye. No matter how tired or sick she felt, she loved doing things for them. She loved seeing them smile and laugh. She loved seeing them happy.*

Carrying Mimi into the family room, I laid her on the couch and dialed 911 as I walked to my neighbor's house.

When my neighbor Christian Degn answered the door, he saw the look in my eyes. "Brad?"

"I need your help. I think Randi died."

"I'm right behind you," he offered.

Returning, there on the porch stood Matt, Adara, and Mimi looking at me.

"Did something happen to Mom?" Adara said.

I could hear Christian coming up behind me, and not feeling prepared to tell them what I already knew, I said simply, "I need you to go with Christian to his house."

Despite their confusion, they followed him.

A Lehi police cruiser pulled up, and an officer got out and quickly grabbed two cases from the trunk. I led him into the house where I pointed the way to our bedroom.

Almost immediately, he returned. "It's no use, she's already gone."

With my head and heart spinning, I knew I needed to go and be with my kids.

On the sidewalk, I dialed my brother's number.

It was about 5:00 a.m. in Seattle when the phone pulled him from a measure of peaceful sleep. "Brad?" Mark said.

"Dude," I said and paused, trying to hold it together. "Randi died. Can you get here?"

"I'm on my way," he said.

I continued down the sidewalk. *How am I going to put this into words so they'll understand?* My heart was breaking open. I knew I couldn't avoid telling them what I knew would surely shatter their little hearts into a million pieces. I was struggling to come to terms with the most difficult conversation I would probably ever have.

They were teary eyed, when I went to them. I could see that Mimi, still sleepy, did not fully understand what was going on. But as I looked into Matt's and Adara's eyes, I could sense that they knew.

I sat between them and wrapped them up in my arms.

"Mom is in heaven," I said softly.

The impact hit them immediately, sending a flood of tears coursing down their cheeks.

I couldn't help reaching over and wiping some of their tears away, as I thought of what to say next. "I need you to look at me."

I found myself staring into innocent eyes.

"I promise you that no matter what, I will always be your dad, and mom will always be your mom. We are still a family and we will always be a family."

"Can we see her?" Adara asked. "I want to say goodbye."

"I don't know," I said. "They're taking her away in an ambulance."

"Does that mean they're going to try and save her?" Matt asked.

"Not this time," I said. "The paramedics already looked at her and said there was nothing they could do."

"I promise you that you will see her again. She always looked after you, protecting and teaching you—sort of like a guardian angel. And from now on, she will be your very own guardian angel for the rest of your lives."

We cried in each other's arms. "We are still a family. We will always be a family."

Later, I began the very unpleasant task of calling family and friends, and in essence, "dropping a bomb" into their otherwise unsuspecting lives. The first call I made was to Jenne, Randi's close friend and roommate from college. I was caught off guard when the call went to her voicemail.

"Hey, this is Brad. I need you to call me as soon as you get this message."

Later that afternoon, my phone rang.

"Hey Brad, its Jenne," she said. "Jenne, I need your help. Randi died."

"Oh Brad, I am so sorry!" Her voice sounded strained with emotion. "I'm in Wyoming at a family reunion. I'll come home as quickly as I can."

"I'm sorry to ruin your time with your family."

"I'll be okay. My parents are here, so I need to go tell them. They really loved Randi. Brad, things will be okay. You know my family loves you, and we will do whatever we need to support you and the kids." Her words reassured me in a way I hadn't expected.

Late that night, alone with my thoughts, I pondered over the last conversations between Randi and me. Those conversations suddenly took on a deeper, more profound significance. I could not think of one conversation, or instance, where I got a sense from Randi of something impending.

The morning of her funeral, July 3, dawned warm and bright. By 9:30, the chapel was already overflowing with neighbors, close friends, and family. The service began with the choir singing "In This Very Room," after which Jenne delivered Randi's eulogy. Then it was my turn to speak. I ascended to the podium and took a deep breath as I looked out over the large congregation.

Despite the gaping hole I felt in my soul, I also had never felt so much love, so powerfully, in any setting in my entire life. It came in waves, from my parents and my brother who were right below me in front. I looked down to where Randi's parents and her two sisters sat in the same pews beside my family. I could see from their expressions they were surprised to see me standing at the pulpit. But somehow, someway, I felt strengthened to say things that only I could, on Randi's behalf.

Noel and Sidney Wells

I spoke about how even though Randi's life was cut short, she still accomplished the most important things, like falling in love and getting married, having children and teaching them to love God by always striving to follow His commandments. She loved animals and passed that love on to the kids. She was fiercely loyal and inclusive to those she loved. At our wedding, I had more than a few fathers tell me to take care of Randi, that I married the gal they had encouraged and secretly wished their sons had married.

How could I sum up someone's life in twenty minutes? I couldn't, but in sharing my thoughts with everyone, a clear impression came to me: that her life, love, and influence would live on in those of us privileged enough to have had an angel in our midst.

At the conclusion of the service, we slowly walked together as a family behind the casket to the waiting hearse, which led a massive procession to the Lehi cemetery.

I picked a spot in a recently opened area in the northeast section of the cemetery. Nearby young trees were dwarfed by much older mature trees near her resting place. Cemetery workers erected a giant canopy tent next to where the pallbearers gently placed the casket amid numerous giant bouquets of flowers.

I picked this spot so the kids, who walked past the cemetery each day on their way to school, could know that their mom would always be close by.

In the days following the funeral, the kids and I spent most evenings with Jenne and her daughter Madyson, swimming at the local pool. It felt odd to be in the house without Randi. And having Jenne close by felt comforting.

One evening, while the kids were getting changed into pajamas, out of the blue Adara looked up at me. "Why don't you marry Jenne?"

"Yeah, Dad," Matt echoed. "You should marry Jenne."

I took a deep breath and looked into their eyes. "You think that's a good idea?"

"Yeah," Mimi said. "That way she could be our mommy."

"Thanks for sharing that with me," I said, stunned by this spontaneous conversation. They seemed to understand Randi wasn't coming back and that they needed a mom—and I needed a wife. "I promise to give it some thought."

Despite my own grief, I couldn't help wondering what Randi would want for me and the kids. Jenne had divorced Mady's dad, Scott, four years before. Despite being bummed about their breakup, I remember telling Randi, "She won't last a year being single. Someone will come along and sweep her up before you know it."

But I never thought it would possibly be me.

A week after Randi's funeral, Mimi asked, "Are we still going to California to see Grandpa Noel get married?"

I had the go ahead from my manager at work to take as much time as I needed. "Yes, we're still going," I reassured her.

The night before our trip, while helping Jen unload some things from her trunk, I figured I should at least say something to her. "Hey, when the time is right—I mean, when things settle down, I would like to see you."

"Okay," she said and sat on the tailgate, where I joined her.

"Do you understand what I'm trying to say?"

She slid her hand inside mine and gave me a smile. "I understand."

The next morning the kids and I loaded the Jeep and headed south on I-15. It felt good to get away, just the four of us.

Out on the open road, we talked. The kids shared their memories of Randi's final few weeks with them. They talked about the good times they had together in those final days of her life.

The time in California was sublime, but passed too quickly. The night before we departed, Noel and I were at a gas station sitting in the Jeep.

"Several months ago, Randi and I were talking on the phone," Noel began. "Randi told me, 'Dad, if anything ever happens to me, I want Jenne to take care of Brad and the kids.'"

I was stunned.

"I played it off and told her, 'You don't need to worry about that, Randi,'" Noel continued. "Everything's going to be just fine.'"

"How could she have the presence of mind to say that?" I asked Noel.

"I have no idea," he answered.

"I can't imagine that she knew something was going to happen."

I shared with Noel that while I was in Arizona, I called home each night. "Numerous times nobody answered. When I spoke to them the following day, they would share with me how much fun they'd had together the day before."

I was grateful Randi felt good enough to get out and do something fun each day, even though I couldn't be there. People who saw her during that time later shared that Randi appeared to feel better and have more energy, a welcome respite from her heath struggles.

Later that night, I called Jen. After some small talk, I took a long pause and inhaled deeply. "Tonight Noel came with me to top off the Jeep. And you're not going to believe what he told me." Then I repeated our conversation.

It was Jenne's turn for the long pause. "She said that to Noel several months ago? What did she know?"

"I don't know, but she had to have known something."

"I agree, she must've known on some level something was going to happen. She never said anything to you?"

"Not a word."

After hanging up with Jen, I kept trying to figure it all out. *She must have sensed something within herself. She had to have known her time was drawing short. Otherwise, why the flurry of fun and memorable times with the kids?* I couldn't remember hearing the kids happier or more excited. *I only wish I could've been there to share in the joy she and the kids experienced in her final days.*

CHAPTER 16

Stepping Through the Door

———————

Back out on the open road, we drove north through Redwood National Park. With the windows down, the kids marveled at the size of the enormous redwoods, right beside the pavement of Highway 101.

Later, as we drove through Ashland, Oregon, the town I was born in, I recognized something within myself: never in my life had I felt two extremes so profoundly—grief and peace. The grief was so heavy that at times I felt physical pain—not only for myself, but also for the kids—knowing that we had to face the rest of this life without her. I struggled with many unanswered questions: *What could I have done differently? Could I have prevented this?* Questions that gripped my heart so tightly, I would lie awake most nights. Then I felt calm, peaceful, reassuring feelings—as if someone were standing beside me resting their hand on my shoulder.

After a month on the road, I called Jenne to tell her we would arrive sometime the next day. I could tell from our conversations a lot was going unsaid, each of us wanting to extend to the other the space and time to sort things out naturally. As much as I still ached for Randi, I honestly couldn't wait to see Jen.

During that time I pondered and prayed, coming to the conclusion that if something were supposed to happen between Jen and me, it could not come about in any possible way other than through divine intervention, approved of and assisted by Randi on the other side. There were times when I swear I could hear Randi whispering in my ear about many things, but especially about Jen.

More and more, I felt my kids, especially at their young ages, needed a mom. And deep down, I could not deny Randi had handpicked Jen for us. Though she may not have shared that insight with me, she shared it with her dad. And for her, I felt those feelings deserved to be honored. When Jen and Mady walked in the door that evening after we arrived home, I took one look at Jen and I knew. It just felt like somehow, someway, this was part of the plan all along.

Over the next couple weeks, Jen and I talked in the evening after the kids were in bed. We considered waiting, but it wasn't as though we needed time to get to know each other.

We settled on a wedding date in mid-November, a little more than three months away. It seemed from the moment we announced our wedding plans to family and friends, a rush of "I knew it!" greeted us from pretty much everyone. Many had experienced their own epiphanies, with more than a few confessing theirs occurred the first moment they saw Jen and I together. Whatever was happening on the other side of the veil seemed contagious to so many loved ones around us.

By mid-August, I returned to work, and after pulling into the driveway after a long day my phone began to vibrate.

"Brad, its Leo," the voice on the other end said when I answered. Sergeant First Class Leo Zachman was the supervisor over the armament section. "This alert roster phone call is to notify you that the battalion has been alerted for an imminent mobilization and deployment." Military units use alert phone rosters, which are regularly updated, to maintain the most current contact info on each soldier for just this purpose.

"Okay, in my case, what does that mean exactly?" I asked.

"Well, I'm not really sure. I will ask and get back with you," he said.

Within a few weeks our entire battalion was mobilized in preparation for a combat deployment. Notwithstanding the action all around me, I was in limbo, not knowing what was going to happen with me until I knocked on the Brigadier General's (one star) office door at state head-quarters late one afternoon. His secretary asked me to wait in his office in a chair next to his desk. I stood as the general walked in carrying some paperwork. He was older, probably in his mid-to-late fifties, even grand-fatherly looking. He asked me to take a seat.

"I've just come from the Adjutant General's office." The Adjutant General was a Major General (two-stars) and leader over thousands of National Guard soldiers in Utah. "He thanks you for your service to our country and extends his sincere condolences for the recent passing of your wife, as do I. In light of your situation, the general signed an uncondi-tional release on your behalf. Your battalion will deploy without you."

I looked into his eyes as we shook hands.

"You get to stay home and take care of your children. They need you now more than ever after losing their mother."

"Thank you, Sir," I said.

"Good luck in the days ahead," he said. "We're sorry to lose you."

I walked out and spent the days leading up to our wedding, seriously considering ending my military career.

On a cool, sunny day in mid-November, Jen and I and the kids were once again surrounded by family and friends at our wedding ceremony in the Mount Timpanogos Temple. Again, I felt an enormous outpouring of love from so many. The laughter, warm hugs, and expressions of love and support filled our hearts to overflowing. The next morning, Jen and I flew to Hawaii, for a week, where we walked on the beach and talked about the kids and our hopes and dreams for each one.

First family photo with Jen and Mady

After the holidays, I was still unsure whether or not I should continue in the guard. I spoke with Air Guard recruiters about the possibility of transferring over, based on my prior radar training and job with the FAA. They offered me a slot in an Air Traffic Control unit, but as I stood in the recruiter's office about to sign the transfer paperwork, I realized I just could not accept being reduced in rank for the slot. I'd worked too hard to get to where I was—promotable from E-6/Staff Sergeant to E-7/Sergeant First Class.

I shook my head. "I can't do it," I said, and promptly walked out.

I was grateful that my good friend and neighbor Major James Slagowski offered me an E-7 slot in the 19th SFG (Special Forces Group) where he was currently serving. To me, it was a no brainer. The more I thought about it, the more the dense fog surrounding my military career seemed to depart. I accepted, and within a month, I was back in uniform. Serving with James and the outstanding soldiers in the 19th SFG felt like it breathed new life into my career.

After completing MOS training in my new slot, I was grateful to pin on E-7 in a ceremony in front of my family. Later, I completed a required physical and received orders to attend the Army's Airborne School, more commonly known as Jump School. Just days before my departure, I learned that I had to postpone Jump School due to previously receiving treatment for kidney stones. It was a setback I was clearly had not anticipated. Nonetheless, I completed medical treatment over the next several months, while remaining physically fit and expecting to attend the course the following year.

We were also extremely grateful that the kids were excited and supportive when our blended family grew. Eliza Sharon joined the family in October 2005, followed by Daniel Bradley exactly twelve months later. The girls loved having a younger sister they could help Jen with, and Matt was no longer surrounded by girls.

In the meantime, the 211th Aviation Battalion returned from what turned out to be a sixteen-month deployment, twelve of those months in Afghanistan. It was great to see everyone, but still bittersweet that they successfully completed a combat deployment without me.

Early one Saturday morning, I glanced across the room and watched as Lieutenant Colonel Bill Cluff, who had just taken over as the 211th battalion commander, walked into the drill hall where we were preparing for a parachute jump that day. I had forgotten that he completed Jump

School years before. Even though he was a new Battalion Commander, and a qualified Apache pilot, he continued to jump periodically to stay proficient and to maintain his jump status. He slowly scanned the room, and the moment he recognized me, his eyes lit up. He made a beeline over to me.

"Sergeant Jones! So this is where you went?" he said as we shook hands.

"Yes, Sir, I transferred here after I found out 1st Battalion would deploy without me. Now that they're back, I heard you were just made the new BC. Congratulations."

"Thank you," he said. "How do you like it here?"

"To be honest, Sir, coming here breathed new life into my career after my wife passed away. I was so close to hanging it up."

"I heard you remarried. Congratulations, I'm happy for you. Listen," he said, his expression suddenly turning serious. "I don't know if you've spoken with anyone back in aviation, but do me a favor and don't get too comfortable here."

"Okay," I said, waiting for more information.

"I don't have time to explain, but I'm going to have Sergeant Major Stearman—the 211th Battalion Command Sergeant Major (CSM)—get in touch with you about some opportunities back home where you belong, okay?"

"Absolutely, Sir," I said and shook his hand again.

"I'm glad I ran into you today," he said. "Expect a call in the next couple days."

"Good luck on today's jump, Sir."

He smiled and nodded before walking away.

Despite being a busy day, I couldn't stop thinking about what he said. *"Don't get too comfortable."* Those words were as exciting as they were intriguing.

I thoroughly enjoyed serving in the 19th SFG, but deep down I had to admit, the thought of returning to aviation felt like coming home. As soon as I got home that night, I shared with Jen what had happened.

"Wow, that sounds like he wants to offer you a promotion to come back to aviation," she said. "Do you have enough time as an E-7 to make E-8?"

"Yes, as a matter of fact I just became eligible."

"Would you go back to aviation if they offered you a promotion?"

"Absolutely," I said quickly.

First thing Monday morning my cell phone rang.

"Hey, Brad, it's Gary Stearman. Long time." Stearman and I spent a lot of time together during our tour in Kuwait before he was promoted to the top (CSM) enlisted spot in 1st Battalion.

"Sergeant Major, it's good to hear your voice again," I said.

Stearman had just gotten off the phone with LTC Cluff and he wasted no time. "Are you interested in coming back for a recently vacated First Sergeant's [E-8] slot?"

"Absolutely," I assured him.

"I will get my people working on the transfer paperwork right away," he said.

"That sounds great. Thanks."

"It will be great to have you back in aviation. Thanks for continuing to serve. I know it was not an easy decision after your wife passed away . . . and then having to watch as the entire battalion deployed for sixteen months."

"It would be great to be back among so many whom I consider family," I said before we hung up. I was grateful for my time in the 19th, the caliber of soldiers and their professionalism was instrumental in my decision to continue serving.

A week later, I received a phone call from the admin section in the 19th SFG thanking me for my service and extending well wishes for my future. I couldn't help but smile. I was back in aviation.

That first drill weekend back was the homecoming my soul needed. I spent the entire weekend shaking hands and hugging so many I had missed. The ribbing started almost immediately, and it was exquisite. A number of times during the weekend I had to fight becoming emotional, feeling I was back where I belonged.

Family photo with young Eliza and Daniel

In March 2009, I was promoted to First Sergeant over Charlie Company. In an Apache Battalion, Alpha, Bravo, and Charlie companies are made up of pilots who fly the eight aircraft, and soldiers who maintain the aircraft.

As a First Sergeant, it was my job to take care of the eighteen to twenty soldiers in Charlie Company, ensuring they had the training and tools ("beans and bullets") to accomplish their jobs. With two simultaneous wars going on, it came as no surprise that we were in a training cycle leading up to another combat deployment.

By mid-2010, we were preparing for a twelve-month Operation Iraqi Freedom (OIF) deployment in the fall of 2011. As the 2011 summer approached, we were in full training mode preparing to deploy to Fort Hood, Texas, for a required three-months of mobilization training, before shipping out for Iraq.

In June we moved the entire battalion to Idaho for simulated combat operations. Our training included new and critical classes to identify

IEDs (Improvised Explosive Devices), as well as vehicle rollover training as a result of the devastating effects IEDs were having on our troops in Iraq and Afghanistan.

During that summer, my son Matt enlisted as a Crew Chief and shipped out for basic and AIT. He hoped to finish in time to join us in Iraq.

Just as we were ready to deploy, and quite unexpectedly, the battalion received word that we were not going. We were being "off-ramped"—a term the Army coined as a way of saying our services were no longer needed.

Many soldiers had made living arrangements with family and employers for the next year, and now that would all have to be rearranged.

As leaders, we spent the following months working to find employment for soldiers who were suddenly unemployed. State leadership worked with local colleges and universities, securing permission for late enrollment for our student soldiers. By the end of summer, everyone seemed to have made the transition back to civilian life.

That September, during a meeting with senior leaders, I was not the only one caught off guard when our Battalion Commander, Lieutenant Colonel (LTC) Greg Hartvigsen, announced, "After we were so recently off-ramped by the regular Army, they're now sending us requests that indicate they want us to find the nearest on-ramp."

Everyone sat in stunned silence.

"We were tipped-off by several requests asking for the readiness status of our personnel and equipment. Apparently the 12th Combat Aviation Brigade (CAB) is set to deploy to Afghanistan by spring of 2012. The brigade already has an attack (Apache) battalion downrange in the Persian Gulf. They need a battalion to fill that gap. I'm betting it's going to be us."

As soon as the meeting broke up, I phoned Jen. "You're not going to believe this. We're being activated for an Afghanistan deployment."

"Shut up!" she said. "When will you be back on orders?"

"They're saying by early December they'll need us back to repack everything we just unpacked, and that we're tentatively scheduled to move the battalion to Fort Hood in mid-January."

"Talk about whiplash. We'll need to sit down and talk to the kids when you get home. Oh, hey, one more thing," Jen quickly said. "Do you think Matt will complete his training in time to go on the deployment with you?"

"I imagine so, if he completes Basic and AIT (MOS training) on schedule, he should be finishing up his training at Fort Eustis sometime before we're scheduled to ship out from Fort Hood."

"Wow, we could have two members of our family serving together on the other side of the world."

"We wouldn't be the only father and son serving together in our battalion," I said. "There are two pilots who are father and son. And get this. They're Joneses too."

"No way! Okay, see you tonight. Love you," she said and hung up.

I leaned back in my office chair and thought about Matt. Two weeks prior Matt had called me during the week. Normally, he was only allowed to call on Sundays.

"Is everything all right?" I asked.

"Not really," he said. "I'm in trouble for being in possession of contraband."

"What was the contraband?" I imagined it was something illegal he'd gotten ahold of, or taken with him, choosing not to use his opportunity for amnesty when he arrived at Fort Leonard Wood, Missouri.

"It was a pack of Skittles."

"Okay, can I talk to your drill sergeant?"

I heard Matt extend the phone. "Drill Sergeant, my dad wants to speak with you."

"GET OUT OF MY OFFICE," she yelled, bringing back many memories of my drill sergeants. "AND YOU BETTER BE STANDING AT PARADE REST OUTSIDE IN THE HALLWAY!" I heard the office door close, followed by the phone being picked up. "Hi, First Sergeant, this is Staff Sergeant Spotted Bear," she said in the most pleasant voice. "I'm Matt's drill sergeant. How are you this fine day?"

I laughed out loud into the phone. "I'm good. So what can you tell me about what's happened?"

"Well, Matt and a couple other recruits were caught with bags of Skittles that one of them confessed to purchasing from a nearby vending machine. Matt says he was only trying to help out his buddy when he panicked and started asking others to help him hide the candy when several of us began searching the barracks."

"I appreciate the job you're doing with our sons and daughters," I said.

"Well, thank you, First Sergeant. When the truth finally came out, I asked them what would their parents say when they told them they had to restart basic again. That's when your son spoke up and said you would not be happy about it because you're a First Sergeant. I just couldn't resist handing him his phone and telling him to call to tell you what he'd done. Other than this incident, he's a good soldier, First Sergeant."

"Thanks, I really appreciate hearing that. I look forward to meeting you at Matt's graduation."

"We will look forward to having you here for Matt's graduation, First Sergeant." Before she hung up, I heard her yell for Matt and the others. "YOU GOT TWO SECONDS TO GET BACK IN HERE. I KNOW YOU DON'T THINK WE'RE THROUGH YET!"

Matt's Basic Training graduation Fort Leonard Wood, Missouri 2011

I smiled at the memory just as an incoming text buzzed on my phone. It was from LTC Hartvigsen. "Do you have a minute to talk?"

"Absolutely," I texted back. *I wonder what this is about?*

His office door was slightly open when I approached, so I knocked. "Sir, you wanted to see me?"

"Brad, come in and take a seat." I'd known Greg since he was a captain. We were close in age, he being only a year or so older than me. We'd worked together closely during more than a few battalion operations, and as far as I could tell, we had tremendous amount of mutual respect for each other.

"What can I do for you, Sir?" I said.

"The reason I wanted to talk to you is I've watched as Charlie Company has put up impressive stats on the number of flight hours and high aircraft-readiness rate. Your numbers consistently lead the battalion."

"Thank you, Sir."

"What do you attribute your success to, if you don't mind my asking?"

"That's easy, Sir. I have excellent NCOs who lead and mentor their soldiers each drill. They're experienced mechanics to begin with, and they get in and work with our younger soldiers' day in and day out."

He nodded thoughtfully.

"The way I see it, it's my job to take care of as many distractors as I can, which allows my NCOs the time and latitude to work alongside their soldiers. I do my best to support them in doing that."

"The real reason I asked you to come here is I need you to further spread that success within the battalion."

"Absolutely, Sir," I said. "How do you see me doing that?"

"As Delta Company's First Sergeant for the deployment. Will you do that for me?"

"Absolutely, Sir," I said, not able to hide my shock. "Where is Delta's First Sergeant going, if I may ask?"

"He just handed me his retirement paperwork yesterday. He's not going on the deployment. He's done."

In a sense I was coming home having previously spent more than ten years in Delta Company.

"We'll make the change prior to everyone going on active-duty orders in December."

"Yes, Sir," I said, knowing I would have to tell everyone in Charlie Company sometime between now and the end of drill weekend.

"Thank you for your willingness to step up for the battalion at such a critical time," he said. "If you think of anything you need or want, do not hesitate to let me know."

"Thank you, Sir, I will keep that in mind."

He rose signaling that our meeting was finished. We shook hands over the desk, and I walked out and immediately called Jen for the second time that day.

"Babe, you're not going to believe this."

CHAPTER 17

Welcome to the Great Place

———————

O utside the armory, the familiar noise of running aircraft filled the air. The aircraft hangar is a large structure about three stories high, and one-and-a-half football fields in length. The hangars' giant doors, when open, provide a panoramic view of the nearby Wasatch Mountain range across the Salt Lake valley.

The hangar is home to twenty-four AH-64 Delta model Apache attack helicopters, each one outfitted with an advanced targeting camera system, powerful enough to zoom-in on skiers descending from Hidden Peak at Snowbird Ski resort roughly twenty miles away.

By their very nature, Apaches are maintenance-intensive. The combination of mechanical and electronic systems requires a tremendous number of man-hours to keep them "FMC," or Fully Mission Capable. Crew chiefs and mechanics perform daily checks and services on each aircraft. The hangar is large enough to comfortably park six to eight aircraft. At any given time, one or two aircraft are undergoing a "phase," which is a maintenance process every 125, 250, and 500 flight hours. During 250 and 500 hour phases, the aircraft is completely stripped of all major components, and inspected for signs of wear and tear.

I stopped just outside the hangar to take in the awe-inspiring sight and sound as eight birds—what we call them—and their sixteen GE T-700 turboshaft jet engines screamed in unison. Each one transferring nearly 2,000 shaft horsepower directly to rotors spinning at 726 feet per second. Mixed in with this thunderous wall of sound, and wafting through the open hangar doors, was the unmistakable smell of JP-8 jet fuel, a sensory overload, that never grew old.

I looked down the length of the hangar toward the shops and offices that would now be my responsibility. The first office was the "QC" (Quality Control) section, staffed by seasoned mechanics who had the critically important responsibility of insuring that maintenance is performed to established standards.

Next was the "PC" (Production Control) shop, which coordinates and tracks all maintenance activities, including on-hand and on-order spare parts logistics.

The Armament, Avionics, Prop and Rotor, Sheet Metal, Engine, and Supply shops filled in the remaining office space.

As I walked through the hangar, shops on one side and aircraft—surrounded by mechanics and their toolboxes—on the other, I couldn't help feeling the enormous weight of responsibility that would soon be mine. In Charlie Company I was responsible for about twenty enlisted soldiers and roughly a dozen pilots. As Delta Company First Sergeant, that number would increase to more than one hundred soldiers.

Of all the sections, the QC section concerned me the most. The technical inspectors (TIs) working in QC have absolutely the most critical role, and everyone, especially the pilots, has to trust in their expertise and integrity.

I crossed the hangar and entered the QC shop. "Hey Top! Afternoon Top." Several TIs, whom I knew well, greeted me.

"Hey, guys, how's your day going?"

Before they could answer, a head peeked around the cubicle at the far end. "Good Top, what can we do for you?" the (E-7) QC supervisor said with an overly friendly, car salesman approach. As he made his way toward me, I felt that uneasy feeling again.

My discomfort wasn't entirely unfounded. Prior to QC, he led the aircraft maintenance section where serious allegations surfaced. Several junior-ranking soldiers alleged that he preyed upon their spouses or girl-friends during parties hosted within the section. I knew I needed someone to lead the section I could trust.

Outside, I watched as the Apaches hovered nearby. *I just can't trust this guy . . . and the BC said if I needed anything to let him know.*

I pulled out my phone and composed a text. "Sir, I need somebody I can trust as the QC section leader. I do not feel comfortable with the current leader. May I recommend Sgt. First Class Brant Burnham? He's a solid and trustworthy soldier and leader." I reread the words several times before pressing send.

Within a few minutes my phone vibrated. "Give me some time to work on this. I will get back to you."

"Thank you, Sir," I replied.

That evening I pulled all three Charlie Company E-7s together and broke the news that I was being moved to Delta Company. Their expressions matched the disappointment I was feeling inside. We had trained together over the last year, making Charlie Co the best line company in the battalion. Through their hard work and dedication, Charlie Co consistently outperformed the other line companies. I wanted to say something to Brant, but for now, I knew I needed to keep my mouth shut.

The text came later that evening. "You deserve the support you feel you need. You will get Burnham before we are ordered to active duty."

I let out a sigh of relief. "Thank you, Sir, I appreciate your support." After hitting send, I called Brant across the street in the hangar and using the same words LTC Cluff said to me, "Don't get too comfortable in your position as Charlie Company Platoon Sergeant." I began.

"Uh, okay, can you be a little more specific, Top?"

"Yes. You're coming with me to Delta Company to be my QC NCOIC. I told the BC that I need somebody I can trust."

"I couldn't agree with you more on that issue," he said. "Thanks for recommending me."

"You earned it, Brant."

Several inches of snow had already fallen by early morning, January 18, 2012, as an enormous crowd gathered inside the hangar. Each company lined up in a battalion formation along the length of the hangar as loved ones looked on. When accountability was established, the formations were allowed to rejoin their families while the Adjutant General delivered remarks to the thousands assembled. Following his remarks several hangar doors were opened allowing windswept snow to accumulate along the floor dividing inside from out. Amid many tears and numerous hugs, soldiers began crossing the divide, leaving family members behind.

I hugged and kissed the tear-streaked cheeks of Jen and the kids one last time.

"Be safe," Jen told me. "I love you."

"I will. I love you too."

When I got to the hangar opening, I looked back at everyone. Brant, standing nearby, was hugging his wife and kids one last time. We were both shook up and teary. I reached over and put my arm around Brant.

"C'mon, Brant, let's do this," I said.

We both turned and walked out into the snow to the awaiting buses all in a row. When all soldiers were aboard, the first bus slowly pulled forward, leaving fresh tracks in the snow for the rest to follow. We slowly made our way across the flight line and through the gate where hundreds had gathered along the road. Many waved American flags, while others stood at attention, saluting.

Fort Hood is home to Third Armored Corps, which includes some of the oldest formations in the Army, including III Corps' 1st Cavalry Division, and before being inactivated, 2nd Armored Division. 1st Calvary Division is one of the most decorated combat divisions in the US Army with a unique history having previously served as a horseback cavalry division, an infantry division, and air assault division and an armored division since its formation in 1921.

The base is massive, covering 214,000 acres. If a soldier gets deployed to a combat zone, chances are they have mobilized, or de-mobilized, following their tour, or both, at Fort Hood. Coming through the main gate, we were greeted with "WELCOME TO THE GREAT PLACE." From there the base sprawls into its own city, where unit offices, barracks, and motor pools, run parallel along Battalion Avenue and Ivy Division Road, for nearly five miles.

The pre-deployment mobilization training pace was like no other we had experienced. Each week, we fixed aircraft and flew missions, followed by weekends testing our weapons qualifications, convoy operations, IED identification, and vehicle rollover skills. Training we had previously accomplished back in Utah.

About a week into training, one of my section leaders called to complain about an issue with another section leader. Following the call, I sent out a text to all six of my section leaders to meet later that evening. With notebooks and pens in hand, we spent the first few minutes sharing the unique challenges, from each of our perspectives.

When the conversation drew to a close, and with all eyes on me, I told them, "I called this meeting to share something important. Each of you is one step away from where I am now."

The silence told me I had their attention.

I looked at Shawn. "I have never worked in PC"—Production Control. Then I looked at Mike, Carl, and Lance respectively. "I have never worked in the Aircraft Maintenance Section, nor Sheet Metal, Prop and Rotor, nor the Engine Shop or Supply." I looked at Brant. "I worked in QC, but only for a short time." Finally, I looked at Heath. "I spent the majority of my career in Armament, and I'm confident I could run that section again.

"I only have experience running one section in Delta Company," I continued, "So, I'm counting on you to lead your soldiers and run your sections based on your experience and expertise. I'm counting on each of you to be the subject matter experts in your particular domain. At this stage in your careers, each of you needs to learn how to tread deep waters." I paused, as each one nodded.

"If you have issues with another section leader, I expect you to take your issue directly to that person, and work together toward a solution. I cannot, and I will not, be the go-between. I refuse to play the role of a parent, or referee, for the next year.

"It's my personal belief that weak leaders tend to consolidate power unto themselves, stifling creativity and initiative. I believe my role is to support and empower each of you to lead and mentor your soldiers. That means I expect you to work together to solve internal issues. If, for some reason, you cannot come up with a solution, then feel free to come see me for guidance."

After the room cleared out at the conclusion of the meeting, Captain Matt Green, came out of his office. "That's one of the best leadership lessons I've ever heard."

"Thanks, Sir. I apologize, I should've asked if there was anything you wanted to add."

"Not at all," he replied. "You said exactly what they needed to hear."

When I came over to Delta Co, Matt and I barely had any time together before we hit the ground running, but I could already sense his support. In that short time, I quickly realized he was easily one of the smartest persons I'd ever met. The first thing I noticed about him was that he reads books at a voracious pace.

Several weeks later, just prior to an evening meeting, I was given a note to pick up several incoming soldiers the next day at the airport. They were flying in from Utah. I quickly scanned the names. Halfway down the list was PFC Matt Jones.

I showed the note to Captain Green sitting next to me.

"Hey, a father and son serving a combat deployment together," he said with a grin.

"He just got home from Apache school last week. That's a quick turnaround, but I know he will be happy. He was worried he wouldn't catch up with us."

The next day, I watched as a group of wide-eyed soldiers walked down the escalator to where I was waiting in baggage claim. Matt saw me and led the group over to where I was standing. I greeted my son with a hug, after which he introduced each new soldier to me.

"This is my dad," he said.

"Nice to meet you, First Sergeant," each one said, as we shook hands.

"First Sergeant," one of them spoke up. "When will we get issued our weapons?"

The question caught me off guard and made me laugh. "All in good time," I reassured him. "You will get your assigned weapon soon enough."

Now that's enthusiasm, I thought.

Two and half months passed like the wind over the hilly farms and cattle ranches of the Blackland Prairies surrounding Fort Hood.

It didn't take long for 21st Cavalry—the unit overseeing our training—to realize the experience level within our battalion. They were tasked with training us, but the irony was, we were sharing knowledge and tactics way more with them.

Fort Hood sunset, the final exercise before departing for Afghanistan

Before departing, I spoke to the company. I wanted to reassure every-one that feeling a measure of fear was normal and natural. "I promise that if you will do your best to focus on doing your job to the best of your ability, things will work out. Don't waste time and energy focusing on something you, or we, can't control. In other words, have confidence in the training and sense of duty, of the other soldiers we will be serving with. Our job is to keep our helicopters in the air where they can and will do the most good.

I related a story I'd heard from a veteran of Desert Storm.

An Apache sat idling while soldier rearmed the bird behind enemy lines in Iraq. With soldiers working below, loading the 30 MM chain gun, pilots spotted several rapidly approaching enemy vehicles. Rather than alert the soldiers—who were low to the ground, and unaware of the approaching enemy—they simply asked over the intercom how close they were to finishing. They were close, so the pilots watched and gaged the timing as the enemy continued to close on their position.

As soon as the soldiers climbed out from underneath and disconnected from the aircraft, without warning, the Apache abruptly leaped from the ground, shooting straight up in the air. The 30MM chain gun suddenly swiveled and came to life, spitting out a rapid succession of thunderous bursts. The destroyed, and now burning enemy vehicles, continued to roll forward before finally coming to a stop not far from the group of soldiers standing there in a state of complete shock and awe.

"This is why we do what we do," I said.

Before dawn on May 4, 2012, we boarded a charter flight to Manas, Kyrgyzstan.

Soon enough we were assembled on the flight line in full combat gear, including IBA (Interceptor Multi-Threat Body Armor System), Kevlar lightweight helmet, several fully loaded ammo clips, individual weapons, and protective eyewear and gloves.

A Boeing C-17 Globemaster pulled up and slowly lowered its tail ramp. With mostly solemn faces and very little chatter, we walked up the ramp and took a seat for the flight. About forty minutes into the flight, a light inside the plane turned from green to red, a signal to everyone that we were now in the combat zone. Our first stop was a base on the outskirts of Mazar-i-Sharif—shortened to Mez—a large city of more than 320,000.

High-altitude snowcapped peaks formed a picturesque skyline to the south. Our destination was a forward operating base (FOB) approximately one hundred miles east of Mez.

After being in transit for several days, I just wanted to get wherever we were going, assess the conditions that would be our reality, and most of all, just get on with it. Get on with doing the job and adjusting to whatever dangers lay ahead.

As I looked at my soldiers, I could not help but notice the expressions of uncertainty on many faces, and I wondered if others saw on my face the same uncertainty I was feeling inside.

CHAPTER 18

Shadow of the Hindu Kush

Military aircraft came and went on Mez's long runway under large gray clouds and intermittent rain showers. All kitted up—Kevlar, ballistic vests, weapons, and backpacks—my soldiers and I had been waiting next to and under three CH-47 Chinook helicopters since mid-morning. The sun occasionally broke through the clouds, temporarily drying us and the concrete.

"Where can we put our gear before the next rain shower?" I asked the aircraft crew chiefs, when they started their preflight checks.

Following a brief conversation, I turned to my soldiers. "Okay, Delta Co, listen up. Grab your gear and stack it neatly into a pile running down the center of each helicopter."

Each pile resembled a mountain dividing the inward facing seats along the sides. The crew chiefs used heavy duty cargo straps to secure the giant mounds to the floor.

We were scheduled for an earlier departure time, but stormy weather and poor visibility on a high mountain pass between the two bases caused numerous delays.

At dusk, we loaded up and sat looking at each other as the Chinooks' powerful dual engines turned the enormous twin-bladed rotor system overhead. I had a front-row seat between the two pilots as we lifted off and cleared the wall surrounding the base below. In front of me, the lights from the instrument panels gave off a glow against the backdrop of darkness ahead. Suddenly, we began a long sweeping turn back toward the lights of Mez.

I tugged at the nearby crew chief's flight suit and gave him the "What's up?" gesture.

He leaned down next to my ear and shouted, "The pass was clear when we took off, but now it's socked in again."

We landed right back where we started.

"If anyone needs to use the facilities, now's the time," I said to the soldiers inside the Chinook.

"Where are we?"

"Are we there yet?"

With no way of orienting themselves to the outside, many didn't realize we'd turned around.

"We're back on the tarmac at Mez, waiting for the weather to clear over the pass," I said.

When dawn's early light began to appear on the horizon, the pilots quickly came out to the aircraft. They'd received word that the pass was clear, and being consummate professionals, they quickly had us airborne again.

Once over the pass, we followed the Kunduz River passing to the south of the city of Kunduz, with a population of more than 268,000. Following above the river, we banked left and climbed a bluff where I could see the FOB airfield below. We circled and landed at last.

We were led to several tents where we were to stay temporarily. As soon as I secured my gear, I had to see for myself what was in store for me and my soldiers. I walked back to the row of clamshell (three) hangars to meet my counterpart, the Delta Co First Sergeant. I stopped and asked two soldiers, "Can you tell me where I can find the Delta Co First Sergeant?"

"You'll find him in that tent toward the back of that hanger," one responded, pointing to the first hangar in the row.

Inside, the hangars were huge, with enough space for several frame tents that served as shops and offices inside—a tent within a tent. I headed toward the tent with a unit flag mounted in a stand in front. The E-4 orderly jumped up to Parade Rest when I stepped through the door.

"Is this the Delta Co operations tent?"

"Yes, First Sergeant," she said smartly, still standing at Parade Rest.

"Please relax," I said, not wanting her to feel nervous. "Is your First Sergeant around?"

"He just stepped out, First Sergeant, but I expect him back shortly."

I stepped around the wall she was standing behind and stuck out my hand to shake hers. "Hi, I'm First Sergeant Jones," I said in a calm voice, looking at her name badge. "Where are you from, Specialist Rodriquez?"

"First Sergeant, I'm from Houston, Texas," she said nervously.

Before I could engage her further, the door opened and in walked First Sergeant Dohrmann, his face lighting up when he realized who I was and that my arrival signaled he and his soldiers' imminent departure.

After shaking hands and exchanging pleasantries, he offered to take me on a tour of the base. Outside, we hopped into a Polaris ATV.

He started it up and drove across the flight line. "This corner of Afghanistan was used as a waypoint—following the 1979 invasion by the Russian Army—for units entering and exiting the country. Just outside the main gate, there are footings and foundations of a large Russian base next to a boneyard of abandoned vehicles they left behind when they pulled out."

We drove along a gravel road just inside the perimeter wall surrounding the base, then stopped at a corner guard shack on the far side of the base.

He motioned for me to follow him up the steps to the elevated guard shack.

"At times you will have to provide soldiers for perimeter guard shifts. Most soldiers don't mind. It breaks up the monotony." He introduced me to the two soldiers inside.

One offered a set high-powered binoculars.

I scanned the area and saw a herd of sheep with a young Afghan kid shepherding them.

"That herd of sheep are not very far away," I commented.

"They sometimes herd them right up to the perimeter wall," one of the soldiers said. "Those kids will come up and talk to us . . . well, mostly they just motion to us."

"What do they motion for?" I asked.

"Extra food and water we may have," he said. "We usually bring extra MREs"—Meals Ready to Eat—"and we always have plenty of bottled water. They're out there all day in the heat and direct sunlight, so we give them whatever we have."

"Wow, I can't believe young kids are the ones herding flocks here," I said.

"Over there on the other side of the airport is a PRT run by the German Army," Dohrmann said, gesturing for me to look just beyond the airport terminal.

"What is a PRT and what do they do?" I asked, looking at a bunch of buildings through the binoculars.

"Provincial Reconstruction Team. They provide services to the surrounding community. Mainly infrastructure projects, such as providing clean running water, electricity, and healthcare services. In this AO—Area of Operation—the Germans run point for the projects, while our infantry provides overall security." I was doing my best to take it all in as we hopped back in the Polaris and continued the tour.

"That's the weight room," he said pointing to a plywood building. "The PX and Post Office are in those buildings over there," he said, pointing them out. "This is pretty much Grand Central Station of the base."

Overall, the size of the FOB was small, compared to larger bases like Mez and Bagram. Thousands of dirt-filled HESCO (barriers) containers, primarily designed and used for flood control, formed the surrounding perimeter wall. I estimated a ten-minute walk from one end to the other.

Dohrmann drove on passed the airfield. "This is the LSA," he said, referring to the Logistics Support Area where we would sleep. He stopped to point out several rows of tents in the middle of a tent city. "These rows are for your soldiers. The row of trailers on the far side are latrines and shower trailers."

Home, sweet home, I thought.

From there we drove to our battalion area where he showed me the location of the Tactical Operations Center (TOC), Medical, Supply/Admin and Morale, Welfare, and Recreation (MWR), and Fitness Center tents. "The MWR tent has half dozen laptops for calling home on Skype," he said pointing to it.

"You'll like the new chow hall," he said, pulling back onto the gravel road. We pulled up next to a two-story tent surrounded by concrete barriers. "It has wide-screen TVs, refrigerators stocked with tons of different drinks, and tables overflowing with CLIF bars, granola bars, and trail mix."

Back in his office, before we sat down I quickly glanced around. It was small but nice, with an L-shaped desk, a locker for my personal things, and a small refrigerator full of bottled water.

"What are the missions like in this area?" I asked.

"Typical missions are CAS"—close air support—"mainly route reconnaissance for friendly forces moving in convoys and infantry units conducting security operations in the valleys and canyons. We also regularly fly support missions for Special Operations Forces (SOF) capturing Taliban HVTs."

"What are those?" I asked.

"High Value Targets," he said. "Then there are the distress calls we get, called TICs, which stands for *Troops in Contact* with enemy forces."

I was sitting on the edge of my seat, listening intently.

"TIC's and CASEVAC and MEDEVAC missions get everyone's adrenaline pumping."

MEDEVAC is using a standardized, well-marked vehicle (helicopter), to medically evacuate injured personnel from a secured (hopefully) landing zone—where the injured has received some level of care and/or stabilization—to a higher-level care facility. CASEVAC, pronounced KAZ-EVAC, is evacuating the injured using non-standard and non-dedicated vehicles, which may or may not have en route medical care, to a higher level care facility. Both are intense missions where speed and timing are everything.

"Nothing will bring a note of the importance and gravity of what we do more than hearing our soldiers surrounded in a firefight, or pinned down and getting pounded in some canyon by the enemy."

I nodded at the reality and gravity of his words.

"We can just shadow each other for the next few days, until you feel comfortable. I'm sure it won't be long before you'll be ready to take the reins," he said.

"That sounds like a plan," I said. "Thanks again."

My soldiers spent the next couple days unloading and unpacking tools and gear, getting things set up. We quickly settled into a routine—twelve on, twelve off, seven days a week—supporting twenty-four-hour operations. Our maintainers quickly began maintaining the aircraft, as our pilots began flying daily flights to orient them to the area and terrain.

Injuries and deaths from AK-47s, RPGs (pocket-propelled grenades), or emplaced IED's (Improvised Explosive Devices) were an everyday threat to coalition troops, and from the moment we took operational control, it became abundantly clear the vital role we played. As coalition forces conducted operations, requests for Apache support flowed in, providing an effective measure of deterrence against enemy forces.

Battalion and brigade leadership quickly pointed out how impressed they were with Delta Co maintenance.

It was during the 250/500-hour phases where my soldiers' efforts stood out. Regular Army Apache units were averaging thirty-to-thirty-five days for a complete phase—with contract maintenance. Our maintainers were completing them in nine-to-twelve days, without contractors.

I couldn't have been more proud of my soldiers, many with very little or no maintenance experience, step up, in the challenging and demanding environment of combat operations. They not only rose to meet the challenge, they set the pace for aviation operations throughout Afghanistan.

Bases and FOBs provide employment opportunities for many locals working to support families, like everyone, just trying to get ahead. We were friendly one with another, despite the obvious language barrier. Locals spoke mainly Dari and Pashto, with more and more learning to speak English. The FOB had a bazaar, run by locals who knew enough English to talk about their lives and families.

They were equally curious about where we came from, what it looked like, and more importantly, about our lives and families.

The younger generation understands and gets why we're here, I realized after a time. *They see and like the things we are doing in this community, which is hopefully improving their lives.* It made me feel grateful to be there.

A sense of nationalism among Afghan citizens is not the same as it is among the citizens of most modern nations. Afghanistan is way more tribal than people realize. Accounts from soldiers serving in other locations, nationalism only existed on the tribal level for most Afghans.

Native Afghan interpreters served with our public affairs forces who regularly engage with the local population. One of the interpreters was a middle-aged woman, who sat across from me one morning at breakfast.

"I see from your patch, you are with the aviation unit from Utah?" she asked.

"Yes, I am," I replied, surprised at the question. "Utah looks a lot like here."

"I've never been there," she said. "My name is Aliah. What's yours?"

"I'm Brad. Where are you from?" I asked.

"I've been living in Southern California for almost ten years now. My husband and I were planning to visit Utah before we volunteered to come here."

My surprise stopped me mid-bite. From my understanding most interpreters were locals. "Where are you originally from?"

"I was born right here in Kunduz," she said.

Again I was stunned. This soft-spoken, nice-looking woman left her life in California to come back to the town of her nativity to provide vital interpreting services for our military forces?

She related how after Russia invaded in 1979, she was taken as a young girl, along with others, to a new life in Russia. In grade school, she quickly picked up the language. After high school, she continued her studies, eventually becoming a schoolteacher. She married another expatriate from Kunduz, and when the Berlin Wall came down, she and her husband immigrated to America. They settled in California, where they raised two children who were now university students.

After 9/11, she and her husband volunteered to act as interpreters, based on their ability to speak English and Pashto fluently.

"Do you still have family in this area?" I asked.

"I do," she said. "But for their safety and security, they do not know I'm here."

I was mesmerized by her incredible story. She related that locals instantly detected her familiar sounding accent, and would ask if she was from the area.

"What do you tell them?"

"I tell them that I'm from a town some distance away, but I can tell they don't necessarily believe me."

"Aren't you nervous that you'll run into a relative?"

"It's a concern that's always in the back of my mind, but I mostly deal with local community leaders," she said.

She expressed the same concern many wives and mothers have—the desire for her children to avail themselves of the incredible educational opportunities available in the United States. She was well aware of how different things were for the people here. "We feel very blessed to be living and raising our kids in America," she said. Then she asked me about my family and life back in Utah.

I pulled out my phone and showed her photos.

"Your son is also a soldier?" she asked.

"Yes, and he's here with me," I said. "He's a helicopter mechanic in my company."

Now it was her turn to be amazed. "I will keep an eye out for him. He's the same age as my son."

"I'm so glad I was able to meet and talk to you," I told her. "Thank you for sharing your amazing story with me."

We both rose from the table. I couldn't help myself; I walked around the table and gave her a hug, which she readily accepted. "Thanks for sitting across from me."

She smiled. "Thank you for the wonderful conversation, Brad. I hope to see you around again."

"Me too, Aliah." I felt a huge wave of admiration for this woman. Her story spoke volumes about how blessed we are in America.

In late August, I received an email from a first sergeant from the Apache battalion scheduled to replace us, asking for advice before they shipped to Fort Hood.

Why, yes, as a matter of fact I do, I thought.

"Twenty-first Cav and 1st Army cornered the market on administering pain." I detailed all the things I wish I had known, before our time there.

Emphasizing the logistical nightmares we faced on a daily basis.

Twenty-first Cav reassured us they had enough vehicles for our transportation needs. We believed them, and with the majority of our organic vehicles sitting in Utah, we continually had issues getting our soldiers around the large base.

"Bring every organic vehicle," I wrote. "21st gave us thirty vans and then informed us they needed us to return half a dozen."

I sent the email and promptly forgot about it.

The weather soon turned to clear and cold. As the holidays approached, snow blanketed the peaks of the nearby mountains, reminding me of home. Sitting in a brigade teleconference meeting, on behalf of our Sergeant Major who was away, the Brigade Commander announced his intention to send us aircraft from other battalions. According to him, there were far too many aircraft down for maintenance, and word had spread about the quick turnaround our soldiers could provide.

Soon enough those aircraft began arriving, and like clockwork, nine to twelve days later we had them ready to fly. Each time, word would come back from the pilots who flew it out that that particular Apache was their best flyer. On one of my work area walk-throughs in each hangar, it suddenly hit me. *All these young, inexperienced soldiers have transformed into seasoned aircraft mechanics before my very eyes.* I was so proud to just be a part of it all.

CHAPTER 19

You Can Still Rock in America

Holidays in a combat zone can be especially tough, being away from loved ones back home and missing family traditions.

One evening during our daily battle update, a major—who was a trained and licensed therapist—briefed us on the counseling services she would begin providing any of our soldiers in need. She also introduced a resiliency evaluation program to identify at-risk soldiers who may be suffering possible issues with depression as a result of the upcoming holidays. The program asked leaders to talk with and get to know each soldier's particular family situation with emphasis on how they were coping with spending the holidays away from home in the stress-filled environment of a combat zone.

As she spoke, I thought of several of my soldiers who were struggling, my son Matt being one of them. As time marched on from his mother's death, I noticed that, at some point, Matt stopped progressing emotionally. In the years following Randi's death, I took Matt to see several counselors, but invariably he avoided opening up and talking about the one issue that now seemed to be taking a toll.

The bottom line was that Matt never mourned his mother's passing. As far as I could tell, his way of coping was to surround himself with emotional walls. He seemed to interact normally with the other soldiers in his section, but for a while now I had been sensing that deep down things were not okay.

It had been weighing on me since he joined us in Texas. No doubt Matt had proven himself to be a hard worker, which was obvious from the output of the team and shift he worked on. The pace during Texas, and for the first few months since arriving, had been so overwhelmingly fast I never felt as though I had the chance to see the emotional growth I expected in him as a result of his experiences in basic and MOS training. Matt worked hard during his shifts, but I also knew that while he was off shift back in his tent, he was isolating himself, even among his tent mates.

As I listened to the major's briefing, I suddenly had the impression that this may possibly be someone Matt might open up to. Without sounding sexist, she was attractive, but more than that, she was bright, cheery, and quick to smile, and her kind and understanding demeanor came through while she spoke.

As soon as the meeting ended, I approached her. "My son is here with me. He's actually in my company, serving in the aircraft maintenance section."

"Is he struggling?" she asked.

"Yes, but it's a bit more complicated," I said and did my best to explain the situation.

"I would be happy to see Matt," she said after I finished giving her the story. "Why don't you bring him by tomorrow after his shift?"

Matt came on shift at midnight, so I waited until after our daily production control meeting at 0700 before making my way to the middle hangar where he was busy working on aircraft components. The noise was loud enough that he didn't hear me approach the bench where he was working. Finally, as if sensing someone standing there, he looked up at me. "Hi, Dad."

"Hi, bud, how are you?"

"I'm good. Just cleaning these parts."

"Hey, I've arranged for you to talk with a therapist who just arrived here to the FOB. I hope you don't have an issue with that."

"I guess I'm okay with that."

I didn't feel the need to tell him that as his first sergeant I could lawfully order him to see a therapist.

"What made you decide to arrange an appointment for me?" he asked.

"Well, I figured since you didn't really like the therapists we sent you to before, maybe it's time to try again. I think you might like this one, and I think it may do you some good."

"Okay," he said.

"I'll meet you here at the end of your shift, and we'll walk over together, okay?"

"Okay, see you then."

I was glad I made the effort, because as it turned out, Matt really liked her, and she set him up—along with a number of other soldiers—on recurring appointments a couple times a week. A good and caring therapist for soldiers in a combat zone is incalculable. All battalions have chaplains that deploy with the unit who are trained to serve in the same capacity as the Major, but she was far and away better than anyone else at helping the soldiers who needed it most.

During the remainder of the deployment, I felt hopeful for Matt. I spoke to the Major a number of times, and she was always quick to say how much she enjoyed working with Matt, that he was intelligent, and they were making progress. She wouldn't elaborate further, nor would I ask her to.

When the advance party from Pennsylvania—our replacements—began arriving, we had already been in the packing and movement phase for a month.

Besides preparing soldiers and equipment for our return, I was working on course material in the US Army Sergeants' Major Academy, a two-year online course I had been selected for by the command. The entire Pennsylvania battalion finally arrived about two weeks after the New Year.

One afternoon a few days from our departure, I looked up from my computer screen, where the Delta Co First Sergeant, Commander, and Maintenance Test Pilot, stood outside my office.

"Can we speak to you?" The Captain (Commander) asked.

"What's on your mind, gentlemen?"

"First Sergeant, we just wanted to thank you for the email you sent," he began.

What email? I wondered.

"You know, that email you sent us about your experiences, and what we could expect at Fort Hood? It saved us a tremendous amount of frustration and pain."

"Oh, that email," I said, trying to act nonchalant.

I soon learned that my email circulated throughout the entire battalion.

For the next thirty minutes, they recounted—with a heaping dose of humor—how they completely avoided having to do double duty under two commands like we had.

Man, this is good stuff!

I had no idea my advice would have the impact on another battalion's experience as it did for them. I was grateful they took the time to personally express their appreciation. Following handshakes, I couldn't help but marvel. *I guess one person* can *make a difference. I'm grateful someone else benefitted from what we endured.*

The dense fog lifted, albeit temporarily, as I looked around the flightline at my soldiers nervously standing in separate groups according to chalk (helicopter) flight manifest. Like me, soldiers would periodically glance skyward, wondering if we were going to make it out before the fog settled again. In one group, I noticed Matt's look of excitement as we prepared to board Chinooks. After twelve months, and being halfway around the globe, we were finally on our way home.

Even the prospect of demobilizing at the "Great Place" (Fort Hood) could not dampen the surge of adrenaline we felt as we began the journey back to the States. After only a few days at Fort Hood, we boarded an early morning United Airlines flight on Sunday, January 20, 2013, for a nonstop flight to Salt Lake City.

When the airplane door opened to a hangar bulging with thousands of people, a roar went up from the crowd like a coliseum full of fans at a rock concert. I made my way down the stairs and waded into the huge crowd. The next thing I knew, a group of people were rushing toward me, and instantly, I felt hands and arms locked around me. Smiles and tears were everywhere.

Then as if on cue, everyone noticed Matt coming down the stairway from the plane. "Matt!" everyone yelled in unison and broke away from Jen and me to smother Matt in a giant sibling hug. Matt picked up Liza and Daniel and held each one for a few moments as they looked at their older brother and me with wide beaming eyes.

Later than night, Jen surprised Matt and me with a party. Many former soldiers and retired leaders I'd served with came. It felt wonderful to be home.

As soon as I returned to work, I looked up a required class I needed and was surprised to see the only class was starting in two weeks, with no classes scheduled for the next eighteen months. The class was full. I called the course manager, who assured me that the class was indeed full and had been for some time.

I explained that I had just returned from a combat deployment and just wanted to double check. When I said that, he offered me the slot they kept for a future instructor.

Following a yearlong deployment, and being home only thirty days, I was back on the road attending a nine-week course in Oklahoma City. Each day I studied in class, and each evening I worked on course material for the Sergeant's Major Academy.

About halfway through the course, I received a phone call from Brian Smethurst, a fellow first sergeant in the battalion.

"Has anyone contacted you?" he asked.

"No. Why?"

"I just heard the Aviation Brigade CSM suddenly dropped his retirement paperwork following some serious allegations, and from what I'm hearing, Cartwright is moving up." Cartwright had been our Battalion CSM since before the deployment. "Word on the street is you're getting promoted as the new Battalion CSM."

I sat stunned. "No way," was all I could say.

The following Monday I received a phone call from Cartwright. "When are you due back in town?"

"This course ends the first week of April, Sergeant Major," I said.

"Well then, we'll see you at drill the second weekend in April, where you're being promoted into my slot as the new Battalion CSM," he said.

Up to that point, at least in my mind, I was sure a promotion to Sergeant Major was at least a couple years away. I'd only served as Delta Co First Sergeant for less than eighteen months, whereas previous First Sergeants served between five and eight years.

I decided to arrange for my mom to fly down from Portland to "pin me" on that Saturday afternoon, the thirteenth of April, in front of my extended family and the entire battalion. Before the ceremony began, Colonel Hartvigsen asked to meet my family. When he met my mother, he smiled. "I heard a rumor you're going to pin on your son's new rank as Sergeant Major. Is that correct?"

"Why yes, that's what I'm being told," Mom replied.

"Now Sharon, the trick is, when I hand you his new rank, in order to really make sure this increased rank and responsibility stick, you're required to give him a good punch to make it stick. Do you think you can do that?"

Mom's face lit up. "Well, I wasn't aware of that tradition, but yeah, I think I can handle that quite nicely."

"Oh, and one more thing. Feel free to dredge up all the things Brad surely got away with in his younger years. Consider this your opportunity to get him back for all the frustration he caused you," Hartvigsen said, cracking up everyone within earshot.

"That I can do," Mom said.

The battalions' six companies—each with a soldier holding the company guidon (flag) out front—lined up side by side and filled the large drill hall. I lined up, along with the other five First Sergeants, one step ahead, and one step to the right of the soldier holding the Delta Co guidon.

From our left, Sergeant Major Cartwright walked with purpose until he was centered on the battalion and stopped before turning to face us. "BATALLION!" he said with authority, signaling the first sergeants to simultaneously come to the position of Attention and issue the preparatory command "COMPANY!" to our soldiers behind.

"ATTENTION!" In one motion the battalion came to the position of Attention signaled by the single stomp sound as hundreds of feet, shoulder width apart, suddenly come together at the heels.

"REPORT," Cartwright said, signaling each First Sergeant to report their respective company. When it was my turn, I said, "DELTA COMPANY, ALL ACCOUNTED FOR," and I saluted.

Following the report, Cartwright did an About Face, signaling to Hartvigsen to walk briskly out to Cartwright, where he stopped and turned to face him. Cartwright saluted. "Sir, the battalion is assembled," he said, turning the battalion over to Hartvigsen, who returned his salute.

"STAND AT . . . EASE," Hartvigsen said, allowing the battalion to go back to feet shoulder-width apart with our heads turned to listen to him.

"It's been more than a few years since we've promoted one of our own to the highest enlisted position in the battalion. As most of you know, Sergeant Major Cartwright came to us from outside aviation, so it's with a great sense of pride I say, FIRST SERGEANT BRADLEY JONES . . . POST."

I walked rapidly to position myself in front of Hartvigsen.

"Sir, thank you for inviting me," I said as I saluted him.

"Brad, this is well deserved."

"Attention to orders!" the soldier at the microphone read. This brought the battalion back to the position of Attention. "The Secretary of the Army has reposed special trust and confidence in the patriotism, valor, fidelity, and professional excellence of Bradley P. Jones. In view of these qualities and his demonstrated leadership potential and dedicated service to the United States Army, he is, therefore, promoted to the rank of Sergeant Major."

In that moment, I thought of those early days—grinding it out as a young soldier. Not once did I ever imagine going from Private E-1 all the way up the ladder like those I admired and respected tremendously—MSG Jack Crumling and CSM Ted Harris. In a split second, my entire military career flashed before my eyes.

Hartvigsen turned toward my family seated off to the side. "I'd like to invite First Sergeant Jones's mother, Sharon, and his wife, Jenne, to come forward."

All eyes watched as they walked out and stood next to Hartvigsen. "Sharon and Jenne, are you ready for this?" he said grinning. With big smiles they both nodded.

"I think so," Mom said.

"Okay, Jenne, I need you to take hold of the rank on your husband's chest and give it a good tug," he instructed.

Jen reached over and easily tore off the Velcro patch.

Hartvigsen then handed my mom the replacement patch, one with a star between the rockers and chevrons. "He's all yours."

Mom took a step toward me and placed the patch where the other one had been. Then she stepped back and curled her right hand into a fist and punched me in the chest. I momentarily rocked back and then forward again. It was beautiful. Even though the entire battalion was still at the position of Attention, I could see by all the smiles that they too were impressed.

Hartvigsen turned to the formation. "AT EASE!" he said.

And with that, the formation erupted. Astonished looks came over Mom's and Jen's faces as they turned toward the source of all the cheering.

I shook a lot of hands and hugged an even greater number of soldiers, as we enjoyed cake and refreshments after the formation was over.

Mom came up and wrapped her arms around my waist. "I'm so proud of you. I can absolutely sense the level of respect these soldiers have for you."

With her arms still wrapped around me, I turned and looked over the large group that still remained, talking and enjoying each other's company. I took a deep breath. *I'm ready to provide the leadership and direction these soldiers need and deserve.*

But then I looked down at my mom. "For crying out loud, Mom, I didn't know you could punch that hard."

"You better not cross me, Bradley Paul, or there's more where that came from."

We laughed.

"Good to know, Mom. Good to know."

CHAPTER 20

Risky Business

The envelope felt thick in my hands, as if the weight of the paperwork inside was some indication of the gravity of the information inside. I opened it and unfolded the sheets. It was a request for PTSD benefits from one of my soldiers. The soldier's statement described a toxic environment within a section of Delta Co, my company, during the deployment. I felt like someone punched me in the gut.

Within six months of our return, this promising young soldier had already been arrested for a DUI.

I thought back on the night when I received word of his arrest, which included additional charges for heroin and firearm possession. All felonies.

No wonder this soldier was struggling.

By all accounts, the soldiers in Delta Company were firing on all cylinders. Over and over, I asked myself, *How could I have missed the toxic atmosphere this soldier described?* I prided myself on knowing my soldiers and their individual circumstances.

When the deployment drew to a close, the efforts of the aircraft maintenance section received the most praise and awards. If this soldier's accusations were true, then a whole other world was going on right under my own, supposed, leadership.

Each drill weekend, usually on Sunday evening, the battalion commander, chaplain, and I were briefed by leaders from each company on all the "at-risk" soldiers within the entire battalion. We relied heavily on section and company leaders to use the STAR template—Significant other, Trade (what they do for work), Activities (what they like to do/hobbies), and Residence (their living situation)—to assess their well-being.

We discussed this particular soldier a number of times. As much as we tried to head off repercussions of this nature, the tragic reality, at least in this particular soldier's case, was our efforts were too little too late. Sadly, his company leaders revealed they had recently received paperwork for a well-deserved promotion to (E-5) Sergeant.

With the involvement of a new and caring chaplain, Captain Tom Berry, our overall efforts were beginning to pay dividends. Like many things, timing was everything. Unfortunately for some soldiers, there seemed to be no forewarning of impending issues.

Surprisingly, many of our soldiers were unaware of the programs and services available to them. Most were surprised to learn help had been there the whole time. We were also well aware of the suicide epidemic going on throughout the military. Clearly, our mission was to intervene before things reached critical mass.

Briefing local leaders and soldier employers before taking them on a
helicopter ride. Also proof that I invented "gangster knife hand"

More than anything, I wanted to talk with this soldier, to hear what
he had to say in the hopes that he still had the desire to get help and turn
things around. Following a deployment, soldiers scatter to their respective
lives and jobs, coupled with no requirement to attend drill for roughly six
months. It's a well-deserved break that I knew from experience, contained
its own set of consequences.

I scanned the faces of those behind me waiting in line at airport security. I almost missed the head nod about four rows back. It was LTC
Hartvigsen nodding and smiling at me. We both yawned as we waited to
board our early morning flight to Phoenix. Boeing executives were host-
ing a three-day convention to celebrate the completion of the final Delta
model Apache, along with the unveiling of the first Echo model to roll off
the assembly line. The convention started with a guided tour of the entire
complex. The Apache program president led the way as we walked from
building to building witnessing the entire manufacturing process from
start to finish. It was quite amazing.

After the tour, we followed the president into a large theater-style room where hundreds of employees—all engineers, we were told—were gathered to hear Hartvigsen speak about our deployment. Before we entered the room, I was expecting a group of engineers gathered around a large conference table. Certainly not a room this size with this many people.

"These are all engineers?" I asked Greg, amazed.

"Apparently so," he said with a grin.

The crowd hushed as the president walked to the podium. "We are grateful to have LTC Greg Hartvigsen and Sergeant Major Bradley Jones with us today. They recently returned from a combat deployment in Afghanistan as part of Operation Enduring Freedom." He then read a list of our accomplishments while performing combat operations: "Seven-thousand, nine-hundred, and thirteen combat hours flown with zero Class A, B, C, or D accidents. Delta Company maintenance completed nine 250-hour and eight 500-hour inspections in nine months of combat operations." He looked up and his face showed that he was impressed. "It's with great pleasure that we present LTC Greg Hartvigsen to personally brief us today."

Amid applause, Greg rose to the pulpit and for the next forty minutes, he highlighted the Apaches' overall ability to mitigate and subdue enemy operations, in many cases, based solely on its mere presence on the battlefield. He praised the tough-as-nails airframe that was the envy of the allied nations we served with. Then he did something I hadn't expected—he began talking about the maintenance accolades the president had listed. And with no prior warning, "To give you a more in-depth accounting of the battalion's maintenance accomplishments, I'd like to bring up Sergeant Major Jones, who served as Delta Company's First Sergeant for the entire deployment. Shortly after returning home I was privileged to promote him to serve as my new Battalion Command Sergeant Major."

Applause erupted in the room as I took a deep breath, swallowed hard, and ascended to the podium to talk about the soldiers I was privileged to lead and how they were primarily responsible for all the awards and accolades.

Amid the convention's activities, I couldn't help thinking of our at-risk soldiers and how they were doing. *I only wish they could all be here to experience all of this.*

Matt, who had spent the summer working for his grandfather Noel—Randi's dad—in Southern California, returned home that fall of 2013.

I took him to lunch to catch up on things from his summer. From Matt's account it was apparent he'd used and built on his experience from the deployment.

It was a good conversation, and when I felt the moment was right, I looked across the table at him. "Matt, how come you never talked to me about the toxic environment you experienced during the deployment?"

He was looking down at his food, when his eyes shot up and met mine. "How did you know about that?"

"While you were gone, a thick envelope from VA arrived in the mail, and thinking it was possibly time sensitive, I opened it and read the contents. It was a copy of your PTSD paperwork. I apologize if you didn't want me to see it."

"Don't even worry about it, Dad."

"How come you never felt like you could come talk to me and tell me what was going on?"

He paused. "Well, one of the things they'd taunt me with after I was mad was, 'Oh, what are you going to do now? You going to tell Daddy? You going to go cry to your daddy for help?' I felt boxed in."

No longer hungry, I pushed my food away. I was livid at his leaders, and frustrated and sad that Matt felt he couldn't talk to me.

"I can only imagine how hard that decision was, but I wished you would have somehow let me know and given me the chance to affect some change in what was going on. You—and they—know full well that I would never stand for leaders treating their soldiers like that. If I had known they were refusing to follow good and sound leadership principles...ones I clearly emphasized, then I would've removed them from their leadership roles."

"I just felt that if I came and told you, you would've dropped a hammer on them, and then I would have to work and live with the aftermath."

As much as I hated to admit it, I couldn't argue with Matt's logic. What troubled me most was the fact that I would soon witness the process that would result in Matt's discharge, and as agonizing as that would be, I knew that had I known, I could've done my job as a leader to mitigate the effects of toxic leaders.

It was heartbreaking to tell Matt that I had already been informed of his impending discharge.

The judge who presided over Matt's case was both impressed and concerned for him. He'd been impressed by his clean-cut appearance and his polite and respectful demeanor. But he was most concerned how the charges would affect Matt's membership in the guard.

The judge's concern proved prophetic. Despite completing a rehab program, Matt received a general discharge. His departure coincided with the normal post-deployment attrition units' experience.

The one bright spot over the next twelve months was ushering in many new soldiers, with their infectious enthusiasm as we prepared for the longest convoy the battalion would undertake that summer of 2014.

During that first year, I felt an unmistakable connection to previous mentors like Jack and CSM Harris and the sixth sense they seemed to possess no longer seemed so foreign to me.

The first leg of the convoy took all day to travel to the halfway point, stopping at a National Guard armory in Las Vegas, where arrangements were made to remain overnight.

As my soldiers positioned their vehicles for an early morning departure, I decided to take a look at where we would sleep.

After seeing the drill hall—a room about the size of a gymnasium—I walked the hallways until I found the bathrooms. Their people had obviously been using the facilities, because they were a mess. The trashcans were full, and the showers, sinks, and stalls all needed cleaning. I made a mental note and looked around for a closet with cleaning supplies. As expected, every door was locked.

Early the next morning, soldiers cleaned up the area as best we could, sweeping the floors and emptying trashcans, leaving the place better than how we found it.

While the convoy commander conducted a briefing with the drivers and co-drivers, I noticed a soldier exit an armory side door and make a beeline toward the huddled group.

I wonder what this guy wants, and why he's interrupting our convoy brief?

"I think I know what this is about," I said to the other leaders with me. "I better get over there."

As we got close to the group, sure enough, the E-7/Sergeant First Class was saying that his boss—whoever that was—sent him out to tell us that we needed to have a crew clean up the mess we'd left in the latrines.

"Here's the deal, Sergeant," I said. "As soon as we pulled in last night, I personally inspected those latrines before any of our people even entered the building, and they were already trashed. I will not have my soldiers be your clean-up crew. If your boss, or anyone else, has a problem with that, you tell them to come out here and talk to me personally."

He stammered a bit, acknowledging that he would pass on the message before heading back into the armory.

I looked around at my soldiers, many with grins on their faces. "All right, let's roll!"

Followed by a resounding, "Yes, Sergeant Major!"

That summer's training exercise in California with local NG units was followed by increasingly intensive training leading up to the summer of 2016, all in preparation for a major training exercise at the Joint Readiness Training Center (JRTC) at Fort Polk, Louisiana. JRTC is one of the Army's three Combat Training Centers (CTC), including the National Training Center at Fort Irwin, California, and the Joint Multinational Readiness Center at Hohenfels, Germany.

A CTC rotation provides unmatched live simulation training, creating an environment intentionally designed to look as close to real combat as possible. The training strategy focuses on improving unit readiness through highly realistic, stressful, joint-and-combined arms training across the full spectrum of conflict, including large-scale conventional operations. A force-on-force scenario where the outcome is never assured and more than likely, but not always, goes to the force that employs timely and inspired combat initiative—the absolute ultimate combat scenario designed to test a unit's ability to function during combat. Our battalion would operate as a CAB (Combat Aviation Brigade) Headquarters responsible for more than twenty-eight aviation airframes—comprised of Apaches, CH-47 Chinooks, UH-60 Blackhawks—participating from New York, Ohio, and Connecticut. New York NG's 27th Infantry Division would be the lead command element, pitting our joint forces against a freethinking, capabilities-based, Opposing Force (OPFOR) that typically overwhelmed and easily defeated (Rotational Training Units) RTUs.

We arrived in Louisiana, on July 10, 2016, to begin our scheduled rotation. It was miserably hot and humid with temps in the high nineties, with equally high humidity levels. Despite the oppressive heat, we immediately inventoried our equipment and vehicles we'd previously shipped from Utah.

Along with our organic equipment, we still had to inventory, check, and sign for a substantial amount of Pre-Positioned (PREPO) vehicles, outfitting each with Multiple Integrated Laser Engagement System (MILES) gear. The entire system was basically the army's version of laser tag.

Each soldier was fitted with a MILES harness, with built-in receivers attached to our web vests covering the torso, along with a belt of receivers attached to our Kevlar helmets. A single laser pulse was generated from a small barrel-mounted box attached to each weapon when activated by the firing of a (blank) round.

A small built-in speaker would emit a high-pitched alarm, signaling that the soldier was either KIA (Killed in Action), or WIA (Wounded in Action), depending on a card in a sealed envelope carried by each soldier. JRTC provided leaders at every level with Observer Controllers (OC's) to shadow them for the entire operation. The OC's acted as referees during and after enemy (OPFOR) engagements. They also provided feedback and coaching to the leaders and soldiers they shadowed. Each OC carried a fob, used to deactivate alarms on MILES gear, at which point they would decide who was KIA or WIA. Sort of a mass-casualty scenario our soldiers would have to react to.

This initial kitting up and preparation phase is called RSOI—Reception, Staging, Onward-movement, and Integration—and it took several extremely long days to complete. There were two separate staging areas for the roughly 4,500 soldiers and equipment that constituted our rotation. The bulk of the 27th ID's infantry and artillery assets were staged at FOB Warrior, with support and aviation (us) assets staged at FOB Forge on an airfield large enough for all twenty-eight aircraft.

Based on the scenario, 27th ID came up with the overall plan of attack, in support of UN resolutions calling for the liberation of a fictitious nation following an invasion by a neighboring nation and subsequent control of that nation's infrastructure (oilfields). Everyone waited for the signal—EX-ROE (Exercise Rules of Engagement)—signifying the commencement of combat operations, the majority of which would take place inside a ten-by-twenty-mile training area known as "The Box."

Word finally came in the early evening on day four. I walked the entire length of the airfield to make sure everyone was made aware that EX-ROE was now in effect, meaning every soldier had to wear their combat gear at all times. After alerting everyone, I walked past the Blackhawk operational cell and noticed they hadn't donned their gear. Several soldiers were sitting out front when I approached. "EX-ROE is in effect, so get your gear on…now."

"Right away, Sergeant Major," they replied.

Coincidentally, that night at dinner with LTC Smith—our Battalion Commander—and the rest of the command staff, Captain Kelly Kimber looked at me. "Sergeant Major, how come I've never seen you have a 'come apart' on someone? As a matter of fact, I don't think I've ever even seen you get mad."

I looked over and noted the rest of the staff waiting to hear my response. "In my experience, having a 'come-apart' is rarely needed, and for me, it's an absolute last resort."

It was dark when we made our way back to our airfield operations center, preventing the aforementioned Blackhawk soldiers from seeing our approach. There they were, the same group, still smoking and joking with no gear on whatsoever.

My eyes narrowed as I executed a hard left turn, crossing the road, and catching them in all their disobedient glory.

I led with my outstretched hand making a chopping motion. In the military this is known as "knife-hand."

"HOW MANY TIMES DO I HAVE TO STOP HERE AND TELL YOU TO GET YOUR GEAR ON?"

They leapt off the stairs and began running in different directions—looking more like the three stooges trying to hide. "THIS IS THE THIRD TIME. NOW, I'M MAD!"

Their Commander, a Captain, finally spoke up. "Sergeant Major, don't you worry. We are getting our gear on right now, Sergeant Major!"

"DON'T MAKE ME USE SOME OF YOUR OWN SOLDIERS AND POST THEM AS GUARDS RIGHT HERE TO MAKE SURE EVERYONE KEEPS THEIR GEAR ON!"

"No, Sergeant Major, that won't be necessary," said the Captain.

As I walked back to where the others stood and watched, Kimber laughed. "I take back everything I said at dinner! That was impressive, Sergeant Major!"

As combat operations commenced that night, I tossed and turned until 2:00 a.m. when I finally climbed out of my sleeping bag. After putting on my gear, I walked back up to the airfield in the warm sticky air. I could not help thinking about the soldiers who should have been there with us. The ones we lost along the way—including Matt. Even though their replacements were performing admirably, I still felt such a keen sense of loss and helplessness for not intervening quickly, or enough, to keep them in the ranks. Even with new faces, I could still see the other faces as I looked beyond the nearby tree line and watched the light rising from the east and its signal of a new day—for me, another privileged day in uniform.

CHAPTER 21

In the Box

T he first twenty-four hours of the operation were a flurry of activity for our ad hoc aviation brigade. To gather intelligence on the battlespace, Apaches flew recon missions over and around the (battlespace) box. On day two the 27th Infantry Division CSM, along with the OC assigned to shadow him, stopped by our aviation CP (Command Post).

"How is the initial phase—shaping the battlespace—of the operation unfolding?" I asked, after I walked them both through our very busy operational planning area, then into a tiny office so we could talk.

"We've been able to insert artillery and some infantry into the box," the CSM said. "But due to transportation issues, one of our badly needed infantry battalions is stuck in the rear."

"Why don't we air-insert them using the eight Chinooks we have sitting out on the ramp?" I asked. "The Chinook planners are begging for missions."

The CSM's face lit up. "That is a fantastic idea!"

"This is what I love to see," the OC said, his first words since the conversation started. "Two Command Sergeant's Major talking through issues and coming up with solutions!"

Five hours later, a convoy of roughly ten vehicles appeared on the dirt road, heading toward us. After parking parallel to the runway, soldiers of Manhattan Island's storied 1st Infantry Battalion of the Fighting 69th began piling out with their weapons and gear to the area where all the Chinooks were receiving their preflight inspections.

I walked down the row of vehicles and sensed the palpable anticipation level among the soldiers.

CSM Tom Siefert emerged from the large group. "Thanks for offering to give us a lift. There's nothing worse than loitering in the rear when all of our soldiers are itching to get in the fight."

Tom and I walked into our CP, where I gave him a brief overview of the operation from the aviation perspective. An hour later, I stood on the airfield and watched as eight Chinooks lifted off in formation with their precious cargo.

The next day, we undertook the monumental task of moving all aviation assets into the box. With twenty-eight aircraft to park, our footprint was enormous, let alone our sleeping and work spaces set up inside the shade of a nearby tree line.

I assigned each unit with area security surrounding their aircraft going all the way back into the dense tree line on our flank. Late that first night, a firefight erupted deep inside the tree line lasting for nearly an hour. We had yet to patrol that far back, but I told LTC Smith, "As soon as it's daylight, I will lead a patrol to find out who is back there, and what all the shooting was about."

Early the next morning, a group of us slowly made our way back into the woods. Suddenly, several soldiers emerged from well-hidden fighting positions, having observed our approach long before we even knew they were there.

"Who's there?" one of them called out.

"It's Sergeant Major Jones from aviation," I called back.

"Proceed Sergeant Major," he said.

"What unit are you with?" I asked.

"We're a squad from the 69th Infantry," he said.

I shook hands with a seasoned Sergeant First Class and his Lieutenant who were leading the squad.

"What happened last night? We heard a ton of shooting," I asked.

They looked at each other and laughed.

"We were hunkered down, minding our own business, when a platoon of OPFOR"—the enemy—"suddenly emerged from over there." He pointed deeper into the thickening trees.

It didn't take a rocket scientist to figure out that we were the primary target the OPFOR were after, and these alert Infantry soldiers unknowingly intercepted them, giving them a welcoming party they were not expecting. *I'm glad I got these soldiers into the fight.*

"Tell me everything, I want to hear it all!" I said, as the squad gathered around.

"They came creeping through the trees," one soldier explained. "So we let them come all the way into our kill zone, and then we opened up on them like a fireman with a fire hose!"

We were hanging on every word.

"They thought they could sneak up on us—that we would be sleeping in our fighting positions. We lit them up in a big way!" The Lieutenant's words eliciting nods and high fives from the group.

"Even with their night vision goggles on, we could see how shocked and freaked out they were when we opened up on them," the Sergeant said.

"From where we are, we heard the horrendous noise from all the weapons and MILES alarms going off," I said.

The OPFOR moved with their own set of OCs, but they were behind the team on the trail and were also caught completely by surprise when things erupted.

"They even had vehicle mounted fifty-caliber machine gun that we managed to take control and turn on them," a young soldier offered.

Finally, the OCs called a cease-fire and gathered everyone around the gun-truck for what's called a "hot-wash"—a discussion of what happened, what went right, and what went wrong. The leader among the OPFOR admitted, "We have never had our butts kicked so badly!"

To which the Sergeant said, "We're from New York, bro. We don't play that game."

They annihilated the OPFOR, who were accustomed to thoroughly overwhelming whomever they attacked. I couldn't have been more delighted and prouder of this group of soldiers who fought with the heart of lions. "Well, on behalf of the aviation brigade, I want to thank you for protecting our flank. Is there anything you need or are low on?"

"We're low on water and ammo," came the reply.

"We got you covered," I said.

The Lieutenant signaled to a few young soldiers who grabbed their weapons.

"Follow me," I told them. I led them back through the forest to our supply truck, where I instructed my Supply Sergeant. "Give these guys anything they need. They lit up the OPFOR last night, protecting our rear flank."

"Roger that, Sergeant Major," the Supply Sergeant replied.

They took all the water and ammo they could carry, trading us several trip flares, which we immediately installed back in the tree line covering a few avenues of approach.

With one of our most experienced pilots embedded with the 27th ID's planning cell, it didn't take long for the overall operational command group to acknowledge and utilize the unique tactics and capabilities an attack battalion provides. During the first several Battle Update Briefings (BUBs) with leaders from every battalion, the overall operational commander (Colonel) flatly stated to everyone in the room, "Right now, the Apaches have the hammer in this fight."

I looked over at LTC Smith and whispered, "That means the OPFOR will be coming for us like a freight train." Smith nodded in agreement.

Later, I spoke to our mission planners in our command post. "The OPFOR was already intercepted and cut off in what I believe was an attack aimed at us. One thing that can further disrupt their efforts is for departing aircraft to fly wagon wheels over and beyond our footprint. But mark my words, they will find a way inside our perimeter to attack us."

The morning of the fourth day dawned like every day since arriving—hot, sticky, muggy, and miserable. We were sure we would be attacked sometime during the previous night, but nothing materialized. Pilot reports from wagon-wheel flights around our AO had seen groups massing deep beyond the tree line, but as the Apaches banked over the groups, the pilots reported that the groups jumped in vehicles and quickly dispersed.

Around mid-morning I learned that the Sergeant Major of the Army (SMA) Dan Dailey would be in the area.

Around noon a motorcade of vans pulled up and parked just beyond the tree-lined hill where the center of our operations was located. I walked down the hill covered in a sticky layer of drenching sweat—my second one for the day. SMA Dailey was friendly and inquisitive about how we were handling the mission, despite the heat and humidity.

I accompanied him into our CP (Command Post) where I explained the impact attack aviation was having on shaping the battlespace. While there, we received word that a group of approximately one hundred pro-testors—local civilian actors—were massing nearby to protest the death of a popular religious cleric reportedly killed in an operation involving our Apaches. The angry mob threatened to storm the hilltop and overrun our CP right in the middle of my effort to fully brief (Dailey) the SMA.

Outside the CP, soldiers were running to secure the hilltop.

Sensing the circumstances, SMA Dailey turned to me. "I'm sure you have some soldiers you would like me to recognize, but at the moment, I can see you have your hands full." He motioned to a young soldier who accompanied him.

The private pulled a handful of challenge coins from a bag and handed them to Dailey, who in turn handed them to me. "Tell your soldiers these are from me in recognition of their dedicated service and professionalism.

One is for you, for your excellent leadership not only to the soldiers in your battalion, but also to the soldiers in this rotation."

As one of the youngest SMA's in my memory, he was absolutely revered and respected by an overwhelming majority of soldiers. It was an honor to receive a coin from him. We shook hands, and I thanked him, before sprinting back to the CP. When I entered, LTC Smith motioned me over to where he was talking to several leaders. "We have a convoy of security vehicles assembled at the bottom of the hill. We have to go talk with the mayor of Dar Salaam—the nearby city—about how we are going to prevent indiscriminate killing of civilians."

"Okay, let's do it." I drove a Humvee with Smith in the passenger seat surrounded by two Humvee gun trucks ahead and one behind.

The city of Dar Salaam was actually a full mockup complete with a traffic circle at the center surrounded by approximately twenty buildings designed to mimic a town square. The mayor's office was just beyond the traffic circle. We parked the convoy along the curb, and Smith and I got out and approached the building while gunners swiveled, scanning the surrounding area, perched up in their gun turrets.

The mayor and several other town leaders greeted us at the door, inviting us into an office, where the air hung heavy, sticky, and hot. I could feel sweat pouring down my back in torrents.

Smith began by apologizing for the mishap, at which point the mayor held up a paper with a giant bullet headline decrying the incident. "Your government tells us you're here to help us, but our citizens' feel like your pilots don't care who they kill."

"I assure you we are here to help liberate your country and we have implemented appropriate measures to ensure this kind of tragedy doesn't happen again," Smith respectfully offered.

"What are we supposed to tell our townsfolk about your blatant disregard for human life?" one of the other leaders asked.

"Please assure them we are here to protect them and to provide for them a stable future by defeating the enemy that invaded this land," Smith said.

I could tell these leaders were not going to give us an inch, and it quickly became a stalemate. We would offer assurances, and they would counter with more accusations of purported incidents by other units operating in the joint coalition.

Up to that point, I let Smith do all the talking, so it surprised everyone in the room when I spoke up. "Mayor, what can we do to repair the damage to the great citizens of Dar Salaam?" Suddenly the ice broke and the stalemate was over.

The mayor perked up as if he had been waiting to hear those words. "Will you agree to an on-air interview by Zazu on our local radio station?"

"Absolutely," Smith and I said simultaneously.

The mayor handed me a card with Zazu's contact info. "I believe if the citizens hear directly from you that you're here to protect and liberate them from the enemy, it will go a long way in repairing this unfortunate incident."

We thanked them for meeting us and made a hasty exit from the town back to our area atop the hill.

I had slept very little over the last four days and sat down at the base of a stump in the shade by my cot and gear. I unwrapped a protein bar and began to eat it. I'm not sure how long it took for my head to bow forward, but it did, and I passed out into a deep sleep, despite being wrapped in sweat-drenched gear and clothing. I awoke to an army of red ants painfully swarming and biting my hands, which still held the half-eaten protein bar.

I shot to my feet and began to brush my lap, shaking my hands to dislodge the ants that were crawling up inside my uniform sleeves. When I finally removed all the ants I could feel and see, I looked down at my hands where the bite marks were already red and swelling.

By that evening, the dozen or so bite marks, which continued to swell and blister, itched like crazy. I had our medics treat them with an ointment that offered little relief. My hands looked grotesque. When I spoke to soldiers and gesticulated as I normally do, I could see their eyes following my hands, trying to figure out what they were seeing. Most would say,

"Those look horrible, Sergeant Major!" as soon as I held out my hands and explained what happened.

That evening I tried to rest for a bit, but as soon as day turned to night, I sensed that something was imminent. Around 2:00 a.m. I got up and dressed in sweat-soaked clothing and gear and walked out to each security check point to check on my soldiers.

Parked out on a rise overlooking the aircraft were two gun-trucks pointing in opposite directions. Each had a fifty-caliber machine gun mounted on top.

I was walking back to the CP from the fuel point with my OC, SFC Green. As soon as we crested the hill, I looked ahead and saw three white passenger vans speeding toward us. It was game time.

I turned and sprinted back to the fuel point. "YOU NEED TO RADIO THE CP AND TELL THEM WE ARE UNDER ATTACK," I yelled at the soldiers in the one of the gun-trucks. "AND YOU NEED TO TURN THAT TRUCK AROUND!"

I hid behind a row of porta johns and watched as the vans came screaming up the road.

I took a knee and fired at the passing vehicles headed toward the Apaches. I ran toward the two gun-trucks, one of which was already firing in the direction of the vans and the OPFOR soldiers now fanning out in groups of two or three.

I had to laugh when I realized the other gun-truck that had yet to fire a single round. I could hear the poor soldier swearing while he tried unsuc-cessfully to unjam the weapon. I couldn't help myself, "FUNCTION CHECKS, GENTLEMEN. FUNCTION CHECKS!"

The OPFOR left no doubt that they were well trained in the art of a commando-style raid. We mobilized our security forces as best we could, but things escalated so quickly, and these professionals knew where and how to inflict maximum damage on our equipment and soldiers. MILES alarms were going off everywhere. The OPFOR had their own OCs who would immediately re-key the OPFOR's alarms, while simultaneously instructing my soldiers to sit down in groups after re-keying their alarms.

When I ran out of ammo, I jumped into the gun-truck with the jammed machine gun and grabbed the radio handset. I stood up in the turret and began broadcasting what I was seeing as the attack progressed. According to OCs, several Apaches were already destroyed by simulated grenades. Several groups of KIA/WIA were growing larger with each passing minute. My suspicions that the OPFOR were monitoring our radio traffic was confirmed when a lone commando jumped out of one of the vans and ran straight toward the vehicle where I was still using the radio to relay info as the battle unfolded.

"SAFETY KILL!" he yelled as he pointed and discharged his weapon toward the floor of the gun-truck, rather than point it at me in such close proximity.

"Sergeant Major," said the OC following him who saw who I was. "You can go wherever you want and further observe the remainder of the battle, but you cannot intervene in any way."

"Fair enough," I replied.

For the rest of the night, I watched the battle from a new angle. I noticed that our soldiers were growing frustrated when the OCs immediately re-keyed the commandos, allowing them to continue as if they had never been wounded or killed. At the end of the attack, somewhere near 5:00 a.m., the OPFOR finally broke contact and retreated back to their vans and sped away, but not before killing nearly everyone in our aviation CP. We barely survived the attack, suffering heavy casualties and a depressing amount of simulated aircraft and equipment damage.

We spent the remainder of the morning with soldiers who survived having to deal with all the KIA and WIA. We ended up with around 20 to 30 percent of our unit KIA and another 10 percent WIA. Dealing with simulated equipment and aircraft battle damage required processes and procedures for ordering replacements. We transferred KIA to a casualty collection point, while WIA were taken to medical facilities, all requiring equipment and manpower that further stressed our unit's resources. Combat, even simulated, is chaos on a grand scale.

Later that morning, the commander, the XO, and I met with leaders from the JRTC Ops Group for an AAR (After-Action Review). Like a hot-wash, an AAR is a more in-depth accounting of what happened, what we did well, and what things we could improve. During the discussion, I spoke on behalf of our leaders and soldiers who were understandably frustrated and, quite frankly, angry, by the fact that the firefight was so one sided.

When I finished, their commander spoke up. "One of the ways we measure a unit's cohesion level is through this type of combat scenario, and what we specifically look for is small bands of individual soldiers coming together and forming groups where somebody steps up and inspires the group to fight back. We witnessed that last night at an exceptionally high level in your soldiers."

I couldn't have been happier to hear that, but I knew our soldiers needed to hear it too. They were out there licking their wounds, trying to make sense of it all.

When the commander finished, I spoke to the group. "What I'm asking each of you is when you return to the leader and/or section you're assigned to, sit down with the soldiers and explain what you just shared with us."

They agreed, and to their credit, they spoke with our soldiers, while LTC Smith and I followed up with each company, to insure their understanding of the purpose.

As I circulated among the soldiers, I could see that insisting on shared understanding helped them process and eventually conclude, that as unfair as the engagement seemed, there was purpose in it. It didn't take long for most to agree, although some reluctantly, that there was a lesson to be learned.

By the end of day seven, the announcement finally came that we had reached the end-of-exercise (ENDEX) for combat operations.

Over the next several days, our command team attended numerous meetings where we analyzed and discussed the different phases of the battle. During one meeting, the OPFOR commander asked, "Who's idea was it to fly wagon wheels around the aviation AO?"

"Mine," I said, raising my hand.

"Well, that couldn't have been more effective. That alone completely disrupted our initial attempts to attack and neutralize the overall effect the Apaches were having on our operating abilities."

Each unit's command team spent the final few days in meetings, while our soldiers worked tirelessly cleaning equipment (MILES) and vehicles for turn in to the PREPO yard.

Each vehicle had to be cleaned, inventoried, and inspected for turn-in. Aviation was only responsible for a fraction of the hundreds of vehicles checked-out by our rotation.

The lines at turn-in were huge, where the civilians inspected each vehicle with a fine-tooth comb. Our soldiers were finding numerous issues with each vehicle, many in addition to the ones we'd already annotated when we signed for them. Some required removal and replacement of major components before they would sign off and accept the vehicle. The heat and humidity were off the charts as our people worked day after day in the oppressive conditions.

Between meetings, I made my way down to the PREPO yard and spoke to one of the civilians in charge. After an intense discussion, he finally admitted that the next rotational unit (RTU) was already arriving and all of the vehicles we were turning in would be issued to them almost immediately.

"So what you're telling me is you lack the workforce to fix all the issues before they're needed by the next unit?" I asked him.

"That's correct, Sergeant Major," he responded.

Our soldiers were being asked to supplement PREPO's inability to prepare an entire fleet of vehicles for the next rotation. I immediately spoke with LTC Smith. "We need to go down to the PREPO yard and let our soldiers know the reason behind all their sweat and effort is there are not enough contractors to get all the vehicles ready for the next rotation."

We drove there with coolers full of cold water and Gatorade and walked the entire yard handing out drinks and thanking our soldiers for their hard work despite the heat and frustrating situation.

We shared how badly needed their efforts were on behalf of the under-manned civilian contractors. Once they knew the reason for their efforts, their attitudes shifted considerably. I was grateful for those soldiers who stepped up and provided additional maintenance, not only to the vehicles we were turning in, but because they helped fellow soldiers from other units work on the vehicles they were responsible to turn in. Watching soldiers work together, I knew deep down that it had been my privilege to serve alongside unique and exceptional individuals from all over this land, truly unselfish volunteers whose service never ceases to inspire me.

CHAPTER 22

Running Down a Dream

The great thing about the military is the inherent culture to grow the next generation of leaders. I had already observed several senior leaders, then serving in the command, who had proven themselves capable and ready to take my position as the senior leader in the battalion. I felt it would be unfair to make them wait any longer. After thirty years, I decided to hand in my retirement letter and step aside for the next generation to take the reins.

My decision couldn't have been more bittersweet. As I stood before the battalion at my retirement ceremony, and uttered the words, "BATTALION. ATTENTION!" one last time, so many memories flashed before my eyes . . .

Standing on the parade field at Fort Gordon, along with thousands of others, silently saluting, as the stars and stripes slowly raised up the flagpole in the distance.

My first sit down with Jack.

Standing below the canopy of trees on that hillside cemetery in that small farming community in Missouri, and with tears in my eyes, saluting

314 | TREADING THE DEEP

the folded flag that would be presented to a grieving mother at the loss of her son and my good friend Roger.

Watching, on that hot and sunny day in early July, as a group of close friends from my unit lifted and carried Randi's casket to the spot above her final resting place.

How hard I slept—and, according to Jen, how loud I snored—that first night back from Afghanistan, knowing that all my soldiers were now safely home.

Standing on a hillside following ENDEX (End of Exercise) and watching our soldiers sweating in the heat and humidity as they turned in equipment at our JRTC rotation on Fort Polk, knowing we had just hit a grand slam in our efforts to affect the overall outcome of the operation.

As my gaze rested on each first sergeant, standing positioned in front of their company, and the platoon sergeants standing behind with their soldiers, I felt I had given my best to mentor them—just as Jack and CSM Harris and others had mentored me. Looking over that group of heroes, I realized that I would gladly do it all over again in a heartbeat.

How do I sum up my thirty-year career? One of monumental amounts of sweat, toil, and sacrifice? In simple terms, serving my country, alongside the bravest men and women I have ever known, has been the privilege of a lifetime. We formed a brother and sisterhood—the bonds of which were forged in the blowing sands of the Persian Gulf, the high mountain altitudes of Afghanistan, and during the hours and hours of training in both the classroom and in the elements on the job. Despite the passing of time, I can still feel those bonds on a visceral level when I think of or talk with someone I served with. There is not one corner of this country where I don't have a brother or sister I served with living in that area.

The soldier perspective has always been a unique one. The military draws from this nation's own citizens, individuals from their respective lives and communities, each one bringing his or her own unique perspective to the tapestry that is the modern military. It then molds these individuals into units and teams with one common purpose—as stated by the majority of those who have served in combat: that of looking out for, and taking care of, each other.

We cannot possibly place a price tag on the effects on our communities, cities, and institutions that our sons and daughters provide through having served in uniform. I am constantly amazed by the caliber of those who have served and continue that attitude of service and sacrifice beyond the military.

My years of service have only deepened my faith and belief that God watches over this nation and His plans for its influence and destiny. As I've traveled the world, I've contemplated how and why America was chosen as one nation under God—a nation that still represents something important to Him. I cannot deny the hand of God at work in the formation of this great country and the Constitution, inspired by men who openly acknowledged God on those hot summer days in Philadelphia.

Like many others, I have to look beyond the vitriol so prevalent in our modern discourse, while acknowledging the many faults of our government and its institutions, and yet still believe in our country's inherent goodness and virtue.

Had President John F. Kennedy lived, he was set to deliver a speech in Dallas containing this quote:

We in this country, in this generation, are—by destiny rather than choice—the watchmen on the walls of world freedom. We ask, therefore, that we may be worthy of our power and responsibility, that we may exercise our strength with wisdom and restraint, and that we may achieve in our time and for all time the ancient vision of "peace on earth, good will toward men." That must always be our goal, and the righteousness of our cause must always underlie our strength.[2]

Why has our nation been lifted up? Could it be that we are to lift up other nations as well? Despite our nation's weaknesses and shortcomings, our nation remains a wellspring of good in many forms. Though the United States makes up a small percentage of the overall world population, we account for one-fifth of the world's Gross Domestic Product (GDP).[3]

America is only 4.2 percent of the world population, yet it holds nearly 30 percent of its total wealth. What does this translate into for others not as fortunate? We are an extraordinarily generous people. Citizens in the United States are among the most generous in the world, according to a recent survey conducted from 2009–2018.[4] In 2019 alone, charitable donations reached nearly $450 billion dollars.[5]

In 2017, my family and I attended a U2 concert in California, where the lead singer, Bono, thanked all American taxpayers for the finances that went directly to fight the scourge of diseases, including AIDS, in third-world countries. Many condemn America, its members, and their faults—but on this occasion, a celebrity, known worldwide for his charitable and philanthropic work, thanked the American people and our government for donating money on a monumental scale to better the lives of those who suffer.

The might of the American economy and the generosity of its people make a monumental difference around the world. No other nation is as willing to sacrifice blood and treasure to create and defend the peace and liberty of other nations. I have stood on a street corner in downtown

Kuwait City and had more than a few Arabic women walk up to me, and say perhaps in the only English words they knew: "I love America!" It was their way of thanking us for sacrificing for their sovereignty.

Despite our faults, this nation is still, as Abraham Lincoln so rightly stated, "the last best hope of earth."[6]

America leads the way: number of Nobel prizes, amount of aid to nations in need, number of service volunteers, number of Olympic medals won, and doctors and hospitals consistently rated as the best in the world.

Chris Stewart and Ted Stewart sum it up well in *Seven Miracles that Saved America*: "From space travel to undersea exploration, from advances in medicine, technology, transportation, education, science, music, and innovations in law—the United States is the world's leader in them all."[7]

Frequently I am asked my opinion on world matters, and specifically the ongoing military presence in both Afghanistan and Iraq. I begin by pointing out the obvious results in the nations we fought during WWII. Who can doubt the economic prosperity following that war of both Germany and Japan? I find it fascinating and miraculous that both of those nations are now among our closest allies.

A very young, rag-tag American militia defeated the British, arguably the strongest, most lethally armed military of its time. Who can deny the hand of God in sending an August morning fog that protected a fledgling army whose defeat was all but assured? That fog allowed them safe passage to Valley Forge and the time to regroup with enough strength to defeat the greatest army on earth.

Since the Revolutionary War, we have fought side by side, shoulder to shoulder with our British brothers and sisters who are the very wellspring of this nation. I have met many of our British (and German) military brothers and sisters, and between us, there is an undeniable bond forged by sacrificing together, each for their respective nation.

We have admired each other's equipment, shared common experiences, and then as a token of our brother and sisterhood, exchanged patches, jackets, and nametags as a token of our respect and admiration for each other.

I believe God looks down on this great nation, and the military that supports and defends it, and is truly proud of the character, demeanor, tenacity, and accomplishments of those serving in uniform.

As is sometimes the case in life, when people who have no prior religious inclinations suddenly find themselves calling out to God while in dire circumstances, almost without question they sense the reality of God and His ability to comfort and ultimately preserve their life. I, for one, have had experiences that give me no doubt that He exists. He brought me comfort in my darkest and saddest hours, a deeply felt sense of peace that surpasses all understanding.

The psalmist said, "The Lord is nigh unto them that are of a broken heart; and saveth such as be of a contrite spirit" (Psalm 34:18, KJV). I've experienced in a very personal way that the power of God and the reality of suffering go hand in hand. If you take from this book one thing, my hope and prayer is that choose to believe in a very real and personal God, and His purposes in setting up this nation as the beacon of light spoken of in Matthew 5:14-16 (KJV):

> Ye are the light of the world. A city that is set on a hill cannot be hid. Neither do men light a candle, and put it under a bushel, but on a candlestick; and it giveth light unto all that are in the house. Let your light so shine before men, that they may see your good works, and glorify your Father which is in heaven.

During my final eighteen months in uniform—and, in part, stirred by our new Commander LTC Matt Badell's inspired command philosophy—I decided to write my own command philosophy. The process led me to write this book for the soldiers I had the privilege to serve with, and for the up-and-coming leaders who would emerge long after my departure. May God grant you His wisdom and strength for the journey ahead.

ABOUT THE AUTHOR

Bradley P. Jones enlisted in the United States Army in 1984 and served until 1988 as a ground control approach radar repairman. Upon completion of his initial enlistment and a break in service, he joined the Utah Army National Guard in 1993. His military awards and decorations include: the Bronze Star medal, Meritorious Service medal, Army Commendation medal (three oak leaf clusters), Army Achievement medal, Good Conduct medal (second award), Armed Forces Reserve medal (with "M" Device), Afghanistan Campaign medal, Global War on Terrorism Service medal, Army Reserve Component Achievement medal (three oak leaf clusters), and the Master Aviation Crewmember badge. His military education includes the Primary, Basic, and Advanced Noncommissioned Officers course, the United States Army Sergeants' Major Academy Non-resident course. In Bradley's civilian career, he works for the FAA as an Airway Transportation System Specialist (ATSS) in the Service Operations Center (SOC) of the Salt Lake Air Route Traffic Control Center (ARTCC). He resides with his wife and kids in Lehi, Utah.

ENDNOTES

1 I am grateful that today, anxiety disorder is no longer in the shadows, with effective treatment options available through understanding medical professionals. There are counseling services and treatment plans available for sufferers. If you suffer from anxiety, there is no shame in it. Reach out to family, trusted friends, and medical professionals.

2 John F. Kennedy, "Remarks Prepared for Delivery at the Trade Mart in Dallas, TX, November 22, 1962 [Undelivered]," John F. Kennedy Presidential Library and Museum, https://www.jfklibrary.org/archives/other-resources/john-f-kennedy-speeches/dallas-tx-trade-mart-undelivered-19631122.

3 "Economy & Trade," Office of the United States Trade Representative, accessed June 10, 2021, https://ustr.gov/issue-areas/economy-trade.

4 CAF World Giving Index, October 2019, https://www.cafonline.org/docs/default-source/about-us-publications/caf_wgi_10th_edition_report_2712a_web_101019.pdf.

5 "Charitable Giving Statistics," National Philanthropic Trust, accessed June 10, 2021, https://www.nptrust.org/philanthropic-resources/charitable-giving-statistics/.

6 Abraham Lincoln, as found at "Lincoln on America: December 1, 1862: Closing Paragraph in Message to Congress," Lincoln Home, https://www.nps.gov/liho/learn/historyculture/onamerica.htm.

7 Chris Stewart and Ted Stewart, Seven Miracles that Saved America: Why They Matter and Why We Should Have Hope (Salt Lake City, UT: Shadow Mountain, 2009), 290.

A free ebook edition is available with the purchase of this book.

To claim your free ebook edition:

1. Visit MorganJamesBOGO.com
2. Sign your name CLEARLY in the space
3. Complete the form and submit a photo of the entire copyright page
4. You or your friend can download the ebook to your preferred device

Morgan James
BOGO™

A **FREE** ebook edition is available for you or a friend with the purchase of this print book.

CLEARLY SIGN YOUR NAME ABOVE

Instructions to claim your free ebook edition:
1. Visit MorganJamesBOGO.com
2. Sign your name CLEARLY in the space above
3. Complete the form and submit a photo of this entire page
4. You or your friend can download the ebook to your preferred device

Print & Digital Together Forever.

Snap a photo

Free ebook

Read anywhere

CPSIA information can be obtained
at www.ICGtesting.com
Printed in the USA
JSHW041350200522
26138JS00001B/15